PATRICIA PEARSON

OPENING HEAVEN'S DOOR

What the Dying May Be Trying to Tell Us

About Where They're Going

Random House Canada

PUBLISHED BY RANDOM HOUSE CANADA

Copyright © 2014 Patricia Pearson

www.randomhouse.ca

Random House Canada and colophon are registered trademarks.

Library and Archives Canada Cataloguing in Publication

Pearson, Patricia, 1964–, author
Opening heaven's door : what the dying may be trying to tell us about where they're going / Patricia Pearson.

Issued in print and electronic formats.

ISBN 978-0-307-36013-7

1. Near-death experiences. 2. Death—Psychological aspects. I. Title.

BF1045.N4P42 2014   133.901'3   C2013-905961-X

Text and cover design by Kelly Hill

Cover image: © Jan Bruggeman / Getty Images

Printed and bound in the United States of America

2 4 6 8 9 7 5 3 1

For my family, and the tribe.
"Blessed are those who mourn."

CONTENTS

AN UNEXPECTED VISION

My father died in his blue-striped pyjamas on a soft bed in a silent house. He wasn't ailing. At three or four in the morning he gave out a sigh, loud enough to wake my mother. A sigh, a moan, a final breath escaping. She leaned over to rub his back, sleepily assuming that he was having a bad dream, and then retreated into her own cozy haze of unconsciousness. Morning arrived a few hours later as a thin suffusion of northern March light. She roused herself and walked around the prone form of her husband of fifty-four years to go to the bathroom.

Downstairs to the humdrum rituals of the kitchen. Brewing coffee, easing her teased-apart English muffin halves into the toaster, listening to the radio. I was being interviewed about a brand-new book. There I was, the youngest of her five children, going blah blah blah with impressive authority about a lawsuit that had been launched by a man who had suffered incalculable psychological damage from finding a dead fly in his bottle of water.

"Did he have grounds?" the host was asking me. Was it possible for a life to unravel at the prospect of one dead fly?

My mother spread her muffin with marmalade, thought ahead to her day. Some meetings, a luncheon, an outing with her granddaughter Rachel, who was visiting for March break. She didn't wonder why Geoffrey, my father, still remained in bed. No heightened sense of vigilance for a healthy man who'd just turned eighty.

In families, one's attention is directed towards crisis, and during the early spring of 2008 we were all transfixed by my sister Katharine. It was she, not my father, who faced death. Vivacious Katharine, an uncommonly lovely woman—mother and sister and lover—now anguished by the wildfire spread of metastatic breast cancer. Katharine's fate had become the family's "extreme reality," as Virginia Woolf once put it.

My father played his role unexpectedly.

"Rachel," said my mother, shaking my niece's slack shoulder as she snoozed in the guest room on the top floor of my parents' house. "*Rachel.*" My niece opened her eyes and glimpsed an expression on my mother's face—wild vulnerability in the visage of the matriarch—that shot her to full waking consciousness.

"Granddaddy won't wake up."

That morning we all received the call, the what-the-hell-are-you-talking-about news that my mother, with Rachel's astonished assistance, dialled to the family. But Katharine, one hundred miles east of my parents, in Montreal, received her message differently.

"On the night of my father's death," she would tell mourners at his memorial service some weeks later, "I had an extraordinary spiritual experience." My sister, please know, wasn't prone to spiritual experiences. Stress she was familiar with, as the single mother of two teenaged boys. Laughter she loved. Fitness of any kind—she was vibrantly physical. Fantastic intellect, fluent in three languages. But she hadn't been paying much attention, in essence, to God.

"It was about 4:30 a.m.," she said of that night, "and I couldn't sleep, as usual, when all of a sudden I began having this amazing spiritual experience. For the next two hours I felt nothing but joy and healing." There was a quality of light about my sister Katharine, a certain radiance of expression, a melody of voice that hushed every single person in the church—atheist, agnostic or devout. She clutched the podium carefully, determined to be graceful while terminal illness threatened her sense of balance. "I felt hands on my head, and experienced vision after vision of a happy future."

Katharine had described this strange and lovely pre-dawn experience to her elder son as she drove him to high school before she received the call about Dad. She also wrote about it in her diary: "I thought, is this about people praying for me? And then I thought of Dad cocking his eyebrow, teasing me about hubris." She hadn't known until the next day how to interpret the powerful surge of energy and joy she felt in her bedroom. "I now know that it was my father," she told the mourners. She said this flat out, without the necessary genuflections to science and to reason, no patience for the usual caveats: *call me crazy but . . .*

None of that. "I feel deeply, humbly blessed and loved," she said simply, and sat down.

Astral father. There, yet not there. Love flowing unseen. A benign companion of some sort, whose embrace is light but radically moving.

*

We are not a family in the habit of experiencing ghosts. Arriving at my parents' house on March 19, the day after Dad's death, I heard about Katharine's vision for the first time and collapsed to the carpeted floor of the hallway, crawling past the coat closet on the verge of hysterical laughter. My reaction wasn't derisive so much as surrendered. Reality was vibrating, pixilating; it was very close to shattering.

"Dad is dead, Dad is dead," I had muttered for twenty-four hours already. Like a child fervently memorizing new instructions about the way of things, crisscrossing the icy park beside my house, pacing back and forth. *Dad is dead.*

Now Katharine had had a vision.

We took it in as an aftershock. But almost immediately it began to make profoundly resonant sense, like a puzzle piece slipping perfectly into place. Without discussing it, we were convinced as a family that he had done something of great emotional elegance. He had died for his daughter. Or he may have died unknowingly but then seized a mysterious opportunity to go to her, to her bedroom in Montreal, to caress her and to calm her before going on his way.

Later I would learn that this sort of experience when

someone has died is startlingly common, not rare. Families shelter their knowledge, keeping it safe and beloved like a delicate heirloom, away from the careless stomping of strangers.

There was much I would learn in the ensuing year about the kept-hidden world all around me, but at the time I understood this much: what a gift this was for Katharine. For the previous twelve months, waking up had meant regaining knowledge of her predicament, which was like an immersive drowning terror in the darkness. How limited we have become, in our euphemistic language, that we speak of patients "battling" cancer without affording them the Shakespearean enormity of their vulnerability, as if they were pragmatic and detached, marshalling their troops, and nothing like Ophelia, or Lear.

I knew my sister better than anyone else in my life, except, perhaps, my children. She was no more or less "brave" than the biblical Jesus when he called out, "My God, my God, why have you forsaken me?" She stood keening in the shower the night that the emergency room doctor dispassionately informed her that she had lesions on her brain; she begged an abstracted universe for ten more years, to see her sons through school and marriage.

Then, suddenly, this astonishment when our father died—*not knowing* that he'd died—of feeling serene, protected and joyful.

For an unspecified amount of time, she wasn't sure if it was minutes or hours, Katharine watched herself—the future beheld in a mirror, a pool?—as she played with her unborn granddaughter on the floor of her bedroom. She somehow understood this to be her teenaged son Graeme's child, a five-month-old baby she knew to be named Katie. Wobbly little creature trying to sit up straight. In her vision, Katharine was supporting this baby girl's back. She

5

was helping her sit and crushing on her sweetness, admiring the wacky little bow in her hair.

"She was *beautiful*," Katharine told Graeme of his distant, future fairy child, when she drove him to his Montreal high school that morning. All will be well, and all manner of things will be well.

Back at the house, the phone rang. My mother, reporting that our father had died.

✳

In early April I flew down to Arizona to visit the Grand Canyon. A scan had shown that Katharine's cancer had spread to her bones, her liver. "Beauty is only the first touch of terror we can still bear," wrote the poet Rainer Maria Rilke. I remember reading that sometime later and thinking, *Ah*.

Along the south rim of the canyon, flies buzzed about the twitching ears of pack mules as they descended the Bright Angel Trail, hooves stepping lively along the steep traverse a few hundred yards ahead of my husband and me. We leaned reflexively into the cliff wall as we followed the party of mule riders, shrinking back from the empty, falling spaces that seemed almost to pull at us, inviting us to swoon and tumble a thousand feet, headlong to our doom.

Were only tourists venturing down that crumbling path, I wondered, or pilgrims too? Intent upon humbling themselves, feeling their way with hands scrabbling rock, confessing to having no knowledge, really, of the vastness that engulfed them, lured by that very admission? When a scouting party of conquistadors first set eyes on the canyon in the sixteenth century, they chose to believe their eyes and determined that the Colorado River, in the canyon's depth, was simply a creek. A thread of blue, easily trudged across at knee's height by their horses in a quarter of an hour or so. They never did grasp that the canyon was ten miles across, rim to rim, and that the river below coursed as wide as a mile.

We understand those dimensions now, but only because the guidebooks make it plain. We fix our eyes accordingly, and when we spy the river, we calculate in relation to what we've been told: if that ribbon down there is actually one mile across, then this height is dizzying. We cower into the Supai sandstone. How do we know what is infinite and what is not? Which do we trust—our eyes or our instincts, our guidebook or our gut?

My sister's death, I felt, was imminent, perhaps a month away, although she hadn't been given a prognosis—didn't want one—and was still working out at the gym. People there were starting to call her the Lance Armstrong of Montreal, and she certainly looked the part, graceful and agile and strong. I was acutely aware of her dying, so much so that it seemed to me the air itself was dangerous to breathe, for each breath demarcated the passage of time. I sensed the clock continuously, how it betrayed me, let go of me, ruined me and broke my heart with every exhalation.

"It's not that soon, do you think?" my husband asked uncertainly, hiking beside me, aware of my fear of the cellphone in my pocket, of its ring. Well, yes, it would be that soon. I'd done the research. Average time to death after brain metastasis from inflammatory breast cancer: three months. But I was alone with this knowledge, because Katharine's oncologist wouldn't say anything out loud that didn't involve metaphors of war. He was currently engaged in bringing out the "heavy artillery," as he called it. Shells were exploding in the rain-dark trenches.

My clock felt increasingly internal and intuitive. When you need to read the world differently, when ordinary channels of information are blocked, what then do you do? About a quarter-mile down the Bright Angel Trail, we stopped to rest. My husband went off to make sound recordings, a passion of his, and I crouched in the scant shade of an overhanging rock, perched uneasily on the slope. The view from there was altered, for the canyon now towered above me. My tilted chin faced an immense wall of stone, as tall as a skyscraper. A red-tailed hawk circled high above me in the shimmering air. What I saw I labelled instantly, unconsciously: a bird of prey, a wall of stone, the quick and apprehensive movement of a ground squirrel. Some tourists, French and German, lumbering along, out of breath, their nylon packs a jarring shade of blue. Someone's dog trotting, the flies, the mules' dung. And far away a helicopter's burr.

What if I had been a Hualapai woman pausing just here a few hundred years ago? Would I have broken down this vista into its constituent material parts? Or would I have seen a landscape rich with portent and spirit, where that bird was not just a bird but a song?

"One has never seen the world well," wrote the metaphysicist Gaston Bachelard, "if he has not dreamed what he is seeing."

Father dead and sister dying. Time to welcome portent and spirit, even while the doctor yaks on, clickety-clack, about the efficacy of the latest round of chemo.

We climbed out of the canyon, stopping frequently to take sucks of water from the clear plastic tubes jutting out of our newfangled backpacks. As we approached the rim, I noticed a rainbow. A perfect, vivid little crescent rainbow hanging in the desert sky as if a child had placed a decal on a window. It was so incongruous, given the arid climate, that I chose to make note of it, and checked my watch. Just shy of noon.

In the evening the sun set breathtakingly, spilling coloured light into the canyon. From an Adirondack chair on the porch of the El Tovar Lodge, I called Katharine in Montreal on my cell. No answer.

"Kitty-Kat," I tell her answer machine, "I'm at the rim of the Grand Canyon." At the end of the world, at the confluence of beauty and terror; here for you, here without you. "I'm thinking about you all the time."

She didn't respond, my sister. At the hour I saw the rainbow in the desert sky, just shy of noon, she was being admitted to hospital in Montreal suffering from acute septicemia, being urged by the doctors to scribble a living will.

A week later I lay entangled with her on her narrow hospital bed in Montreal's Royal Victoria Hospital, watching CNN on the hanging TV in her curtained-off ward cubicle. She, sipping Pepsi through a straw, bald as an eagle in her wisp of a hospital gown, hands bruised from multiple IV punctures and her legs looking too pale and slender. My face tanned from the Arizona sun, while my beautiful sister's was puffed by steroids and flushed from the blood infection that was slowly being brought under control.

She was finally on morphine, and for the first time a little smile played at the corners of her mouth, after a week-long stretch of pained affliction due to wave after wave of intense headaches. Nothing had been offered by the hospital but Tylenol, because they were treating her for the infection and had lost track of the other medical team that had been treating her for cancer. Katharine's characteristic grace and composure had masked the degree of her suffering from the nurses and doctors on ward rotation, until I had a Tasmanian devil–style tantrum at three in the morning, threatening—I am not proud of this—to saw off the nurse's legs and offer *her* Tylenol if she didn't stop making that the only option "allowed" for "Mrs. Pearson."

So that was where we were, my sister and I, holding hands on her bed and watching coverage of the 2008 U.S. primaries, when her oncologist—finally aware of her presence on this ward, being treated for septicemia—came in to break the news that he was transferring her to palliative care. No more chemo. No further radiation. The guns would go silent. It was time now, he said, to "manage the symptoms."

Katharine moved to the hospice on May 14, 2008. The palliative care physician guessed that she had weeks, at the outside margin, but nobody told her that. She was left to envision a horizon without end, distant or near, bright or dark. She didn't ask. Instead she became a peaceful queen presiding over her court as fifty or more friends, relations and colleagues came for one last conversation, a final kiss. The short hallway of the hospice seemed to be streaming to and fro with weeping executives in tony suits and well-heeled women with red-rimmed eyes carrying bottles of Veuve Clicquot. Just one more toast, another laugh.

The hospice nurses were fascinated, they told me later, for they were more accustomed to small family groups visiting elderly patients in a quiet, off-and-on way. They watched as we cracked open Champagne and played Katharine's favourite songs while she swayed dancingly in her bed, and brought her foods for which she had a fleeting craving, and offered her lilies of the valley to bury her nose in. Never have I seen human beings so exquisitely emotionally attuned to one another as we were when we spent those last days in May with my dying sister. When she wanted the volume of energy up, we turned it up. When she wanted it down, we brought it down. The calibration was so precise that when visitors barged in, all innocence but with the wrong energy level, we tackled them like a rugby team. Get out, *get out!!* You're too chipper/too sad/too alpha/too can-do.

When I kissed my sister's cheek, she would kiss me back and behold me in a manner that was so loving it startled me. Generous love, released from need. Often we sat about wordlessly as she slept—my other two sisters, my brother and me. Sometimes we massaged her hands with cream and sang softly. Her sweetheart, Joel, played his guitar. My mother, awash in two waves of grief, read Katharine the love poetry that our father had penned for her in the early fifties.

One afternoon, Katharine's ex-partner came by with a vast bouquet of spring flowers that, he explained, had been left anonymously on their formerly shared doorstep. "Everybody in the neighbourhood loves you, Katharine," he said, with fervent sincerity.

"Surely there's someone who doesn't love me," she responded with dry amusement.

She spoke very little in those final ten days of her life. A few sentences here and there, more often just a word or two. Yet it was clear from everything she said that she was present, and observing. Which was why it grew more remarkable to us that she seemed so content. She enjoyed our company and the music we played, and gazed admiringly at the garden beyond her window and the light playing in the curtains.

"Wow, that was strange," she remarked once upon waking up, her expression one of smiling delight. "I dreamed I was being smooshed in flowers."

All this appeared to interest her—to interest and to please her, as if she were engaged in a novel and agreeable adventure. She looked gorgeous, as if lit from within. Sometimes she would have happy whispered conversations with a person I couldn't see. At other times she'd stare at the ceiling of her room as a full panoply of expressions played across her face—puzzled, amused, skeptical, surprised, calmed—like a spectator angled back in a planetarium, watching a heavenly light show.

I watched her ardently, but she couldn't translate it for me. The sister with whom I'd shared every secret had moved beyond words. "It's so interesting," she began one morning, and then couldn't find the language. "It must be so frustrating," I said quietly, "to not be able to say," and she nodded. We touched foreheads. I was left to guess, or to glimpse what she was experiencing in the accounts of others, others who'd recovered their voice. I would read later, for example, about the Swiss genealogist Albert Heim, who fell off a mountain and wrote, in 1892: "No grief was felt, nor was there any paralyzing fright. There was no anxiety, no trace of despair or pain. But rather calm seriousness, profound acceptance and a dominant mental quickness."

We could say, *Well, she has forgotten that she's dying.* But she hadn't. "Is Mum all right?" Katharine might ask me with concern. Or, "You guys must be falling apart faster than I am."

Indeed we were. My brain was a computer in meltdown, a car shoved into neutral, an old black-and-white television whose brightness had narrowed to one fizzing star. It is difficult to describe, in truth, because I was not capable intellectually of observing my own disintegration. I was lost, but Katharine wasn't. She knew very well that she was dying, and more than that. Forty-eight hours before she died, she told us she was on her way. Literally, as in "I am leaving." How did she know? Hospice could have lasted two months or six months or two years. If nothing else, hope could have swayed it that way; she'd subsisted on hope for the first eleven months of her illness. A study conducted by Harvard researchers found that 63 percent of doctors caring for terminally ill patients wildly overestimate how much time their patients have left. The patients themselves, however, become crisply precise, sometimes nailing their departure to the hour.

Katharine woke up one morning and, looking decidedly perplexed, said to Joel, who lay in wild dishevelment on the cot beside her, "I don't know how to leave." As if the difficulty of the task at hand was akin to learning to water ski, or the trick to making bread dough rise. Clearly she didn't feel the way we felt anymore, with our thirsting, ecstatic joy to find that she was still alive when we raced to her side each day. She teased Joel that in his hollow-eyed disarray he looked like a drug addict. She remained present, but also elsewhere. Katharine had removed herself to some new plane of consciousness where we were now unable to follow.

That afternoon she gazed through her French doors for a long time, with a look that seemed to me, sitting beside her and stroking her hand, to be slightly exasperated. Vexed.

"What are you looking at?" I asked her.

She lifted her arm languidly and pointed in the direction of the garden, remarking, "*Hapless* flight attendants."

We all laughed in surprise. Just then a hospice volunteer wheeled in a trolley of snacks.

Katharine turned alertly to this new visitor and asked, "What's the situation?"

Said the hospice volunteer with brisk cheer, "Well, the situation is that we have lemon tarts, Nanaimo bars and oatmeal cookies. All home-baked." She seemed pleased.

My sister regarded her as if she were insane.

"I mean," Katharine clarified, clearing her throat, for her lungs were becoming congested, "when do I leave?"

Joel, masterfully suppressing his raging grief at losing the love of his life after only three years, assumed a comical Indian accent (they'd met in New Delhi) and, wobbling his head, offered, "That is for you and God to decide."

Katharine left the next night, in silence and candlelight, while I lay with my cheek on her chest and my hand on her heart, feeling her breathing slow and subside like the receding waves of an outgoing tide. Joel sat on one side of the bed, my sister Anne on the other. The nurse came in, barefoot and with a flashlight, to confirm death with a deferential wordless nod, and we anointed Katharine's body in oil and wrapped her in silk. The staff lit a candle in the hospice window. My mother, and Katharine's godmother, Robin—three thousand miles westward in Vancouver—awoke in their beds, attuned to some new-sounding clock.

All the world should weep at the loss of such a lovely girl, Robin found herself dreamily thinking, as the curtains shifted and rustled in the shadows of that dawn.

✳

I remember holding my face to the wind when Katharine died, feeling the air, the coolness and fluidity, the urgency. Every day, wind in my face, capturing my attention in some fundamentally new way. I was aware of breath, of what the ancient Greeks called *pneuma,* of a soul-filled world. I gulped the air.

"Welcome to our tribe," someone said to me wryly that summer, speaking of the crazy shift in perspective that comes with grieving, and that is exactly how it felt. Suddenly there were people who understood how you could feel as if you were constantly gulping air. It was a bond that was fiercely intimate; even if we had nothing else in common, we had death in common now. It's less hard to imagine this being the basis for tribal belonging two hundred or five hundred years ago, when death and its rituals were shared. So much about it now seems taboo. The experience of grieving is so socially fractured. We have no universal consolation to offer, such as "Your father and sister are with God now." Instead, people feel awkward around you, while those who know all about your wild, unhinged reconfigurations say, "Yup, I get it, my friend." Stuff gets weird. You respond to new-sounding clocks, you gulp air.

For a subset of this tribe—perhaps half of its members—something else unites them as well. Even more quietly, almost invisibly: the sense that we have encountered a radical mystery. We have learned from the dying about additional channels of communication that we hadn't been aware of before, that enable us to know things in mysterious ways, to *connect* in mysterious ways with one another, with the dying and with the dead, along uncharted or long-forgotten paths.

The sense that the dying might open a door to us that leads elsewhere came first in hushed confidings. During the summer and fall of 2008, people began to tell me things. Some were friends and colleagues I'd known for years; others were people who sat beside me on an airplane or met me for the first time in a bar. If I told them what I'd witnessed with my father and sister, they reciprocated. Almost invariably, they prefaced their remarks by saying, "I've never told anyone this, but . . . " Or, "We've only ever discussed this in our family, but if you think you might do some research . . ." Then they would offer extraordinary stories about deathbed visions, sensed presences, near-death experiences, sudden intimations of a loved one in danger or dying. They were all smart, skeptical people. I had had no idea that this subterranean world existed all around me.

The director of a large music company drove me home from a dinner party, and when I explained that I was thinking of investigating what my family had gone through, he parked the car outside my house, not ready to say goodnight. He told me that, as a boy, he had come down to breakfast one morning and seen his father, as always, at the kitchen table. Then his mother broke the news that his father had died in the night. He briefly wondered if she'd gone insane. "He's sitting right there," he'd said. It was the most baffling and unsettling moment of his life.

On a hot summer afternoon I stood chatting with a woman on a sidewalk in Pittsburgh. We were waiting for some fellow tourists on a shared weekend trip to the Carnegie and Warhol Museums. I explained what had happened to me, and she nodded, then offered the story of her sister, who had woken one night to the sensation of glass shattering all over her bed, as if the bedroom window had been blown inward by a tempest. Adrenaline rushing, her sister leapt out of bed and felt around gingerly for the shards of glass she expected to find on her blanket. There was nothing there. The window was intact; all was quiet. The next day she learned that her daughter had been in a car accident in which the windshield had shattered. We spoke a little more, about another death in her family, and by the time the other tourists rejoined us, tears were filming her blue eyes. It struck me again how powerful and raw our experiences around death are, how carefully we keep them concealed and yet how close to the surface they stay.

In the late nineties, the palliative care physician Michael Barbato designed a questionnaire for family members of patients. He realized that neither his unit nor most other hospice facilities had ever formally investigated how common such experiences were. To his surprise, he found that 49 percent of his respondents had undergone an uncanny encounter that couldn't be easily explained away. "Even if we cannot understand the basis for these phenomena," Barbato argued in a subsequent journal article, "the weight of evidence suggests we cannot continue to ignore them." Certainly you cannot ignore them when they happen to *you*.

There is pain in loss. And then—in our culture—there is further pain in the silence born from fear of being dismissed or ridiculed when that loss entails something unexpectedly wondrous. Tell someone that your sister felt a presence in her bedroom on the night your father died, and at once the explanations come. Hallucination. Wishful thinking. Coincidence. And the implied condemnation: *Know what? Yer kinda credulous.*

I attended a Christmas party with old university friends, and caught up with a man I hadn't seen for years, who works in information technologies for a bank. I told him about losing Katharine and Dad, and some of what transpired. He said gently, "I don't mean to be unkind, but it is very likely that she was imagining all those things."

Walking home, I mused about why he had found it necessary to say that. Here was someone who hadn't taken a single psychology course in his life, as far as I knew, much less acquainted himself with hospice care, who felt he could speak with complete authority on the subject of what the dying see. More to the point, he had casually stripped the meaning from one of the most sacred moments in Katharine's life. Just like that. Would he have jumped up while she was speaking at my father's memorial service, this specialist in IT for banks, and said, *Oh, excuse me! I don't mean to be unkind . . .*

When I stopped feeling angry, I wondered how he explained away his days. We are meaning-seeking creatures. We dwell among stories and myths; we don't do well when we are chained all around by a materialist frame and then, for good measure, are labelled as fools when we grieve.

I love you, a man whispers to his new wife at their wedding reception. A scientist barges into the celebration. *Prove it!* she commands. *Prove that you love your wife. Do you have an MRI scan?*

Prove your anger, prove your empathy, prove your sense of humour. Nobody ever asks you to do that scientifically, of course, because love, anger, empathy and wit are considered common elements of human nature, even if they are not all that measurable beyond locating possible neural correlations. Spirituality used to be considered an ordinary part of the human experience as well, but now it qualifies as an extraordinary state requiring extraordinary evidence. Why should this be? It has nothing to do with what has been proved or disproved.

In 1979 a survey of more than 1,000 college professors in the United States found that 55 percent of natural scientists, 66 percent of social scientists and 77 percent of academics in the humanities believed that some sort of psychic perception was either a fact or a likely possibility. Only 2 percent felt it was outright impossible. This was before the rise of biological psychiatry in the 1990s and 2000s, and the deepening assumption that all human experience would be explained by understanding the workings of the brain.

In 1999 the psychologist Charles Tart put up a website called the Archives of Scientists' Transcendent Experiences, to serve as a place for scientists to anonymously confess their uncanny or spiritual experiences without risk of career blowback. Tart described it as a "safe space" for these scientists, as if they were admitting to a lifetime of boozing or wearing women's underwear. Engineers posted, chemists posted, mathematicians and biologists posted. These scientists, and many like them, put the lie to a very persistent belief that only credulous and sentimental people fall prey to certain imaginings. A recent study in the *British Journal of Psychology* showed that there is no difference in critical thinking skills between people who have had uncanny experiences and those who call themselves skeptics; other studies confirm this lack of difference.

The Princeton physicist Freeman Dyson wrote in 2007:

> If one believes, as I do, that extrasensory perception exists but is scientifically untestable, one must believe that the scope of science is limited. I put forward, as a working hypothesis, that ESP is real but belongs to a mental universe that is too fluid and evanescent to fit within the rigid protocols of scientific testing.

What he meant was that the tools we have designed to map the genome and determine what makes wheat grow cannot be applied here. The paranormal or spiritual experience comes unbidden. We cannot put my sister in a lab in California and wait for my father to die one more time.

Dyson received flack for his assertion, but, like many of us, he'd witnessed inexplicable phenomena within the confines of his own extended family. His grandmother, he wrote, was a "notorious and successful faith healer." A cousin of his had been the long-time editor of the *Journal for the Society of Psychical Research*. Skeptics warn that such people are either con artists or their credulous victims, and likely a few of them are. But when you know people—when you respect their intelligence, their groundedness; when you witness their discomfort with what they're picking up by unknown means—that characterization is simply unpersuasive. As Dyson said of his cousin and grandmother, "Neither of them was a fool." Nor are the people who have been coming out of the woodwork to tell me about what they encountered. Nor was my sister.

Private moments of conversion—from assuming that the universe operates by one set of rules to suddenly suspecting there might be other forces at play—can happen to people "like a jolt," as University of California psychiatrist Elizabeth Lloyd Mayer said after her own encounter with perception that seemed to draw on some unknown sense. In Mayer's case, the jolt came as a result of an act of clairvoyance, which is the ability to somehow glean information across a distance. Her daughter's rare and valuable harp was stolen near San Francisco in 1991; neither the police nor the family's public appeals managed to recover it. After several months, a friend suggested to Mayer that she had nothing to lose by consulting a dowser. "Finding lost objects with *forked sticks?*" Mayer scoffed. But her friend gave her the phone number of the president of the American Society of Dowsers, a man by the name of Harold McCoy, who lived in Arkansas.

"I called him that day. Harold picked up the phone—friendly, cheerful, heavy Arkansas accent." She told him she was looking for a stolen harp in Oakland, California, and asked, dubiously, if he could help her locate it. "Give me a second," he said. "I'll tell you if it's still in Oakland." He paused, then said, "Well, it's still there. Send me a street map of Oakland and I'll locate that harp for you." Mayer sent the map by express post. Two days later,

McCoy phoned back to tell her precisely which house in Oakland contained her daughter's harp.

Feeling as though she'd surely lost her mind, Mayer put up flyers within a two-block radius of this house, which was in a neighbourhood she was unfamiliar with. She soon received a phone call from someone who had seen the harp, and he was able to get it back to Mayer. "As I turned into my driveway [with the harp]," she later wrote, "I had the thought, *This changes everything.*"

Mayer needed to completely re-examine her understanding of how the world worked. After my father and sister died, I felt much the same way. I wanted to understand what we know and what remains unclear, unexplored, about these controversial modes of awareness. It wasn't enough for me, as a journalist, to accept the officially received wisdom. It certainly wasn't enough for me, as a sister, to ignore Katharine's intelligence and discernment and what she was willing to put on the line at our father's memorial service in favour of some information technology guy saying, *Oh, she was just making shit up.* Sorry, too much at stake here, in terms of defending her integrity and of respecting our collective experience.

So I tried to pursue these questions. Why had my sister had a powerful spiritual experience in the hour of my father's unexpected death? How did she sense a presence in her bedroom and feel hands cupping her head? Why did she enter into her own dying experience afraid, only to become increasingly joyful? What was she seeing, what was she learning, what would she have told me if she could have, after she could no longer converse?

What I learned in the ensuing few years was far richer and more mysterious than I ever imagined. By sharing it with you, I am hoping that I open a door.

WHAT THE DYING SEE

The Phenomenon of Nearing-Death Awareness

The dining room of the West Island Palliative Care Residence is, improbably, a rather cheerful place. When my sister lay dying, it was presided over by a budgie named Blueberry, who hopped from perch to floor to swing to wall and gabbled at all and sundry. On any given day, the sundry include several volunteers who sing along to light rock on the radio while they bake scones and whiz up fresh fruit smoothies for the dying to sip through straws. It has been three years since I ate the delicious soups and tourtières served here to shell-shocked families. Now I am back, in a calmer frame of mind, to talk to Monique Séguin, one of Katharine's nurses, about a phenomenon that hospice staff throughout North America call "nearing-death awareness."

Monique, a middle-aged woman with curly dark hair and an aquiline nose, had seemed bossy to us in our overwrought emotional state, as she shooed a crowd out of Katharine's room one afternoon so that my sister could rest. I even began a letter to her at the time, shouting via big, sloppy cursive handwriting that it was none of her business, that no one who was about to sleep forever needed to sleep in the interim. I never gave her the letter, and I'm glad of that. It would be months before I understood that hospice nurses and doctors see their patients differently than most families—brand new to dying—can see their beloveds themselves.

This wouldn't have been the case historically, when everyone was in agreement about the spiritual import of dying. But now nurses such as Monique find themselves becoming passionate advocates of the need to create a hushed, listening space around the dying, because they have learned from experience that the men and women in their hospice beds will begin to undergo subtle transformations in awareness and mood. Resting her elbows on the wooden dining room table, Monique tells me that most of the people she's cared for over the years have come to know, at a certain point, exactly when they will die. For the nurses this certitude is uncanny. "We all know we are going to die . . . one day," Teresa Dellar, director of the residence, told the Montreal *Gazette* in an article I found after Katharine died. "This is different."

Within roughly seventy-two hours of the end of their lives, many dying people in hospice settings begin to speak in metaphors of a journey. They are not being euphemistic—they are far beyond the task of making everyone feel better. They often haven't said a word in days, and then suddenly they say something focused on travel. They sincerely want to know where their train tickets or hiking shoes or tide tables are.

Monique offers me an example. "We had a patient who was agitated. It was a Friday evening. She keeps saying, 'I want to go shopping.' In life she was a real shopper. I said, 'When do you want to go shopping?' She said, 'Monday.' I said, 'Fine, let's go shopping Monday.' For me, she was telling me, 'I'm going.' And actually she died that Monday evening."

To families, the desire to go shopping on Monday would have been delusional talk, febrile mutterings of no importance. Far more significant to them, perhaps, would be the anticipated deathbed pronouncement, something for which they had a cinematic sense—a whispered "I love you" or "Take care of the children" before the head falls back upon the pillow. But hospice staff know that when their patients begin to talk about travel, they are announcing their departure. They do not behave like perishing characters in Hollywood movies. Instead of offering some eleventh-hour contemplation of their lives, they request tickets, or boats. Some ask for their coats, others inquire about the bus schedule. They're caught up in the busy preoccupation of leaving, not reflecting upon what they're leaving behind. In my sister's case she asked, "When am I leaving?" after dismissing her flight attendants as hapless. She asked it the way I might double-check my flight time to Newark.

David Kessler, chair of the Hospital Association of Southern California's Palliative Care Committee, has observed this phenomenon countless times, in his own work and in conversation with medical colleagues. "The notion of the dying preparing for a journey isn't new or unusual," he writes in his book *Visions, Trips and Crowded Rooms*, "although, interestingly enough, it's always referring to an earthly journey. People talk about packing their bags or looking for their tickets—they don't mention chariots descending from heaven or traveling to eternity in some other manner."

Kessler recalls a ninety-six-year-old man who suddenly woke up in his hospice bed and told his daughter, "Gail, it's time to go."

"Go where?"

"Out! Let's make a run for it—I have to be free."

"She didn't know what to say," reports Kessler. "She helped him sit up, as he seemed to want to get out of bed. 'Is the car ready?' he asked. When she assured him that it was right outside the hospice, he said, 'Good. I'm ready. Are you?' She asked him where they were going, and he said he wasn't sure. 'I only know that I've got this trip in front of me, and the time has come.' He decided to rest a bit before 'the trip,' and died that morning."

There is no known medical reason for the dying to have such an acute sense of timing about their demise. Palliative care conferences often devote sessions to how to improve doctors' ability to prognosticate about death. When patients make their announcement about going off on a trip, rarely are there physical signs of imminent decline, such as a marked deterioration in blood pressure or oxygen levels. On the contrary, the bodily symptoms take place afterwards. "I'm going away tonight," the soul singer James Brown told his manager on Christmas Day, 2006, one day after being admitted to hospital for a pneumonia that wasn't considered fatal—whereupon his breathing began to slow.

In the most comprehensive cross-national study ever done of deathbed experiences, the psychologists Karlis Osis and Erlendur Haraldsson confirmed that such intimations of departure occurred even in people who weren't considered by doctors to be terminally unwell. Here is a case reported by one of the physicians to the researchers:

> A male patient in his fifties was going to be discharged on the seventh day after an operation on a fractured hip. The patient was without fever and was not receiving any sedation. Then he developed chest pain and I was called to him. When I came, he told me he was going to die. "Why do you say so? Having a little pain in the chest does not mean you are going to die." Then the patient told how immediately after the pain in the chest started he had had a hallucination, but still remained in his full consciousness. He said he felt himself for a few seconds to be not in this world but elsewhere . . . "I am going," he said, and departed a few minutes later.

Paramedics see this puzzling interior knowledge displayed in their ambulances en route to hospital, as one explained on the radio program *Coast to Coast AM* with George Noory. "It's very unnerving," he said. "They know, for whatever reason. They have a prescience. It's a definitive feeling that they have that they are gonna die, and I would say 95 percent of the time they end up dying in front of me. And it's very disturbing to me." Why does he find it so disturbing? Because it eludes medical logic and thus defies his training. "There were many cases where, really, I did not think that they were ill enough, and then, for whatever rea-son, they would suddenly have a cardiac arrest and I would say, 'Oh my God, he told me this [was going to happen].'"

Is it a failure of modern medicine to document the mind–body processing of death? "My patient said, 'Yeah, I'm going to die today,'" a palliative physician recalled in a 2010 report in the *Canadian Medical Association Journal* about the impact of dying on the personal lives of doctors. But the physician thought, "There is no way that he should die . . . and [yet] he died within 48 hours. I marvel at that. There's a mystery there." His reaction, and that of the paramedic, apparently isn't unusual. "Several medical observers expressed amazement and surprise when confronted with cases in which patients died . . . despite good medical prognoses," reported the two psychologists who com-pared American and Indian dying experiences.

> For example, a patient in his sixties was hospitalized because of a bronchial asthmatic condition. His doctor's prognosis predicted a definite recovery. The patient himself expected to live and wished to live. Suddenly he exclaimed, "Somebody is calling me." He paused, for it caught him up short, but he tried to dismiss it at first, telling his family, no worries. But, within ten minutes, he had died.

Florida-based palliative psychologist Kathleen Dowling Singh has described this *way of knowing* as something akin to a transition in modes of consciousness. Sometimes it is fast, and so unexpected that there isn't time to understand what has hap-pened. Other times, with a slow terminal illness, it is like a dawning awareness that another realm awaits. She recounts sitting with a nurse colleague who was herself now dying, and apparently in a coma. Somewhat rhetorically, Singh asked the nurse how she was doing, patting her arm lightly. Surprisingly, the woman answered, "I'm halfway there." Writes Singh:

> I . . . will never know whether her words . . . referred to time—i.e., the unfolding of events from Saturday [when she was hospitalized] to Wednesday [when she died]—or whether they referred to her psycho-spiritual movement from tragedy to grace. I do know that she was referring to a process she was aware she was enduring and that that process had, for her, a referential beginning point and end point by which she could measure her halfway point.

Assuming that there is something about dying that is qualitatively different from any previous experience in a person's life, shouldn't that make the process unfamiliar, not measurably certain? Ask a woman giving birth to her first child if she knows what to expect moment by moment, if she can tell you with confidence that the baby will come "on Monday." Of course she can't. Why do some of the dying know when they will die?

"Does my wife understand about the passport and ticket?"

This question was put, in a hoarse whisper, to Maggie Callanan, a hospice nurse in Virginia, by a well-travelled man who was succumbing to the ravages of pancreatic cancer in the 1980s. She knew what he meant—*Does my wife understand that I'm about to die?*—but she couldn't account for the way he was asking, not at that early stage in her career. Callanan first started working with dying patients a scant decade after the hospice movement began, to provide families with an alternative to heavily medicalized hospital death. Trained as an ER nurse, she found that in the quieter realm of the home she could observe a distinctive pattern of behaviour in her dying patients that didn't correspond to the idiosyncratic nature of drug-induced hallucinations, which she had more commonly witnessed in hospital. But no one seemed to be discussing such behaviour in the nursing literature. The pioneering research of Osis and Haraldsson, which they'd published in 1977 in a book called *At the Hour of Death*, had been classified as parapsychology and didn't find its way into the hands of medical staff. The famed psychiatrist Elisabeth Kübler-Ross pioneered hospice care during this decade and had introduced the psychological concept of the five stages of dying, which was really more about overlapping states of mind: denial, anger, depression, bargaining and acceptance.

Callanan had read the Atlanta psychiatrist Raymond Moody's groundbreaking research on near-death experiences (NDEs), which he published in 1975. Certainly people in palliative care settings can have NDEs days or weeks before they actually die. But what Callanan and her colleague Patricia Kelley were observing didn't really have to do with Moody's classic account of losing consciousness, seeming to drift out of one's body, becoming immersed in a powerful white light, and the other features he described. This was more about what the dying saw and said and seemed to feel while still anchored in full consciousness, in this world. She began to canvass fellow hospice nurses and physicians to find out whether they had noticed these things as well. Uncanny foreknowledge of death's arrival? Visions of deceased friends and relatives in the room? A peaceful radiance? The use of language pertaining to a journey? Colleagues had certainly noticed these patterns but hadn't known what to think of them either. Elisabeth Kübler-Ross was making observations about this in lectures in the 1980s. "Suddenly someone will bid you farewell when you are not thinking that death will arrive soon," she said in a speech in Switzerland in 1982. (And this puzzled noticing continues: a 2009 study of five hospices and nursing homes confirmed that 62 percent of physicians and nurses had encountered what might be called paranormal "deathbed phenomena" during the study year, but many still considered it taboo to openly discuss what they had witnessed.)

Callanan and Kelley decided to frame what they had observed as a distinct state of consciousness, which they dubbed "nearing-death awareness." It was critically important to them that families understood what was being communicated by their dying loved ones, rather than dismissing potentially important messages by attributing them to medication or delirium. In 1992 the two nurses published a book titled *Final Gifts: Understanding the Special Awareness Needs and Communication of the Dying*. It is a bit like a modern *Ars moriendi*, a version of the treatises on the art of dying well that had once circulated through medieval Europe. Only here, Callanan and her co-author hoped, nurses and doctors would learn to watch for some of the psycho-spiritual transformations of dying that are no longer discussed in our culture.

A charismatic Irish-American with a keen sense of wit, Callanan continues to see herself as "death's best P.R. person," spreading enlightenment about what the dying process really entails, which she thinks is far less frightening than most of us tend to believe. "I think we have a moral, ethical and human responsibility to tell our stories, no matter how many times they fall on deaf ears."

Hospice nurse Monique Séguin agrees. "We have to create an opening to be able to listen. If you don't believe in that, well, you're doing your work as a nurse, but you're missing a few things." Making her rounds at the West Island Palliative Care Residence, Séguin now makes a point of asking her patients about their dreams. It is another way for them to convey how they feel, what they sense is coming. They've told her that they dream of riding in a yellow bus, uncertain of where their stop is; of floating in a sailboat on a calm pink sea. The woman who had that dream told Séguin, "My [deceased] father was in the boat. My father is coming to get me." Sometimes they dream of being unable to get their message through to their distraught family. A woman in her eighties dreamed of trying to jam a corn cob into a too-small opening, wild with frustration.

Whether they speak of a journey or through dream logic, Séguin tries to translate for the family when she can. "I remember we had a patient who kept telling her son, 'Take me home,' and he would just argue with her: 'Mum, you know you're too sick.' She would get more and more frustrated. One evening I tried to tell him, 'Maybe you should ask her, *Mum, when do you want to go home?* Maybe she's trying to tell you something.' He didn't listen, he was not interested." She smiles and gives a quick shrug. Staff, she says, "must tread on eggshells." The woman died a few days later.

One intriguing aspect of nearing-death awareness is the tendency for some of the dying to hallucinate visions of deceased family members, friends, and iconic spiritual beings in the days and hours leading up to death. Forty-one percent of the dying patients in a study done by University of Virginia psychologist Emily Williams Kelly in 2000 reported a "deathbed vision." Are these the kind of sensed presences my sister encountered on the night my father died, there to comfort imperilled, frightened souls? Fifty-four percent of staff in the five-hospice study had patients who had experienced a "visit" from a deceased relative very close to the time of death. Informally, nurses often use these visions as a gauge for impending demise.

"When a patient says that they have been visited by a dead loved one, you know that their time has come," Penny Sartori, a former critical-care nurse turned academic told me. She described the first time she encountered this phenomenon. "When I was a student nurse, I remember crossing over with the night shift, and they said, very matter-of-factly, 'So-and-so has been chatting with his dead mother for the last five hours, so he'll be off soon.' I thought they were joking: 'Are they saying that now because I'm new and they are trying to freak me out?' I kept going to check on him, and he *was* talking away to someone I couldn't see. He had a big smile on his face. He died later that day. That spooked me, but I soon realized it was common."

Dianne Arcangel, former director of the Elisabeth Kübler-Ross Center in Houston, recalls a case where she was paying regular visits to an octogenarian weakened by congestive heart failure. He wasn't at death's door, as far as anyone knew, but one day he had his daughter call Arcangel and ask her to come and see him. When she arrived at his house, he explained somewhat sheepishly that he'd had a visit from his long-deceased uncle. The relative wanted to reassure him that all would be well, and told him to "ask Dianne what it's like here. She knows." Arcangel was taken aback; she had had a near-death experience several years earlier, and had to assume that was what the apparitional uncle was referring to. Was it? Or did a mysterious hallucination collide accidentally with an enigmatic dream? Whatever was going on, she decided to describe her NDE to the patient, assuring him that he was destined for a beautiful place.

In Osis and Haraldsson's research, of the 10 percent of dying people who were conscious in the hour before death, the majority reported seeing such visions. Eighty-three percent of the visions were either of deceased people or of religious archetypes such as angels (in the United States) and death spirits (in India.) It isn't clear what the remaining 17 percent were—gnomes? elephants? pots of chocolate? But the dying have a clear orientation towards the spectral. Sixty-one percent of the patients in this study had received no medical sedation, and 20 percent had been given only weak doses.

"Such experiences can happen to patients who are convinced that they will recover and who are not at all ready to 'go,'" the researchers discovered.

A cardiac patient, a fifty-six-year-old male whose consciousness was clear, saw the apparition of a woman who had come to take him away. . . . he did not seem to be repulsed by [her], just slightly frightened." He said, "'There she is again, she is reaching for me.' He did not particularly want to go, but he did not make a fuss. He became calmer. This experience made him serene. He died a day later."

Searching for other correlations, Osis and Haraldsson determined that less than 10 percent of the patients had a high fever, which can ignite hallucinations. Twelve percent had a "hallucinogenic disease process" such as stroke, brain injury or uremic disease. But impaired cognition caused by such diseases "drastically reduced the number of benign apparitions," the researchers found. The more confused or medicated patients were, the *less* likely they were to perceive a consoling or beckoning presence. It is estimated that about half of all Americans who are dying enter (at some point) a state called "terminal restlessness," featuring agitation, anxiety and flickering psychosis. Some of the factors include organ failure and "opiate toxicity." Here I conjure the memory of my mother-in-law, ravaged by liver and kidney failure in a Nova Scotia hospital, cowering from the onrushing menace of black bears. Her disoriented anguish haunted my husband for months.

These two states of consciousness—nearing-death awareness on the one hand and terminal restlessness on the other— are radically different, for the former is experienced in an oriented and clear state of consciousness, imparts a profound sense of calm, and oftentimes features information about the time of departure. As one nurse in a U.K. hospice study described it,

> When they have a high temperature they see things and it's
> an anxiety-based thing. You can see there's an underlying
> fear because they don't understand it . . . Whereas with the
> end-of-life experience it's like a process and once they
> have experienced it, they move onto a different level. It's
> like a journey.

What does that mean? What process? It seems to be an
exposure to something, to some state or realm that profoundly—
radically—reassures and illuminates the path. In nearly 80 percent of Osis and Haraldsson's cases, the apparent purpose of the
deathbed vision was to accompany or take the patient away.
They didn't find a single instance of an apparition evincing this
"take-away" purpose when the vision involved a still-living person or animal. The bears that menaced my mother-in-law in
her toxin-induced psychosis did not turn around and invite her
across the River Jordan.

Pondering other angles, the two psychologists examined
what they called the "mirage effect." Could these visits from
sisters and uncles and angels be the kind of wishful projection
that a thirsty desert traveller conjures as a shimmering pool of
water? Unable to face self-obliteration, do the patients project a
companion to accompany them to the abyss? A couple of factors
made that a less straightforward explanation. Patients in a distressed or anxious state were less likely to see apparitions than
those in calmer moods, the data showed. Also, again, several
patients who had such visions hadn't expected to die.

Are families and staff who witness deathbed visions predisposed to see supernatural narratives and coax them along on any pretext? No. In fact, many families are primed in the opposite direction, by what our medical culture dictates to them as true. Consider the case of Barbara Cane, who provided this account to the neuroscientist Peter Fenwick: Cane was sitting with her ninety-year-old mother, who had been hospitalized for treatment of pneumonia in December 2005. The lady was lucid, her oxygen levels and blood pressure were stable, according to the nurses, and her family was discussing Christmas plans, among other subjects. At the same time, however, her mother became aware of "these people" who were in the room. She referred to them periodically as they apparently drew closer and closer to her bed—not in a menacing way, but gently and incrementally. Finally, Cane told Fenwick, "she said she wouldn't be there the next day, as 'these people' would 'pick her up when she fell and take her on a journey.'" The following day, which was Christmas Eve, the ill woman died. The Cane family hastened to reassure Fenwick: "We think that there is probably a medical reason why the dying hallucinate—poison in the brain, medical drugs or a lack of certain chemicals in the blood—but it was so strange that it was amidst totally normal conversation, and that she knew so much about her impending death."

What's strange, actually, is that we inhabit an era in human history when a family's response to their own observation that their mother wasn't dying alone is to reassure a doctor that there's a medical explanation.

*

One summer afternoon, I went to interview Audrey Scott, a woman I'd never met before. What connected us was that I was beginning to research this book and she was dying of cancer. She had invited me, through mutual friends, to come and talk with her. The afternoon was suffocatingly hot, and I found her tangled in a light sheet on a borrowed hospital bed in the middle of her living room, squeezed in between some creaky couches and piled-high tables, her face hidden beneath a cooling washcloth, her body as slight as a bird's. It felt as if the house she had lived in for decades was quietly absorbing her.

It was a cluttered bungalow in a tiny town, the property shaded by maple and pine, house cats languishing in the heat as an occasional car rumbled by. Audrey was fading in body—of a cancer metastasized to the bones—but at eighty-three she remained sharply aware. She was preoccupied, on the day I came, with getting a book she'd written about some early adventures in her life back from the local print shop before she lost consciousness forever. She wanted to approve the final version.

I pulled a hard wooden chair beside her bed and sat down. She lifted the washcloth slightly to appraise me with keen blue eyes. Her skin was smooth and translucent. The temperature was thirty-five degrees Celsius and her forehead shone with perspiration.

"I'm honoured that you've allowed me to come," I told her. We clasped hands and regarded one another frankly. Dying has a tendency to dissolve all pretension.

We spoke for a few minutes about her book, the unit cost of privately published books, and other pragmatic matters, as if we were meeting in a coffee shop rather than at her deathbed. "I don't want to just give my book to friends and family," she emphasized. "I want it to be a bestseller."

It was, apparently, a collection of her letters home from Europe when she was a college graduate making the grand tour. She'd titled it *Bobbies, Blisters and Beaux*. Later I would learn that her European tour had sparked in her a lifelong ardour for architectural history. She'd even created a colouring book featuring the Victorian-era buildings of Wayne Gretzky's hometown, Brantford, which was a few miles down the road.

Was this comment about bestsellerdom a genuine lunge for glory at the end of her life or a wry joke? There was no way for me to know. I was learning who she was just as she was taking her leave.

"What do you want people to know about dying, Audrey?" I asked.

"There should be no fear," she said without hesitating. (After the effort of discussing her book, she had repositioned the washcloth over her eyes and was beginning to cough.) She spoke declaratively, with a touch of impatience, hinting at a lifetime of answering the questions of her fourteen natural and adopted children. "Life is laid out from birth to death; it's all just part of the process."

"Are you experiencing . . . or seeing . . . anything unusual?" I wondered, having bugged out the night before trying to figure out how in the hell to word this question.

She eased the washcloth up onto her forehead and studied me, a note of caution in her expression. "I see things twirling in the room," she offered. "It's quite pleasant, actually." After a pause she added, "My son Frankie has been visiting me. He sits there." She gestured towards an armchair to my left.

Our mutual friend Judy, who had been standing discreetly near the window so as not to interrupt the conversation, reached up to the window ledge behind Audrey's head and selected an old seventies-era varnished frame containing the photo of a smiling young man with thick, square glasses and flat bangs. This was Frankie, a boy that Audrey and her husband had adopted after he'd been disabled in a car accident. He had died of cancer in 2002 at the age of thirty-five, Judy later explained.

I angled the frame towards Audrey so that she could see too, but she evinced no interest, clearly feeling no need for nostalgic glimpses in picture frames if the young man had been sitting right there in the armchair. I tried to find a clear table surface where I could set down the picture, to no avail. I held on to Frankie uncertainly.

"Is this a dream you are having, or are you awake?" I asked.

She shrugged, determined to remain pragmatic. "I don't think I can tell the difference with all this morphine."

"Is he talking to you?"

"We've been talking about my books." Audrey was the sort of person—and I can't say I've met many—whose curiosity was so intense that she seemed to be listening even when she was talking. She wasn't seeing or dreaming about anyone else, she said. Not her late husband or any of her living children or friends. No bears or Virgin Marys. For whatever reason, she was encountering Frankie.

I asked if there was anything she wanted to know about my research, whether she wanted me to describe, for instance, what

I knew at that point about near-death experiences. Her attention seemed to quicken, and she nodded. She wasn't much of a one for "Sunday school stuff," as she put it, but she hoped she was heading to a "place of well-being." Without pain. She studied me from beneath the washcloth. A cat wandered through the room. Cicadas kept up their whirring chorus in the yard.

I told her what others had conveyed about what they'd gone through on the brink of death, how the light felt encapsulating and loving, how it felt safe. At some point in this brief description, it occurred to me that I was vibrating. It was a curious sensation. It wasn't in my throat or voice, where grief lives, but more in my torso. It had the thrumming feel of an impersonal energy rather than the riled-up rush of nerves. I didn't— and still don't—know what to make of the sensation. We frame experiences almost instantaneously according to known categories. *This is nausea, this is anger, this is pain.* If a sensation doesn't immediately make sense to our brain, the nature of it quickly becomes elusive. Was it vibration or am I just assigning that description for lack of a better one? Maybe I was suffused with the gravitas of what I was saying, my responsibility to a dying woman who was regarding me with listening hope.

Later, a friend who had been volunteering in hospices described a weird sense of surrounding energy. He had almost passed out from it once, as did my sister's best friend at one point in the West Island Palliative Care Residence, come to think on it. She was massaging Katharine's temples and she suddenly realized that if she didn't sit down, hard, on the floor, she would faint. It's like being too close to a whirlpool or a rip tide. Maybe it has to do with the life force receding.

"Thank you for that, Patricia," Audrey said. "I'm going to have a nap now." Judy and I went out into her garden, carrying a box of her unpublished papers and books, which we sorted through in the shade. She had written and illustrated a number of small books about her adopted children. Her drawings were accomplished and charming, and the accompanying verses were sweet. I realized that she had devoted a large part of her life to refashioning the life stories of injured, broken people: a blind, mentally disabled child from India; a girl, now middle-aged, with the mental age of a six-year-old; Frankie. Had he come back now, to help her on her way to some new healing?

Audrey died, at her home, ten days later.

A year after the deaths in my own family, my mother and I flew to France. We landed in Paris, where Katharine had been born. My mother wanted to make a kind of pilgrimage; she needed to re-experience the trajectory of her daughter's life, and I was the witness. Here, on Rue de Bellechasse, was the flat where Mum found herself pregnant with her second daughter in the summer of 1957. Here was the little park she'd wheeled Katharine to in her pram. Here the narrow road where her "quicksilver child" had a first tantrum. And here was the school where my sister, ever charming, won a very French prize for *coquetterie*.

We took the train to Bordeaux and then drove to the limestone caves of mid-southern France where so many famous prehistoric paintings have been found. One morning the rain poured down as we scurried into the shelter of a cave and, shaking the wet out of our hair, looked around. This was a maw, a wide, shallow entrance to a cavern that penetrated for a mile into the rock body of France. There was a little electric cart to run us along tracks into the light-less interior, run by guides who periodically went insane, we were told, from their mole-like travels underground.

The trolley juddered from the entrance into the darkness, following a rickety track, every now and then whirring to a halt. The guide would disembark with her flashlight and illuminate the nearby cave walls. The pale beam of light showed that some-one had scratched graffiti on this rough limestone during the French Revolution. "Pierre was here"—that kind of thing. A shiv-ery spark of time warp. It was another half-mile into enclosing black before the true depth of history began to reveal itself in the dancing flashlight. Cave bears had built nests here, scraped-out hollows of stone wide as Jacuzzis. Seventeen thousand years ago, humans lay in these hollows and sketched brilliant, perfect art on the ceiling. The guide's flashlight washed back and forth across this ancient overhead and we stared wonderingly. The images above us were utterly commanding. Clean, bold lines—there is no redo option when you're working with charcoal on limestone by rag light. One chance only to evoke an aged mastodon with an obvious limp, a horse with an evident temper. Perspective, dynamism, a sort of Sistine Chapel of the natural world.

Who knows what their purpose was, doing art so profoundly deep in a cave. Had they seen the art at Chauvet, in France's Ardèche region, created at least fifteen thousand years earlier? The artists weren't amateurs, that much is clear. Some research now suggests that their drawings involved an early version of animation, with multiple legs etched in such a way that flickering torchlight would depict exquisitely fluid movement. These minds were intelligent. Later we visited France's museum of prehistory and saw an exhibit that argued that "cavemen" did not, in fact, galumph about with shaggy, indifferent hair. They had styled haircuts. Well, of course they did. If they could do art that way, and could carve and play ivory flutes, they could visually conceptualize style.

It hit me then, full force, that a great prejudice of our time is to assume that pre-Enlightenment humans were stupid. Caught up in a notion of evolution as some sort of linear progress from hunched-over dumbo to straight-backed citizen of the Age of Reason, we have lost the capacity to believe that the men and women who preceded us could actually have been observant and skeptical and humorous and wise. Thus it becomes possible for us to assume that spirituality was invented as a hedge against death anxiety by a superstitious populace. The idea that the spiritual world was evident to people—to the dying, to their families, to their shamans—lost traction in scientific minds. It was in France's limestone caverns that I began to wonder if that was based on evidence or prejudice. What do we *really* know about spiritual experience?

"When it comes to the mind," science journalist Jeff Warren, who has written extensively about neuroscience and consciousness, told me, "we just do not know whether the brain is a producer or a transmitter. Does the brain generate the mind, like a lamp produces light? Or is it more like a prism or a lens, refracting a pre-existing phenomenon into the full spectrum of our personality? Many philosophers have argued that it is at least theoretically possible that 'mind'—the capacity for experience—is some sort of fundamental cosmic property, like space or time. There is nothing about neural activity, per se, that can tell us which of these types of functionality is true."

So how do we pursue the inquiry? The earliest scientific investigators, at least those for whom we have records, weren't trying to determine the soul's existence. They took that for granted; what interested them was where it was anchored. Where was the "prism" or "lens"? In the third century BCE, the Greek physician Herophilus of Alexandria became the first known man to dissect a human corpse out of pure curiosity. Part of his mission was to find the locus of the soul. He decided that it was in the fourth ventricle of the brain. This was a radical departure from the classic Egyptian understanding, that the heart contained the soul. The heart-centric view was the basis upon which mummified corpses had their (irrelevant) brains pulled out while their hearts were carefully kept within them, to be weighed by the god Anubis.

In the first century CE, Emperor Hadrian asked Rabbi Joshua ben Hananiah to show him the "soul bone" that some Jewish spiritual authorities claimed existed. It was called the *luz*, this bone, and was located somewhere along the spine. The hallmark of the *luz* was that it was indestructible.

"He had one brought," Hadrian later wrote, "and put it in fire, but it was not burnt. He put it in a mill, but it was not ground. He placed it on an anvil and struck it with a hammer. The anvil was broken and the hammer was split, but all this had no effect on the *luz*." This account caused men for several centuries to hunt for the *luz*, at various times nominating the sacrum, the coccyx and the sesamoid bones of the big toe.

In the second century, the Roman physician Galen, a doctor to gladiators (he peered into their stabbed torsos when he could), theorized that the soul animated consciousness in a manner that was mechanically similar to how Roman bathhouses were heated. Humans drew into themselves with their breath the soul force of the world, and this *spiritus* flowed through pipes and organs and was heated and cooled and performed various functions such as digestion.

René Descartes devoted hundreds of hours to rummaging around in the carcasses of cows looking for the precise whereabouts of the soul. At length he decided that it resided (or was somehow received and transmitted) via the pineal gland, which we now understand to govern levels of melatonin in the body. Descartes believed that spirit flowed to and from the pineal gland through a nervous system that he modelled on a church organ, with microscopic bellows.

The early nineteenth-century anatomist Franz Gall of Vienna was one of the first to theorize that consciousness was more diffusely located. His hunch was right but his details were a bit off. He proposed, for example, that there were twenty-seven distinct organs in the brain, including an "organ of poetical talent," an "organ of metaphysics" and an "organ for the instinct for property-owning and stocking up on food." Whichever organs were most developed would place outward pressure on the skull and create telltale bumps. Gall had a collection of 221 skulls, which he used to demonstrate his vision. As evidence for the location of the "organ of belief in the existence of God," he cited a series of Raphael paintings in which Christ appears to have a noticeable prominence at the crest of his cranium. His theories led to the explosive popularity of phrenology.

In the mid-nineteenth century, an enterprising American doctor named Duncan MacDougall decided to try to locate the soul by weighing it. He managed to procure the co-operation of some patients dying of tuberculosis in a home for consumptives in Dorchester, Massachusetts. As death approached his first subject, he moved the patient to a cot mounted on a scale and then waited patiently for the last exhaled breath, whereupon his eyes shot to the needle on his giant scale. The soul, he determined, weighed three-quarters of an ounce (hence the Hollywood movie *21 Grams*).

At around the same time, in the mid- to late nineteenth century, other investigators began to turn the question on its head. Instead of assuming that the soul existed and trying to locate it physically, they tried to prove that it existed at all. To do this, they turned to inferential observations. The nearest analogy in terms of scientific measurement is probably the methods used in astronomy. Men and women peering through telescopes don't actually see black holes. They infer their existence by observing that something is exerting a massive gravitational pull on planets and stars in certain parts of the universe. What could it be? Likewise, palliative care doctors and researchers are observing that something is having an effect upon dying people, and that something is inconsistently related to medication, body chemistry or any given psychological state. What, then, is it?

✳

The first modern report of deathbed visions was written by Lady Florence Barrett, a pioneering feminist obstetrician who was married to a physicist at the Royal College of Science in Dublin. On January 12, 1924, Lady Barrett attended the birth of a child whose mother, Doris, lay dying from complications and blood loss. "Suddenly," Lady Barrett later wrote,

> she looked eagerly towards one part of the room, a radiant smile illuminating her whole countenance. "Oh, lovely, lovely," she said. I asked, "What is lovely?"
>
> "What I *see*," she replied in low, intense tones.
>
> "What do you see?"
>
> "Lovely brightness—wonderful beings." It is difficult to describe the sense of reality conveyed by her intense absorption in the vision. Then—seeming to focus her attention more intently on one place for a moment—she exclaimed, "Why, it's Father! Oh, he's so glad I'm coming, he is so glad. It would be perfect if only W. [her husband] would come too." Briefly, Doris reflected to those in the room that she should, perhaps, stay for the baby's sake. But then she said, "I can't—I can't stay; if you could see what I do, you would know I can't stay."

At this point Doris saw something that confused her: "He has Vida with him," she told Lady Barrett, referring to her sister, whose death three weeks earlier had been kept from her because of her advanced pregnancy. "Vida is with him," she said wonderingly.

Hearing about this experience from his wife, Sir William Barrett decided to investigate formally. He solicited written accounts of Doris's apparent vision from Lady Barrett; an attendant nurse; the resident medical officer, Dr. Phillips; Matron Miriam Castle; and Doris's mother, Mary Clark of Highbury, all of whom had been in the room. The descriptions corroborated one another, which prompted Sir William, by this time retired from the Royal College of Science, to pursue other cases, which he published as a compendium in 1926, titled *Deathbed Visions*. It was this book that later inspired psychologists Osis and Haraldsson to compare American and Indian deathbed visions. (Like most people who come to this research, Osis's own experience with such a phenomenon originally motivated him to study the dying. As a teenager in Lithuania, he had witnessed the deathbed visions of his aunt.) Ever since, research interest seems to have proceeded in dialectical waves: a wave of scholarly curiosity in the late nineteenth and early twentieth centuries, followed by a wave of backlash; a wave of inquiry in the 1960s and '70s, then another wave of backlash.

One phenomenon that caught attention originally in the burgeoning insane asylums of the nineteenth century was "terminal lucidity," a state of consciousness in which patients with severe chronic mental illness or dementia suddenly become clear just before death. Their psychotic or amnesiac symptoms resolve. They recognize family members for the first time in years. They are able to orient themselves and to say goodbye. Several alienists, as asylum doctors were then called, made careful note of this, in Germany, France, and America. Then discussion disappeared until a paper on the phenomenon was published in the USSR in the 1970s. Nurses and physicians began to notice it after hospice treatment became more common in the United States.

Elisabeth Kübler-Ross corresponded with Karlis Osis about their shared observations of schizophrenics and stroke patients who suddenly became oriented, direct, crisp, the timing ranging from an hour to a day before they died.

In 2007, the physician Scott Haig wrote an account of his patient David, who had lung cancer that spread profoundly and aggressively to the brain. David's speech grew slurred and then he became incoherent. As the cancer cells replaced normal brain tissue he lost the ability to speak, and ultimately to move. A brain scan done by his oncologist showed that there was scarcely any brain left. "The cerebral machine that talked and wondered, winked and sang, the machine that remembered jokes and birthdays and where the big fish hid on hot days, was nearly gone," wrote Haig, "replaced by lumps of haphazardly growing gray stuff." *Lung* cancer cells. For days, his patient had "no expression, no response to anything we did to him."

When Haig made evening rounds one Friday, he noticed that David had lapsed into what is known as agonal breathing—the gulping and gasping that accompanies the active dying process. But, an hour before David's death, he woke up, and talked calmly and coherently with his wife and three children, smiling and patting their hands, before returning to his dying.

As Haig wrote, "It wasn't David's brain that woke him up to say good bye that Friday. His brain had already been destroyed." So what was it?

In another example, reported by the psychiatrist Russell Noyes, a ninety-one-year-old woman had lost her capacity for speech and movement as a result of two strokes. Yet she suddenly broke through those walls before her death. She smiled excitedly, turned her head, sat up without effort, raised her arms and called out happily to her deceased husband. Then she lay back down and died. Whether or not she was hallucinating her husband, the far more difficult and astonishing fact for observers to explain was that she'd regained her speech and mobility.

Colorado hospice physician, Pam Kircher, wrote about her first encounter with terminal lucidity in the 1990s, although she didn't have a label for it when it occurred (with a patient who had advanced dementia) because nothing in her medical training had alerted her to the possibility. "That was a very important learning experience for me," she recalled. "I had always assumed that someone that demented would not be able to have any other human contact in this lifetime."

Hospice care still serves only a portion of the dying population, although it has been steadily increasing since Maggie Callanan and Patricia Kelley coined the term *nearing-death awareness* in 1992. That year, 28 percent of dying Americans were able to pass away in a hospice setting. By 2011, 44.6 percent had done so. The United Kingdom lags behind: less than 20 percent of British citizens passed away in non-hospital settings in 2008. In Canada it's about 30 percent. Nevertheless, slowly, the hospice movement is beginning to return families to a forgotten experience of intimate death, and those families, along with attending staff, are starting to challenge twentieth-century assumptions arising out of the machine age.

Interestingly, we may owe something *to* the machine age for this shift. What differs at the twenty-first-century deathbed from previous centuries is the level of medical and pharmaceutical expertise in pain control. We may well be entering a unique period in human history, where we can calm distress without damaging alertness. The dying may finally be able to convey to us what they are feeling, and where they have glimpsed themselves to be going.

And who is telling them where they are going? That is the next question, as unsettling as it must be. Is it the dead? What actually happened on that early spring night when my father died?

SIGNALS AND WAVES

Uncanny Experiences at the Moment of Death

A humid night in summer; no sounds but the incandescent humming of the street lamp, the tick of an invisible clock on an antique dresser. Ellie Black rouses quietly to consciousness at around three, her eyes unfocused, mind placid. Not time to get up yet, nothing troubling her sleeping child. There is a smell of August grass and last evening's cigarettes. In the stillness, a movement at the end of her bed commands her attention. There, amazingly, she sees her father. Why is he here, she wonders with fully quickened alertness, this difficult man from whom she's so long been estranged? Why here, in her bedroom? And what on earth is he wearing? Is that a top hat and tails? Her father gazes back at her happily, tips his hat

53

and bows with a flourish. He is bidding her—his audience?—some sort of farewell. Then he's gone. She blinks. Her bedroom reverts to shadow and silence.

The following morning, Ellie relayed the experience—whatever it was, perhaps a waking dream—to her daughter at the breakfast table. My childhood friend Michele remembers that breakfast conversation with her mother clearly, because she was so surprised when the phone rang later that day, bringing news of her grandfather's demise.

That seeming whisper across the universe, a susurration or hint transmitted by some unknown current, the way birds bend their wings in unison or ants follow their invisible queen: humans clearly and repeatedly encounter some kind of unexplained attunement. Research done in Wales, Japan, Australia and the United States shows that between 40 and 53 percent of the bereaved experience "anomalous cognition" when someone close or connected to them has died. Usually this takes the form of sensing a presence, or sometimes seeing or hearing one. Psychiatrists call these experiences "grief hallucinations," although they have never been studied neurologically. Then there are the intimations received as the first signal, the gleaning before the knock on the door. An estranged father at the foot of the bed. We don't know what to call those.

In 1991 the British neurosurgeon J. M. Small wrote to the medical journal *The Lancet* to describe a perplexing experience he had had. "Sir," he began, "what are those waves of communication, that extra sense not yet understood? Something remarkable happened to me." He went on to describe a Sunday morning:

when crossing the hall to the kitchen to make tea, a pre-sentiment of doom beset me and I feared we had been' burgled. When I opened the kitchen door all appeared normal, but then there seemed to be a curious descending dark shimmer in the far part of the kitchen, immediately gone—but I knew it was death and female. I thought some catastrophe to one of our daughters-in-law. Disturbed by these suppositions and deciding not to tell my wife, I made the tea and took the tray to the bedroom. As I reached the bedroom, the doorbell rang and I was not surprised to see the village policeman.

One of the two elderly sisters who lived next door to Small had just died in hospital. The policeman had received the message on his radio and thought Small or his wife might know the surviving sister and could help him break the news. Small was shocked. Why him? Had the dying sister been trying to recruit his help for the living one? "Was that the cry? My wife and I did have to support the sister, a woman we did not know who had a considerable disability." To the *Lancet*, he concluded:

As a neurosurgeon my mind has been pragmatically directed and I had had no interest in telepathy or extrasensory perception. Here was the reception of information from a source I did not know nor comprehend when it declared its nature, female death . . . For me to have received such a message remains astonishing. It would be valuable if declared telepathic communicators could be investigated by scanning and electroencephalography to find which areas of the brain are involved with inception, reception, and onward conscious recognition. There was a message in my mind. How it reached there is not defined; although at first confused with fear, it was so very clear.

In 2012, psychologist Erlendur Haraldsson reported a comprehensive study he had done on 340 cases of extraordinary encounters around dying and death. They had happened to men, to women, to young and old, to scientists and sailors, to the bereft and to the content. They happened at night and in the day, waking or napping, travelling or working. Most commonly, people encountered their fathers or mothers, as if the parental impulse to connect and to reassure continues past death. About a quarter of his subjects saw or heard the deceased person either at the hour of death or within the day. In 86 percent of those cases, they hadn't yet become aware of the death by ordinary means. Thirty-eight percent of the subjects had not considered that such an encounter was even possible.

A musician, Rory McGill, sent me a letter that captured this sense of being absolutely mystified and at the same time moved by the symbols and portents of spirit. "The night my dad died," he wrote,

I dreamed about him passing. I had last seen him three weeks prior. He had suffered something like a stroke. He was unable to speak or otherwise communicate, apart from some signs of recognition in his eyes, and the touch of his right hand. He was also completely naked, lying under a sheet, for his own comfort, and his scalp was shaved clean on one side for medical purposes. So, he had a striking new look, which remains vivid in my mind's eye today.

When I left to return to university, the doctor's prognosis was for a fairly good recovery. Three weeks later, I dreamed of my father. He was lying on a hospital bed, on top of the sheets, and he was wearing beautiful new yellow pajamas. Rich yellow, like the color of zucchini flowers. And he had a full head of hair. I was delighted. I climbed on to the bed and held him in my arms, but in an instant I was standing alone in the room, he was gone and the bed was now empty and neatly made, set in a different corner. The beautiful new yellow pajamas were folded on the pillow.

I woke up perplexed by the dream but, strange to say now, I didn't make much of it. It didn't trouble me much, oddly, but stayed in my head and colored my day somewhat. When I returned to the rooming house in the late afternoon, I found a handwritten note pinned to the front door. It said, RORY CALL YOUR MOTHER.

I went immediately back down the street to the nearest phone booth with my heart speeding and my throat beginning to close. I dialed my mum's phone number and my head started to spin. I had no conscious idea of what would come next as the phone rang, but then the instant she picked up at the other end, I started to sob and I just knew. My dad had died while I slept and dreamed of one last visit.

Cross-cultural surveys show that "about half of all spontaneous [telepathic] experiences occur in dreams, and many of them involve accidents or the death of a family member," according to

Dean Radin, a scientist at the Institute for Noetic Sciences in Petaluma, California, who is arguably the most accomplished investigator of psi phenomena in the world today. (*Psi*, short for *psychic*, refers to a number of cognitive abilities that can't be accounted for through identified senses, including clairvoyance, telepathy and precognition. Don't look these up on Wikipedia, because there's an interesting cultural subplot going on at the moment in which paranormal topics are edited by activist skeptics in a manner that presents them as having been officially debunked.) Odds against chance in a review of spontaneous telepathy studies have been calculated, Radin says, at "22 billion to 1." Meaning that it *could* be a coincidence that you had that particular dream on the day when someone you loved died . . . but it is very, very unlikely.

"I've never experienced that sort of communication so intensely before or since," Rory concluded in his letter, "but it made it abundantly clear to me, for all time, that the signals and waves are transmitting."

In the late nineteenth century, the German psychiatrist Hans Berger, creator of the electroencephalogram (EEG), was prompted along the path towards his invention because he wanted to locate the "psychic energy" that had somehow enabled his sister to know when he was almost run over by a horse-drawn cannon, a day's distance from where she lived. Picking up on her brother's acute terror in the moment of near collision, she had been abruptly beset by an urgent certitude that her brother was in danger. She begged their father to contact him, refusing to relent until he sent an inquiring telegram. Berger was fascinated by his sister's response. Do we have a form of consciousness—a way of knowing—that has yet to be charted? he wondered.

In 1929 Berger unveiled the first technique for "recording the electrical activity of the human brain from the surface of the head," using electrodes to detect and transmit to a graph electrical signals, or brainwaves. Because he was a relative unknown within German medical circles, he was greeted with skepticism, but his measurement technique was eventually tested by others and was soon in use around the world, laying the foundation for modern neuroscience. It would be another three decades before the EEGs of distance-separated twins were studied and tentatively found to correlate. Berger would have been thrilled, but it was to be several decades more before those twin studies were considered even remotely reputable.

One of the first twin studies showed that when one twin being monitored by EEG was asked to close his or her eyes, which causes the brain's alpha rhythms to increase, the distant twin's alpha rhythms also increased. Twin studies using the EEG were subsequently performed more than a dozen times, with refining of protocols and controlling for design flaws, and they continued to confirm subtle correlations in the brains of the separated siblings. In 2013, a study of British twins found that 60 percent reported telepathic exchanges, and 11 percent of identical twins described themselves as having frequent exchanges with their sibs, including shared dreams. What can science contribute to those claims? After reviewing the methodology of all the EEG experiments done over a decade or so, Czech neurophysiologist Jiří Wackermann concluded in 2003: "We are facing a phenomenon which is neither easy to dismiss as a methodical failure or a technical artifact, nor understood as to its nature." What, indeed, is its nature? How else to get at this question?

In the early 1960s, University of Virginia psychiatrist Ian Stevenson began to investigate what he referred to as "telepathic impressions." Like Hans Berger, he was interested in determining how it was that people could know that someone emotionally close to them but physically distant was dying or in distress. Unlike Berger, he hadn't had such an experience himself, at least that we know of, but he was aware that the Rhine Research Center, established by Duke University in North Carolina in the 1920s, had collected and archived thousands of such "spontaneous psi" cases. The Rhine Research Center is generally better known for its efforts to study telepathy through controlled experiments such as card-guessing games. But its researchers have also been interested in spontaneous cases that arise from the rough, swift-moving emotions of human life. Stevenson wanted to know more about the collection. What did the cases mean? Could they be verified and analyzed? Would a pattern emerge?

A quiet and meticulous scholar, originally from Montreal, who would go on to head the University of Virginia's Department of Perceptual Studies, Stevenson decided to start by reviewing the first collection of spontaneous telepathy cases known to have been investigated: 165 reports published in the late nineteenth century by Cambridge scholars Frederic Myers and Edmund Gurney. One of the criteria that Myers and Gurney used for including cases in their book was that some action had to have been taken because of the experience, but *before* the corresponding event was learned of through conventional channels—for instance, suddenly declaring before others, "So-and-so has died!" in advance of the news arriving by cable or messenger, or insisting on sending an inquiring telegram, as Hans Berger's sister had. Myers and Gurney felt that such actions were a means to validate the report.

They also included rare cases of collective perception they had come upon; for example, a man and his son simultaneously saw the face of the man's father near the ceiling of their parlour at precisely the time (they later learned) that the father had died. The man's wife witnessed the reactions and comments of her husband and son, although she did not herself perceive anything unusual. Another instance of shared perception involved distress—a storm at sea—rather than death. This one was investigated by Edith Sedgwick: "Mr. Wilmot and his sister Miss Wilmot," the researchers reported,

> were on a ship travelling from Liverpool to New York, and for much of the journey they were in a severe storm. More than a week after the storm began, Mrs. Wilmot in Connecticut—worried about the safety of her husband—had an experience while she was awake during the middle of the night, in which she seemed to go to her husband's stateroom on the ship, where she saw him asleep in the lower berth and another man in the upper berth looking at her. She hesitated, kissed her husband, and left.
>
> The next morning Mr. Wilmot's roommate asked him, apparently somewhat indignantly, about the woman who had come into their room during the night. Miss Wilmot [the sister on board] added her testimony, saying that

the next morning, before she had seen her brother, the roommate asked her if she had been in to see Mr. Wilmot during the night, and when she replied no, he said that he had seen a woman come into their room in the middle of the night and go to Mr. Wilmot.

This would, of course, have seemed terribly inappropriate in the mid-nineteenth century. *A woman in their room?* Good heavens. Mrs. Wilmot, back in Connecticut, was equally bothered by the impropriety: "I had a very vivid sense all the day of having visited my husband. I felt much disturbed at his [the man in the upper berth's] presence, as he leaned over, looking at us." Still, the experience or dream or whatever it was seems to have moved her. "The impression was so strong that I felt unusually happy and refreshed."

In carefully reviewing such collected curios from nineteenth-century England, Stevenson found that Myers and Gurney's cases were distributed roughly equally between men and women. Eighty-nine percent occurred when the person was awake rather than dreaming or dozing. (Oliver Sacks steps lively over this research in his recent book *Hallucinations*, noting simply that "one suspects" the percipients were mostly snoozing. They were not.) Two-thirds of the gathered cases involved news of an immediate family member. Eighty-two percent pertained to death or a sudden illness or accident (or, in the Wilmot case, a storm). People did not, apparently, pick up on one another's good tidings. "Is it that the communication of joy has no survival value for us, while the communication of distress has?" Stevenson wondered. It was impossible to know.

In assessing thirty-five of his own, contemporary cases, Stevenson discovered that a third involved violent death, whereas only 7.7 percent of all deaths in America that year (1966) had been violent in nature. (His findings were replicated in 2006, when researchers for a study in Iceland again found a dramatically higher number of abrupt or violent deaths in telepathic impression cases.) Perhaps, Stevenson mused, there was something in the emotional quality of the event—a thunderclap of fear or pain—that carried like a sound wave across water.

Stevenson was careful with the cases that he chose to research himself. He excluded "instances of repeated gloomy forebodings which on one occasion happened to be right." He refused to consider accounts without witnesses who could confirm what the person had felt or seen. He interviewed those involved separately, then cross-referenced their descriptions of what had happened. In more than half the instances, "the percipient's impression drove him or her to take some kind of action apart from merely telling other people about it." A phone call, a frantic trip, an abrupt change of holiday plans. One woman drove fifty miles home in the middle of the night after suddenly sensing that her teen daughter was in urgent trouble; it turned out that their house had been broken into by armed intruders while the daughter was inside.

A South Carolinian named Janey Acker Hurth provided Stevenson with this account:

When my five-year-old daughter came home from a birthday party, she was disappointed to find that her father and brother had gone to the Walt Disney movie without her.

The Rivoli Theatre is a block and half away. I told Joicey that her father expected her to join them there, so she waved goodbye and skipped towards the corner. I returned to the dinner dishes still unwashed in the kitchen sink. Quite suddenly while I held a plate in my hand an awesome feeling came over me. I dropped the plate. For some unexplainable reason, I knew Joicey had been hit by a car or was going to be. I was quite conscious of her involvement in an accident. I immediately went to the telephone, looked up a number, and shakily dialed the theater. I gave my name and said, "My little girl was on the way to the theater. She has had an accident. Is she badly hurt?"

The girl answering the telephone stammered, "How did you know?" Joice Hurth was not seriously injured in the accident. She later wrote her own letter to Stevenson: "I was so terrified [as it happened] . . . I made a silent plea for my mother." Was the child's plea important, Stevenson wondered, to whether her mother caught wind of the event? Reviewing the cases, he found that it wasn't crucial that the "agents" be focusing on the percipients in terms of the latter picking up their signal of distress, but it did affect whether the percipients took action. Notably, they responded to cries for help.

How people can feel confident about the telepathic impression they receive is a further mystery. Stevenson found that a "feeling of conviction" was one of the characteristics that separated telepathic impressions from ordinary dreams and anxious imaginings, but it's hard to imagine what that feels like if you haven't experienced it. In a series of email exchanges with a businessman from northeast England, I explored this feeling of conviction.

When he was twelve, Max Bone had a vivid and distinctive nightmare that spurred him to do something that remains unique in his life experience. The dream concerned a house his father had bought, which he was planning to convert into an office. "I awoke in terror," Bone told me, "in the early hours of one morning, after having what seemed like a nightmare, but the content of which had a noticeably different and unusual quality."

It had been very windy that night, and I had dreamt that I was outside the rear of this property in Borough Road, standing on the pavement and facing directly towards the rear yard gate. This green-painted wooden-panelled yard gate off the street was unfastened and was opening, then banging shut, again and again in the wind. I approached the gate and the gate opened; the peeling paint and grain of the grey and denatured timber was shown in incredible detail. As the gate swung open, revealing the small back yard, I noticed that the white half-panel kitchen door had been pushed completely open, leaving just a dark rectangular hole in the wall. The top pane of the small kitchen window was also broken, and partly open. As I moved through the open gate and across the yard towards the empty door, fear started to build in me. My vision centred on the small kitchen step. As I reached the threshold I was looking right down at the step, and the fear became incredible, and as I began to cross the threshold I woke up in terror.

The next morning (I believe it was a Sunday morning), I still recalled the dream in detail, and I did something unusual—I acted on the dream (I have never acted on a dream before or since this event). I immediately went downstairs and told Dad about the dream whilst he was having his breakfast. I explained the dream's unusual quality, and made clear that I believed that something had happened to the property, pestering him to drive over to it immediately.

Dad finished his breakfast and decided to indulge me, as he hadn't checked on the house for a while anyway. My two elder brothers, overhearing the story and I think sensing something exciting, wanted to come along too. So my dad, myself and my brothers drove over to the house. We pulled up at the rear of the property, opposite the green gate, which was indeed blowing open and shut in the wind. When we all saw this, both my brothers turned to look at me in the car and pulled 'spooky' faces at me.

We left the car and entered the back yard through the gate, to find the kitchen door wide open; it had been pushed right back against the kitchen units so that it was not visible, just like in my dream. The top pane of the kitchen window was also broken and slightly open, again just as in my dream. We entered the house to find water gushing through the ground floor ceilings, and the beginnings of mould on the dining room carpet.

It became clear that the house had been broken into some days before, and the thieves had been returning to remove fixtures, fittings and lead piping over some period of time. We secured the house and turned off the water. Dad refused to talk about the incident for many years, although he does talk about it now. My two brothers found the whole affair creepy and unsettling and recall [it] to this day.

"I have thought deeply about the incident for the whole of my life, and drawn the best conclusions I can to explain it." Bone keeps an eye on theories and speculations in paranormal and neurological research, and he is convinced that there is something in the electromagnetic field that enables thoughts and perceptions to travel between minds. He doesn't think he literally went out-of-body in his dream; he suspects that he saw, somehow, what the thieves saw, tapping into their perception of the back of the house. He does not accept that the dream was a coincidence. I pressed him about why he couldn't accept it as coincidence:

My dreams tend to be sort of softer, still plenty of visual detail but they don't have the hard-edged detail of this dream. I had absolutely no problem in recalling the dream and remembering I needed to do something about it. That's not typical in my experience. It was almost as if the memory had been lodged somewhere it shouldn't really be lodged. Almost as if "raw" unprocessed imagery had been laid down, accidentally bypassing my normal visual pre-processing, having what I considered to be almost silly levels of recorded detail, like the peeling paint on the gate.

As the sole inhabitants of our heads, we are generally the best judges of a strikingly different perception. It is invariably the clarity and specificity of the impression that seems to prompt people to act.

Ian Stevenson found that there were two other factors that made people sit up, wide-eyed, and reach for the phone or the pen. One was if the agent—the person in crisis—specifically focused on the percipient during the moment of danger. This seemed particularly true for parents responding to children, although that would make sense, because children would be most likely cry out to an absent parent. The second factor was, possibly, a higher degree of gift for picking up such signals in the first place; a number of his cases involved people who had formed "telepathic impressions" at key moments more than once.

Janey Acker Hurth, for example, who sensed her daughter's imminent collision with a car, also twigged to her father's sudden and critical illness. "It must have been sometime after midnight, January 23," she said,

> when I awakened with a feeling of deep sadness, an impression that something was wrong. I did not want to disturb my husband, so for a long while I stared wide-eyed at the ceiling of the bedroom, which was barely visible in a dim, shadowy light. I remember the terrible ache in my heart. I started to cry and sobbed softly into my pillow. My husband was immediately awake and asked many questions, to which I had no answers. I repeated over and over to him that I had a feeling that something was wrong. His

efforts to console me were futile and I did not sleep the rest of the night.

This experience took place three months into the marriage, when the Hurths were visiting his parents.

The next morning when we went downstairs to breakfast, my in-laws were shocked at my appearance—swollen red eyes and haggard expression. They accused us of having had a "lover's quarrel," but I assured them that this was not the case. I told them I had no explanation for my mood of depression. They were much concerned. I put bread into the toaster, and while waiting for it I suddenly wheeled around and exclaimed, "It's my father! Something is terribly wrong with my father!"

A phone call to her parents' house within moments of this exclamation confirmed her sense that she was homing in on the matter. Her father, her mother said on the phone, had fallen into a coma after his kidneys failed in response to a sulpha drug (he died shortly afterwards). Stevenson was struck by how information sometimes gradually came into focus for people. "The percipient's mind," he mused, "may scan the environment for danger to his [or her] loved ones and, when this is detected, 'tune in' and bring more details to the surface of consciousness."

Stevenson's findings from the 1960s are echoed in cases collected three decades later by British neuropsychiatrist Dr. Peter Fenwick, of King's College, London. A long-time specialist in epilepsy, he has an abiding curiosity about unusual perceptions and experiences around death, sparked when one of his patients described a near-death experience. Fenwick, now in his late seventies, has amassed more than two thousand accounts of what he calls "death-bed coincidences." (One does wish that everyone would settle on just a single label for these events.) Based on letters solicited from the British public, Fenwick's research is less exacting and more exploratory than Stevenson's, but the accounts give a rounded flavour of what people seem to encounter.

One woman wrote to Fenwick about her husband, from whom she'd recently separated and who committed suicide in February 1989.

> I woke up crying at 3 o'clock in the morning after a very "real" dream in which Vincent was sitting on the end of my bed and telling me not to cry anymore and that it was all over and that he was finally at peace. I got up, "on auto-matic," did some work I needed to do; two clients phoned me around 8 o'clock and I freaked them out completely, as I told them I would be taking some time out because my husband had just died.

She didn't yet objectively know this to be true, but she *knew* it was true. She went over to his flat with Merlin, their dog, and discovered the body. "The coroner's report was that Vin had indeed died around 3:00 a.m." Here, the agent in distress didn't seek help by focusing on the percipient, but rather sent a message of reassurance after all was done. He was dead.

Richard Bufton, a college lecturer and commercial diver,

was aboard ship when he learned of his grandfather's death via unconventional means. He wrote to Fenwick:

> I was lying in the bunk in the forward cabin in a sort of half-asleep state, when what I can only describe as a vision similar to seeing a teletype ribbon went past my eyes. The words, which I read in my mind, simply said, "your grandfather is dead." I jumped up and climbed the three or four steps into the main cabin, saying to my friend that I had to make a radio-telephone call. I put out a link call through Bahrain Radio to my mother in the UK, and when she answered the phone she said she had some bad news. I interrupted to tell her that the reason I had rung was that I knew my grandfather was dead.

What's interesting about Bufton's experience is that, according to neurologist Dominic ffytche of King's College, London, one of the world's leading experts in visual hallucinations, when people hallucinate text, they don't see meaningful messages. The hallucination is visually incoherent, either a rough approximation of text or a random assemblage of letters. So if Bufton was hallucinating, how did he see words stating clearly that his grandfather was dead? In the one case that ffytche has found where a woman was actually visualizing written-out "command hallucinations"—suggesting that she should throw tea in a family member's face, for instance—he discovered that she wasn't actually reading the words, in the sense of visually scanning each word. Instead, she was inferring the meaning. And that seems to have been the case with Bufton. It was as if he were picking up a message about his grandfather in some other way and then imaginatively projecting it as a teletype ribbon. Some researchers propose that people intuit these death and distress events, garnering the raw information, and then their brains instantly assemble a representation of what they intuited, in much the way that in our dreams we impose meaning on external sounds like a ringing alarm clock.

When someone appears at the end of the bed, are they reaching out to you *post mortem* or are you perhaps sharing telepathically in their dying experience of calm and peace? Impossible to know. Several people have reported the strange joy that my sister Katharine felt, as if she had received from my father not news of his death but a shared sense of his final elation. "I can remember feeling incredibly content and happy," a woman named Kath McMahon recalled the night she learned that her father had died. There was no information attached to this feeling; she didn't know as a fact that her father had died. She merely experienced an abrupt emotional shift. Likewise, another woman described the startlement she felt when she realized that both she and her daughter, in separate houses, had awoken suddenly at the hour of her mother's death and felt extraordinarily and buoyantly happy.

A sailor named Raymond Hunter appears to have shared both the pain of his father's illness and the peace that followed. Of the evening his father died of lung cancer, he said, "I cannot possibly describe the feelings of love and great peace I experienced." But these emotions flowed after a much more bizarre and intense interlude in which he felt as if his lungs were collapsing and he could scarcely choke in a breath. This abrupt and violent experience of another's dying symptoms has been noted by some researchers, although it remains almost completely unexplored. Ian Stevenson came across it in his cases and suggested that it could be a kind of telepathic extension of a more commonly documented phenomenon, in which people who live together sympathetically take on one another's symptoms or moods.

"The syndrome of couvade in which a man imitates the symptoms of his wife's labor pains and delivery has been well documented with numerous examples," Stevenson noted.

> I once studied a middle-aged woman who complained of severe pain in her right shoulder for which physical examinations could discover no cause. Eventually I learned that shortly before her illness began, her son had died of cancer of the gall bladder, and that irritation of the diaphragmatic nerves had referred the pain induced by the cancer to his right shoulder . . . Pain due to identification and mediated normally through the senses raises the question whether a similar identification can take place by means of extrasensory perception.

A particularly vivid instance comes from an interview conducted by journalist Paul Hawker in 2010. A woman in her late thirties told him:

> I was awoken around 2:00 a.m. by the sound of my heart breaking. I know that sounds really odd, but that's what it was. I heard it crack and felt my chest sort of splitting. It

was massive, sudden and explosive. The next morning I did all my usual early morning things and got into the car to drive to work. I was sitting at a set of the traffic lights when I became aware of or felt this pressure on the side of my face. I distinctly remember that the pressure was that of a cheek lightly pressed against mine, sort of cuddling me. The feeling I was filled with at this time was one of love and support—it felt fine. I then felt a hand holding my hand and "felt" it had no middle finger. I knew this because there was no pressure in this area. And then it dawned on me. I realized it was my dad's hand; he'd lost his middle finger in a building site accident when I was a little girl.

I continued on to my first appointment which was a short one and I returned home after an hour to be met by my husband's words, "Your dad's gone." Apparently he'd died from a massive heart attack during the night. I wasn't at all surprised.

The idea, often advanced by mental health professionals, that these experiences are wishful imaginings of events after the fact is a miscasting of their intensity, their clarity and their power to unsettle. They take place on a rather different plane than the cool realization that you've just been thinking of someone when they call on the phone. Consider the sailor Raymond Hunter's description: "I remember grabbing my mouth, forcing it open to help me breathe. I was fighting for all I was worth but the pains were now unbearable." *Unbearable.* That is not something you shake off as a strange bit of dreaming, particularly when you learn that your father died in that moment of your panic and pain.

Sociologist Glennys Howarth of Plymouth University, who researches rare cases of shared illness symptoms across distance, observes that this sort of event creates a kind of crisis of identity as you pass from one mode of being in the world to another. "If the person sharing such experiences is to make sense of them, for him or herself and for others, a plausible explanation is crucial." In other words, someone tell me what the heck just happened! Without an explanation, the person will be stranded "in a stigmatized explanatory world of hallucinations and madness." That's not a comfortable place to be.

"When I was eighteen," a man named Derek Whitehead wrote to Fenwick,

> I was in the Merchant Navy crossing the Pacific Ocean on the way to Australia. One night I was on my bunk reading a magazine—Mayfair or Playboy I think. I looked up and my grandfather stood next to me, looking at me. Well, I shot off the bed, I did scream, and he was still there looking at me. I ran for my life up to the bridge shaking like a leaf.

Whitehead would later learn by post awaiting him in Australia that his grandfather had died that night. He found this highly alarming. "I don't know what these things are—fantasies, dreams, wishes, delusions—I don't like them. They make my sense of reality wobble."

This sense of destabilized reality is, of course, one of the reasons why people sometimes fiercely resist the idea of anomalous experiences. A particularly arresting story, beautifully told, comes from Harvard-educated surgeon Allan Hamilton, a professor of neurosurgery at the University of Arizona Health Sciences Center, who had the following experience during his years as a medical resident in Boston. In 1982 he was doing a rotation in the pediatric burn unit of Massachusetts General Hospital. A ten-year-old boy named Thomas was brought in after falling from a high-voltage tower onto a power line. The only skin that remained on his body was in patches in the folds of his joints and at his groin. "In the initial phases of critical burn care," writes Hamilton in a memoir titled *The Scalpel and the Soul,*

> the victim must be covered with new skin. This is first accomplished with grafts taken from fresh cadavers. Although the skin is dead, the thin strips of dermis and epithelium work beautifully as temporary skin. Soon the patient's immune system rejects the foreign grafts. The hope is that the cadaver grafts will buy enough time that the remaining pieces of the patient's own skin . . . can be gradually harvested to resurface the body.

In this case the boy's fragile frame kept rejecting the grafts, and Hamilton and his colleagues were losing hope that they could keep him alive long enough to regenerate his skin. He remained in a coma, precarious, barely there. Then his forty-two-year-old father, wildly distressed, collapsed and died of a heart attack. Suddenly the medical team had an almost imponderable opportunity. Genetically, his father's skin would be a closer match than that of the previous cadavers; there was a chance that the boy's body wouldn't reject it.

"The decision was made to take Thomas to the operating room and cover him with his father's skin," Hamilton recalls. The grafting took nearly twelve hours. After the operation,

> I went into the call room and fell asleep instantly. I had been on the move for more than forty-eight hours straight. Only seconds seemed to pass before I woke up angry and disoriented. A nurse was knocking loudly on the call room door. I looked at my watch. I'd been asleep for over two hours. The nurse was hammering, and it suddenly flashed into my mind that Thomas was probably dying.

Instead Hamilton found his young patient—who would indeed survive—roused from his long coma and scrabbling madly with mittened hands at the endotracheal tube in his windpipe. He wanted to talk. Hamilton removed various bits and pieces of equipment from the boy's trachea and mouth. "He coughed violently a couple of times. Suddenly, he spoke. His voice was perfectly clear. 'What happened to my father?'"

Stunned, Hamilton's impulse was to lie. He assured the child that nothing had happened, that his father was fine. The boy found this answer confusing. "My dad's just standing there at the end of my bed. Why doesn't he say something?"

Hamilton craned his neck to look for an image or silhouette beyond the hospital curtain that might be tricking his patient, but there was nothing there. He and the attending nurse broke the news to the boy of his father's death, as if it were more important to disabuse him of disconcerting illusions than to protect him from sorrowful news. If the boy was shocked, the doctor was bowled over. He writes: "Here was my own fragile moment of awakening. It left me tingling all over, as if sparks were dancing off my skin."

Fragile awakenings, private startlements, moments of utter confoundment. For my Irish and Scottish Highland ancestors, the reality of an extraordinary way of knowing things was always there, embedded comfortably within their culture and nothing suppressed about it. Our sense of awakening and confoundment is a very new reaction to a deeply ancient experience.

One summer afternoon, my elder aunts and cousins—women in their eighties and nineties—gather around the dining table at our cottage, Lochend, on Ontario's Stony Lake, a gathering spot for the Mackenzie clan on my mother's side since we went into exile from the original Loch End, near Inverness, during the Highland clearances. Here, in a hundred-year-old cabin in the North American forest, my grandmother painted a saying directly on the wall: *Fra' ghosties and ghoulies and long-leggedy beasties, and things that go bump in the night: the guid lord deliver us.* A playful nod to the Gaelic the clan once spoke; a nod to our witchy Celtic ancestresses. But now that I'm writing this book, we clan ladies have come to talk seriously of such things for the first time, over lunch.

Aunt Bea, who is ninety-three, still drives herself four

hours to spend summers on an island at the lake. She reads
the *New York Times* and has a thing or two to say about British
foreign policy and climate change. She keeps her grey hair in
a bob with bangs and gazes at you intently from beneath the
fringe, always curious and probing. As we finish up our summer salads and talk of the latest books, she recalls how
great-grandmother Maude always went about with an absolute confidence in her mysterious way of knowing things.
"Granny would be sitting in the living room reading a book
or something, and she'd suddenly slam it down and mutter,
'Damn! So-and-so is coming and I don't want to see them.'
And sure enough," Aunt Bea says in bemusement, her arms
clasped lightly across her belly, "so-and-so would show up ten
minutes later."

The Norwegians have a word for this uncanny anticipation
of visitors: *vardøger*. We call it "second sight," which was the
term our Highland ancestors would have used. (As an interesting aside, many Highlanders have Norwegian DNA, and these
are the only two European cultures I'm aware of with folk
names for this particular precognitive trait, so perhaps there is
a genetic predilection.) In any event, culturally it was *understood*, and nobody who had the second sight felt treated like a
fantasist or a liar. Great-Granny Maude was tiny, a slender
woman just shy of five feet. When she intuited the approach of
some bore or crank at the cottage, she sometimes hid in the
painted wooden chest on the porch. Years later, when my
grandfather telephoned his mother to report her husband's
fatal heart attack on his sailboat in Lake Huron's Georgian Bay,
Maude replied, impatiently and disconsolately, "I *know*."

After Maude, with each successive generation, talk of "second sight" receded into private silences as members of the family merged into the rising secularism of the twentieth century. It was only during this afternoon of lunch and reminiscence that Bea, our eldest relation, spoke of Great-Granny Maude, and more besides. Cousin Marion offered that she had been working at a resort hotel in Banff, Alberta, as a teenager—"this would have been in the late forties"—when the hotel caught fire, prompting her mother in Montreal to wake in high distress and make an urgent call to her. Cousin Sonny confided that she had drifted into the mystic after an allergic reaction to penicillin, and that later, on the very afternoon when her ex-husband died, she had been suffused through and through with a warm, hard-to-describe "glow" of emotion. My mother, the über-rationalist, conceded that, "come to mention it," one morning in university she had awoken suddenly and hurried to the dormer telephone to call my grandmother, whom she *knew* to be in crisis. Granny was—her dearest friend had died that night.

Each experience was different, but all were ways of knowing—or modes of being—that tilted the world on its axis, if only for a moment. Yet we had never shared them before. It was amazing in a way. Here we had all been walking past that Gaelic incantation on our wall (*fra' ghosties and ghoulies . . .*) and completely ignoring that lore's reference in relation to our own experiences. We had long since internalized the masculine, left-brained Scottish Enlightenment philosophy of our patriarchs, most of whom (since emigrating to North America) had been soldiers, Anglican clergymen and scholars. Ghosties, ghoulies and witchy Celtic women—be gone with you!

What goes missing when we silence the conversation about our impressions and visions? We no longer have the old models for understanding them, and "models help us think," writes Berkeley psychiatrist Elizabeth Lloyd Mayer, the one who was bowled over sideways by the dowser finding her daughter's harp. "Without a conceptual home, observations that don't fit our existing models may be intriguing and entertaining," at least for those hearing the stories, if not for those living at the powerful centre of them, she writes, "but they have the ultimate impact of writing on water. Without a model to contain them, we have no place to put new and unfamiliar things while we try to figure them out."

History, of course, is littered with examples of mainstream science deliberately overlooking "new and unfamiliar" things. It's worth pausing to consider the record. The French Academy of Sciences in the eighteenth century scoffed at meteorites because, how could rocks fall from the air? Museum curators across Europe promptly jettisoned the meteorites they had in their collections, embarrassed that they could have been seduced by something so fanciful. In the late nineteenth century, Hungarian obstetrician Ignaz Semmelweis pointed out that if doctors washed their hands before delivering babies, the rates of infection in mothers went down. In fact, he demonstrated this by having the lowest fatality rates in Europe on his maternity ward. But his proposition was deemed absurd and he was ridiculed into obscurity, eventually dying, unhinged, in an insane asylum. John Snow was belittled for proposing the existence of germs when all the smart people knew better.

My favourite example is the one that novelist Hilary Mantel pointed out a few years ago in the *London Review of Books*:

> From 1904, the Wright brothers made flights over fields bordered by a main highway and railway line in Ohio; but though hundreds of people saw them in the air, the local press failed to publish reports because they didn't believe the witnesses, and didn't send their own witnesses because it couldn't be true. Two years after their first flight, *Scientific American* dismissed the feats of the flying brothers; if there had been anything in it, the journal said, would the local press not have picked it up?

About ten years after Ian Stevenson began investigating telepathic impressions at times of crisis, three psychologists developed a method of measuring telepathy in the lab that came to be known as the "Ganzfeld technique." *Ganzfeld*, roughly translated from the German, means "whole field"; the premise is that you can widen your field of perception and tap into subtler sources of information by quieting everyday sensory input. It is not dissimilar in principle to hushing a noisy group of hikers who are with you in the woods so you can listen for, and finally hear, the snapping of a twig by some small concealed animal. "The ordinary waking state is largely driven by sensory awareness, so anything that disrupts that awareness will probably improve psi perception," Dean Radin, who has run several Ganzfeld experiments, writes.

In typical Ganzfeld experiments, the people being tested as receivers settle in a comfortable chair with halved table-tennis balls over their eyes. Their eyes remain open and a red light is shone at their face, so their visual perception is of a mellow red glow. They also wear headphones, so their only auditory stimulus is the rhythmic whooshing of unpatterned sound. In this calm, reduced-stimulus state, they are left to settle for a quarter of an hour or so. Meanwhile, in a separate room, the volunteer playing the role of sender opens an envelope containing four distinctive images. Choosing one, he or she attempts to mentally project the image to the receiver for a period of thirty minutes.

Here is an example, from an experiment run by Radin in his lab at the Institute for Noetic Sciences in Petaluma in 2010: The pictures that a participant named Tom could choose to project included a grassy field with blue and yellow flowers, a bird's nest with four golden eggs, the Great Pyramid of Cheops, and a plain asphalt road flanked by telephone poles in a flat landscape. The receiver, Gail, was told to vocalize her impressions without naming or analyzing them. Gail was recorded as saying:

> Keep feeling like looking up at tall. I'm looking up at tall. . . . Something about texture. Texture. . . . I feel like something has a rough texture. . . . Tall, very tall impression, looking up high. Feel as if I'm walking around observing something, like when you would walk in an art gallery or in a museum and you would look at something. . . . Wow. . . . First I'm feeling like tall trees, and then I'm feeling like a tall building . . . And then I'm like a Yosemite kind of image of a tall rock or a tall, some kind of a very tall solid stone

something. . . . Seeing browns and grays. . . . Something like a feeling of walking around, looking up and being in awe . . . In awe of something. . . . Monolithic, or I don't know what the word is.

Of the four pictures he'd found in his envelope, Tom had opted to mentally project to Gail the one depicting the pyramid of Cheops.

Between 1974 and 2004, nearly ninety Ganzfeld experiments were conducted and published by a number of scientists around the world. Overall, randomly selected pictures were described correctly 32 percent of the time, which is 7 percent above what you'd expect to see by chance. In other words, the odds that someone like Gail would describe an image approximating the picture Tom chose *by chance*, and do so 32 percent of the time, have been calculated at 29 million trillion to 1. It can be difficult to get one's head around these kinds of statistics. Seven percent above chance doesn't sound like a lot, but it's enormous: it shouldn't be happening above chance *at all*. If telepathy is a gift for attunement similar to musical genius or mathematical intelligence, and you're sampling a random number of university volunteers, none of whom are picking up on resonant echoing distress or death calls from their families—just mundane stuff like pictures of an Egyptian pyramid—then 7 percent above chance is extraordinary.

If you are new to this research, as I was, it's worth reading Dean Radin's books. He takes readers step by step through the history of the research, the refinements of protocols, the selection of subjects, the "file-drawer effects," the calculation of odds, and so on. Suffice it to say that even psychologists like Richard Wiseman, a popular skeptic of paranormal phenomena in the United Kingdom, have publicly conceded that the best of these experiments "meet the usual standards for a normal claim" in science. It's just that telepathy is an "extraordinary claim," so the usual standards aren't sufficient.

As long ago as 1988, the National Research Council of the National Academy of Sciences commissioned Harvard psychologist Robert Rosenthal to scour the research for methodological flaws. Were the results biased by poor study design or faulty analysis? After sifting through the studies, Rosenthal and a colleague reported that "the Ganzfeld ESP studies regularly meet the basic requirements of sound experimental design." Furthermore, they said, it would be "implausible" to say that these telepathy findings resulted from chance. What did the NRC do with Rosenthal's assessment of telepathy research? According to Rosenthal, they requested that the research be withdrawn.

"It is a scandal," said Cambridge scholar Henry Sidgwick,

> that the dispute as to the reality of these phenomena should still be going on, that so many competent witnesses should have declared their belief in them, that so many others should be profoundly interested in having the question determined, and yet that the educated world, as a body, should still be simply in the attitude of incredulity.

Sidgwick made that protest in 1882. One hundred and twenty years later, much progress has been made in studying these signals and waves, but little has changed with respect to what is considered official truth.

Cambridge physicist and Nobel Prize winner Brian D. Josephson told the *New York Times* in 2003: "There's really strong pressure not to allow these things [psi phenomena] to be talked about in a positive way." Harold Puthoff, a physicist at the Stanford Research Institute, appointed to oversee the CIA's remote viewing (clairvoyant) experiments in the 1970s and '80s, described this pressure in a series of emails to psychiatrist Elizabeth Lloyd Mayer. "The evidence we had [on clairvoyance] was rock hard," he wrote to her.

> I saw that. But I also saw that it didn't eradicate my doubt. That made me see my doubts weren't the problem. On the contrary, the problem lay with my beliefs. I was having terrible trouble giving up my beliefs about how the world worked, even in the face of evidence that said my beliefs were wrong.

By the time of the first EEG twin studies, physicists had discovered the quantum universe, where subatomic particles were breaking all the rules of classical physics and demonstrating a phenomenon called "entanglement." Two particles with no physical link to one another could somehow remain connected, or entangled, exerting influences upon one another at a distance. This is by now well-established and discussed. Physicists have grown to accept "non-local" connectivity as a real, if totally mystifying, phenomenon at the subatomic level. In 2011, physicists at Oxford took quantum entanglement to the macro level by briefly entangling two separated diamond crystals that were visible to the eye.

Neuroscientist Michael Persinger, of Laurentian University in Sudbury, Ontario, thinks that he may have demonstrated the entanglement effect between people, although his experiment needs to be replicated. "What we have found," he reported in 2009, "is that if you place two different people at a distance and put a circular magnetic field around both and you make sure they are connected to the same computer so they get the same stimulation, then if you flash a light in one person's eye, the person in the other room . . . will show changes in their brain as if they saw the flash of light." Scientists such as Persinger (who used to be an adamant skeptic about all things paranormal) are increasingly at ease with the findings in this new world. "Quantum theory and a vast body of supporting experiments tell us that something unaccounted for is connecting otherwise isolated objects," says Radin. "And this is precisely what psi experiences and experiments are telling us. The parallels are so striking that it suggests that psi is—literally—the human experience of quantum interconnectedness."

Scientists based at Princeton are exploring this mysterious force of connectedness as well, through what they call the Global Consciousness Project. Beginning in the early 1990s, faculty at Princeton's Engineering Anomalies Research (PEAR) lab began placing electronic "random event generators" at collaborating universities around the world. REGs are essentially like coin tossers: they generate heads or tails—ones and zeros—

following nothing but the laws of chance. Preliminary lab experiments had determined that REGs could begin to behave less randomly if they were the focus of the researcher's willed intention. Pursuing this idea that human consciousness could somehow exert an effect on material systems, lead investigator Roger Nelson and his team began monitoring data during events of global significance, such as the 1997 funeral of Princess Diana, which is estimated to have been watched by 2.5 billion people, and later the calamitous unfolding of 9/11.

"We asked if groups of people brought by circumstances into resonance or coherence might share a group consciousness that would register in the data from our random devices. The answer was yes," writes Nelson. For seventy-two hours, beginning on the morning of 9/11, the REGs were feeding patterned data from all around the world into the Princeton lab. You can see what this looks like—how random data shifts to patterned data—on the PEAR Global Consciousness Project website. It makes for an eerie kind of art. They have even converted the data into sound, creating a dirge for 9/11.

"The overall statistics for the project," Nelson says,

indice odds of about 1 in 20 million that the correlation of our data with global events is merely a chance fluctuation. And we can exclude mundane explanations such as electromagnetic radiation, excessive strain on the power grid, or mobile phone use . . . . We don't yet know how to explain the correlations between events of importance to humans and the GCP data, but they are quite clear. They suggest something akin to the image held in almost all cultures of a unity or oneness, an interconnection that is fundamental to life.

In 1919 American naturalist William Long published a book titled *How Animals Talk*, reporting his observations of wolves in the Nova Scotia wilderness. The pack he was studying appeared to be able to range beyond the threshold of hearing and smell yet still keep track of one another. Long found this interesting, although he was in no position to prove anything, one way or another, about what it meant. It would be another sixty years before the maverick former Cambridge biologist Rupert Sheldrake picked up on Long's field observations and applied them to a study of dogs.

Sheldrake designed a series of experiments to test how dogs know—or seem to know—that their owners are coming home (this would not include my sheltie, which once barked incessantly at an album cover featuring Glen Campbell). Controlling for scent, the sound of the car on the road, the routine time of day, and all familiar sounds, Sheldrake was able to establish that dogs begin to anticipate their owner's arrival regardless of the sensory cues. There appears to be a force that binds and alerts social animals over distance, Sheldrake concluded. Later he would realize that traditional human cultures took this for granted, although it hadn't been widely studied by anthropologists for obvious reasons of taboo (who's going to give you a research grant to study telepathy in indigenous tribes when it isn't supposed to exist?). Instead, intriguing glimpses appeared here and there in field reports. South African journalist and author Laurens van der Post described African Bushmen who knew when a hunting party would return with a kill; they explained to him that it was like the white man's wire (telegraph), but—they gestured at their chests—"in the heart." The Iroquois of North America refer to such communication as using the "long body," which denotes the means by which they stay connected to the group, to their tribal lands and to objects on that land. Like an outsize shadow, the long body sees further.

Reading this, I realized with a start that I'd encountered similar stories myself, in the summer of 2010, when I flew more than a thousand kilometres north of Toronto to visit Ojibwe and Cree people on their traditional lands in the boreal forest near Hudson Bay. The elders there were born in the forest and followed an age-old way of life. They had scarcely more contact with modernity than the tribes of the Amazon or the Andaman Islands. (Americans of European ancestry tend to think of North America's "Indians" as a homogeneous mass whose intermingling with them dates back to Pocahontas. But until you fly across the oceanic vastness of northern Ontario, you can have no clear sense of why it might be possible for some groups to remain largely uninfluenced by Western ideas, even if they did conduct sporadic trade, until their children were brutally forced into boarding schools as late as the 1970s.)

The elders spoke of their shamanic "shaking tent" ceremony and tried to explain that it was what they had used, for all intents and purposes, as a radio. The shaking tent is difficult to describe. It consists of long strips of hide over a framework that forms a narrow cylinder, almost like a closed umbrella. The shaman stands inside it, its width barely greater than his body. As he enters a trance, the hide strips begin to flutter, as if he's creating some kind of energy field. But, the elders explained to me, the shaking tent isn't merely a ritual means to commune with the spirits. It was how they learned what was going on before they had telephones—what the weather was like, what hunting conditions other families and groups were encountering hundreds of kilometres up and down their main waterway, the Severn River. As with the Bushmen and their "telegraph," there was—there always had been—this other way to know things.

How to interpret that? Were they just making it up? When I'm standing in the midst of an unutterably huge spruce and pine forest, I lose any armchair skepticism and grow humbly curious. How did human beings evolve and maintain a culture and economy over such inconceivable distances, patrolled by bear and wolf and wolverine? Well, there are many answers, of course, but one starts to appreciate the evolutionary advantage of developing an alternative means of perceiving or communicating, a sixth sense, not only for humans but also for timber wolves and herds of caribou. If an extra sense could transcend distance limitations, then it sure as hell would have been the belle of the evolutionary ball.

Factoring in the number of Ian Stevenson's telepathic-impression cases that were akin to distress calls rather than simply intimations of death, the evolutionary advantage becomes all the more clear. "It is altogether probable," Stevenson concluded,

> that important unrecognized exchanges of feelings through extrasensory processes are occurring all the time to most of us and perhaps significantly influencing our emotions and behavior. . . . To believe in some universal binding that

joins us all is not, of course, to deny that for most of us this union is never manifested consciously. But even if we can only observe it occasionally, and usually between persons united by love and during a special crisis to one of them, this should arouse our curiosity and our efforts to find out why this is so.

✳

Dean Radin offers one theory about what might be going on to facilitate our detection of danger. "At a level of reality deeper than the ordinary senses can grasp," he ventures,

> our brains and minds are in intimate communion with the universe. It's as though we lived in a gigantic bowl of clear jello. Every wiggle—every movement, event, and thought—within that medium is felt throughout the entire bowl. Except that this particular form of jello is a rather peculiar medium, in that it's not localized in the usual way, nor is it squishy like ordinary jello. It extends beyond the boundaries of ordinary spacetime, and it's not even a substance in the usual sense of that word. Because of this "non-local jello" in which we are embedded, we can get glimpses of information about other people's minds, distant objects, or the future or the past. We get this not through the ordinary senses and not because signals from those other minds and objects travel to our brain. But because, at some level, our mind/brain *is already coexistent* with other peoples' minds . . . From this perspective, psychic experiences are

reframed not as mysterious "powers of the mind," but as momentary glimpses of the entangled fabric of reality.

He goes on: "Particles that are quantum entangled do not imply that signals pass between them. Entanglement means that separated systems are *correlated.*" If you grow alert to the fact that someone you cherish is in danger, "it would appear to be a form of information transfer, but in fact it would be a pure correlation. That is, within a holistic medium we are *always connected.*"

We are always in a position to feel what others feel and to learn of their joy or distress, even to react to that joy or distress without knowing why, but most of the time we're not paying attention. We can't; if we did, we'd be overwhelmed by the signals and waves. It would be like straining to hear your name being whispered in a nightclub at two in the morning. For survival's sake, the brain has evolved to filter out most information. So, even when the signal flares, we may be unclear about what we're responding to.

"When we were students at Bristol in the late 1960s," a woman wrote to the neuroscientist Peter Fenwick in London,

> my fiancé was estranged from his mother who was a doctor in Nigeria and he was living with his father. Around New Year, we were both attending a dinner party at my parents' house when he suddenly began to cry uncontrollably and was consumed with grief. He went out to the kitchen to wash dishes, trying to give himself something to divert his mind, but nothing worked, and eventually he gave up and drove back to his father's house, where he

was met by a policeman who told him that his mother had been killed that evening . . . he was not at all an emotional man, quite the opposite, and this strange episode has remained as one of the most inexplicable episodes of my life.

In 2010, Cornell psychologist Daryl Bem published research in the rigorously peer-reviewed *Journal of Personality and Social Psychology* establishing that people are able to unconsciously intimate events a few seconds in the future. Recruiting more than a thousand student volunteers, Bem conducted nine separate experiments on well-established psychological effects, such as reacting to subliminal or arousing images. But he time-reversed them. For example, in one experiment, the volunteers were told that they were going to be shown two pictures of curtains side by side on a computer screen. They were told that one curtain had a picture behind it and the other had a blank wall. The volunteers, who thought they were being tested for ESP, were asked to choose the curtain that they felt had the picture behind it; they were also told that the curtain would then draw back to reveal whether they were correct. In fact there was no picture behind either curtain. Once the volunteers had made their choice and clicked, the computer randomly assigned a picture— either neutral or erotic—to each curtain. And here's what happened: the volunteers clicked on the erotically arousing, rather than neutral, pictures at an above-chance rate, *before* the pictures were there. In other words, they reacted to the appearance of an erotic image by clicking on it before it was actually there to arouse them.

The nine experiments were, according to colleagues, impeccably done, notwithstanding the fact that no one could believe the results were true. As one of Bem's peer reviewers, Joachim Krueger of Brown University, put it, "My personal view is that this is ridiculous and can't be true. Going after the methodology and the experimental design is the first line of attack. But frankly, I didn't see anything. Everything seemed to be in good order."

Bem tested for personality traits in those who performed particularly well in his experiments. Two things caught his eye. One was that the better performers scored high in the trait known as extraversion. Such people tend to be stimulus seekers, restlessly scanning the environment. Maybe, he speculated, they were more apt to pick up on remote or obscure signals. The other element Bem noted was that people who did well with precognition tests also tended to be very quick at processing subliminal data. Both of these traits would have, Bem theorized, a considerable evolutionary advantage, all the more so if people could pick up on cues across time and space. "The ability to anticipate and thereby to avoid danger confers an obvious evolutionary advantage that would be greatly enhanced by the ability to anticipate danger precognitively," he wrote. "It was this reasoning that motivated [our] experiment on the precognitive avoidance of negative stimuli. Similarly, the possibility of an evolved precognitive ability to anticipate sexual opportunities motivated [our] experiment on the precognitive detection of erotic stimuli."

Bem was building on the insights of psychologist Hans Eysenck, who argued that "psi might be a primitive form of perception antedating cortical developments in the course of evolution." If so, he wrote, the later evolution of "cortical arousal might suppress psi functioning. Because extroverts have a lower level of cortical arousal than introverts, that provides another reason [besides enhanced stimulus-seeking tendencies] for predicting that they will perform well in psi tasks." All evolutionary psychology, even when it includes parapsychology, is purely speculative, bear in mind.

Recent experiments in presentiment have also been done by measuring nervous system response to stimuli—a scary face, for instance. The face might trigger a physiological reaction such as changes in skin temperature (blushing or blanching) or accelerated heart rate. But in these experiments, such responses were triggered a few seconds *prior* to the scary face actually appearing. Research done by Spanish biologist Fernando Alvarez in Seville found that Bengalese finches showed alarm up to nine seconds before the video monitors next to their cages actually displayed a horseshoe whip snake apparently approaching them. Other experiments in presentiment continue apace all over the world, studying (in no particular order) college students, earthworms, zebra finches and Zen meditators.

In 2012, Northwestern University neuroscientist Julia Mossbridge and colleagues published an article in the journal *Frontiers in Perception Science*; it concluded that carefully sifted studies dating back to 1978 established a small but statistically significant incidence of precognition in experiments without methodological flaw. Before agreeing to publish Mossbridge's article, one of the peer reviewers for the journal requested that a line be inserted to say that this phenomenon was due to natural physical processes yet to be determined, Mossbridge told me. This must be the materialist science version of genuflecting to the powers that be, muttering such phrases as "Praise be to God." And it's unnecessary. There is no reason to assume that presentiment is anything other than a natural physical process; it's just a process we don't understand.

What one hopes is that this kind of research will one day explain the premonitions and presentiments that people and animals live with almost daily. "You know," my husband said to me as I was working on this chapter, "Abraham Lincoln dreamed of his death three days before Booth shot him. He wrote a letter about it. Did you know that?" No, and now that I know, I don't know what to do with the knowledge. There's no model.

"I'm reading this fascinating book," says my mother, who is always reading fascinating books, "about a love affair between two Russians during World War II." Prisoner-of-war Lev Mishchenko dreamed of his lover, Sveta, in a white dress, kneeling by the side of a little girl. The dream recurred when he was in Stalin's gulag in 1949, a time of horrible pained isolation and torture when he didn't even know if Sveta was alive. Then, in 1962, biographer Orland Figes writes,

> Lev and Sveta were staying with the children at Uncle Nikita's dacha at Malakhovka. One day, they were walking to the lake across a field that skirted the forest. Lev was in front, Sveta behind him with Anastasia, who was then six. "As I reached the edge of the forest," Lev recalled, "I had this feeling . . . I turned around and behind me I saw Sveta in a white dress kneeling on the ground to adjust

something on Nastia's dress. It was exactly what I had seen in my dream—Sveta on the right and, on the left, our little girl."

Does this explain my sister, in the quiet of her bedroom, having a vision of her unborn future grandchild? Somehow the universe connects us and consoles us. The dying reassure us— and are reassured. Sometimes, as I explore next, we are even pulled back from the brink.

ASTRAL FATHER

The Phenomenon of a Sensed Presence

ignal Corps officer Alex Watson stands guard in front of a British naval regiment in Calcutta, India, in May 1943. His helmet is tight, his face risingly hot. Desperate for even the slenderest touch of shade, he angles his rifle butt above his head. And then, all of a sudden, he's not there.

Watson finds himself instead on a cold, wet field in what appears to be Europe. Soldiers stagger by, carrying and dragging wounded men towards a Red Cross tent. Looking down, he is astonished to see his best friend from childhood, John Wilmhurst, bleeding and unconscious in the grass. The rescuing troops are moving away—they don't realize that Wilmhurst is alive. Watson bends down, picks up his friend in a fireman's lift and carries him into the tent. At once he is back in the scorching sunlight of his station, blinking in surprise that he somehow fell asleep and dreamed a dream on his feet.

Two years later, at war's end, the friends reunite in a London pub. While sharing some lagers, Wilmhurst confides to Watson that it sounds crazy—he certainly knows that—"but I believe you saved my life during the war."

"How's that?"

Wilmhurst explains that he was wounded in France. "I was somehow outside my body, looking down, and suddenly you appeared. You picked up my body and carried me across this field and you put me in the medical tent."

Alex Watson nods, sips his lager, says nothing.

"Did you tell him your side of the story?" Watson's daughter Janice asked her father some decades later.

"No, I didn't."

"*Why not?*"

"It didn't seem necessary."

Thinking people tend to keep a lid on such tales.

War is a theatre for ghosts. Filled with corpses and fraught with danger, the frontlines are nightmare places with moments of unexpected grace, where "the signals and waves are transmitting" like mad. There are many accounts of families receiving the "three a.m. news" when their boys were felled in the murderous struggles of the two world wars, which accords with the research conclusion that violent and accidental deaths result in more telepathic impressions. But intriguing tales also abound of soldiers themselves sensing a guiding presence alongside in battle. Those who are dying or in peril seem, then, to encounter these presences regardless of whether they are lying quietly in bed or crouching in a rat-infested funk-hole. The "grief hallucination" is at the same time a guardian angel; the "deathbed vision" also a guide.

In his memoir about fighting in the First World War, journalist William Bird described what for him was the most extraordinary chapter in the battle. He was in France in April 1917, sleeping beneath a groundsheet amidst the muddy and maze-like trenches after the Battle of Vimy Ridge. In the cool darkness he was awoken by the grip of someone shaking him. He tried to pull away, exhausted and irritable, but the grip held with some urgency. So he opened his eyes and saw, to his confused surprise, his brother Steve, who had been reported missing in action two years earlier.

"Steve grinned as he released my hands, then put his warm hand over my mouth as I started to shout my happiness. He pointed to the sleepers in the bivvy and to my rifle and equipment. 'Get your gear,' he said softly."

While Bird tried to work out in his mind how in hell his brother had even located him, he obediently followed Steve away from the other sleeping men, down the trench. By the time it occurred to him to ask where they were going, his brother had rounded a corner—and vanished. Bird searched for him frantically but eventually reconciled himself to the conclusion that he had been asleep on his feet, dreaming. His brother, come to think on it, had been kitted out in the uniform and cap worn in 1915; it was two years out of date—a dream for sure. Bird gave up in despair, crawled into a nearby funk-hole and fell asleep where he was.

The next morning he was awoken by his battalion mates, who were excited to find him alive. They took him over to the bivouac where he'd been sleeping when his brother appeared to him. It had been hit by a high-explosive shell, the men there mutilated beyond recognition. The incident was such a profound part of his war experience that Bird titled his subsequent memoir *Warm Hands*.

"The supernatural and the uncanny seemed natural and explainable in these sites of mass death," writes military historian Tim Cook. No soldier dismissed his own experience as a product of sleep deprivation or madness, for there was often an element of being assisted or rescued. George Maxwell wrote, for example, of being separated from his platoon in no man's land on a lightless evening, lost and uncertain of the contours of the enemy lines. Terrified, he was about to bolt in a random direction like a maddened horse when a voice commanded him: "Be seated and await deliverance." Brought up short by the authority of this unseen speaker, he obeyed, kneeling in a crater, which is where one of his comrades located him and led him to safety.

This experience of a sensed presence was also encountered in the extreme environments that Europeans and Americans were newly exploring at the turn of the previous century, in particular the Arctic and Antarctic. "Who is the third who walks always beside you?" wrote the poet T. S. Eliot in 1922. "When I count, there are only you and I together / But when I look ahead up the white road / There is always another one walking beside you." These lines from *The Wasteland* allude to the uncanny experience of Sir Ernest Shackleton, who made a desperate, exhausted trek across a mountainous stretch of Antarctica in 1916. The expedition's boat had got mired in the ice and provisions were running low. Leaving the remaining men behind with the stranded boat, Shackleton and two of his crew members climbed and staggered forty kilometres in search of rescue. At some point in the arduous, freezing journey, all three men became aware of a presence, another companion, accompanying and guiding them.

The presence—to Eliot, "the third man," though in reality a fourth—seemed to escort them safely to a whaling station and then departed. None spoke about it during the trek itself, each thinking that he alone sensed the extra companion. Later, when Shackleton was asked about this, he refused to surrender such a sublime experience to ridicule. "None of us care to speak about that," he said. "There are some things that never can be spoken of. Almost to hint about them comes perilously close to sacrilege."

His reticence has been shared by the great many explorers, sailors, divers and mountaineers who turn out to have experienced the Third Man in the midst of duress and danger. These companions have sometimes been visible, sometimes not, have sometimes spoken aloud and other times not, but always they have comforted them, and in some cases they have led them to safety.

Early scientific explanations tended to focus on the location. Soldiers in the First World War were presumed to have been sleep-deprived. Mountaineers were thought to be suffering from the effects of altitude, lack of oxygen and cold stress. Victims of shipwreck, who had plenty of heat and air, were assumed to have hallucinated because of sunstroke and dehydration. Polar explorers had been tricked into the illusion by monotony and sensory deprivation—a world of white in which "the brain attempts to create the perception of a person from partial sensory stimuli." (In fact, as has been demonstrated by the Ganzfeld telepathy experiments, sensory deprivation may be an ideal environment for enhancing receptivity to subtle information.)

Meanwhile, men traversing the rich and varied terrains of jungles and forests were also encountering the Third Man. When Henry Stoker (cousin to Bram) and two fellow British sailors escaped a Turkish prison during the First World War, they wandered for days through the wilderness; the Third Man stuck by them until they found rescue. "We had all three been sensible of his presence throughout the most trying part of the night; we all three agreed that the moment he left us was when we had put the danger behind. I cannot exaggerate," Stoker wrote, "how real his presence was, how content one felt—despite the mystery of it—that he should be there."

Three of the World Trade Center survivors of 9/11 later claimed that they were guided to safety by sensed presences. One was prodded through a wall of fire he would otherwise have shied from, fearful of the flames, and led down the stairs of the North Tower; another was comforted as he lay beneath the rubble. A third, trapped beneath concrete, received encouraging visits from a presence that she perceived, for some reason, to be a monk.

In 1989, two mountain climbers, Lou and Ingrid Whittaker, experienced the same visual hallucination: of a kind middle-aged Tibetan woman who stayed by them on India's Mount Kanchenjunga. Lou Whittaker was leading an American expedition when he became aware of the woman—"a friendly spirit"— at base camp. She kept him company each evening for three months. Whittaker's wife, Ingrid, meanwhile, was trekking down from the summit to base camp with her own expedition group when she developed altitude sickness. For several days she lay in her husband's tent, where she found herself being attended by a Tibetan woman. "She was wearing a headscarf and a long dress. She was shadowy and two-dimensional, like a silhouette." It was "very comforting." Both husband and wife had experienced this woman but made no mention of the vision to one another until months later.

Over the past decade, Swiss neuroscientists have tried to replicate the sensed presence in their labs by using electrodes to stimulate a part of the brain called the left temporoparietal junction (TPJ). Olaf Blanke, lead researcher at the Brain Mind Institute in Lausanne, implicated this area of the brain because it "integrates sensory input into a cohesive picture." For Blanke, any dysfunction in this area, for example, due to "disruption of the oxygen supply," might cause a person to become disoriented as to self versus other, or here versus there.

Blanke's research is pioneering, but unfortunately there isn't any evidence yet that people encountering the Third Man are all experiencing a disruption in the normal functioning of this part of the brain. They might be, for reasons as yet unknown, but so far no scientist has managed to place mountain climbers

and lost soldiers in laboratories to test the theory that distur-
bances to the TPJ are creating these experiences out in the
quixotic world. "Explanations of the sensed presence phenomenon abound, which is paradoxical, given how little systematic
research has been done on the subject," notes clinical psychologist Peter Suedfeld, a leading expert on human cognition in
extreme environments. "How these hypotheses explain the
repeated and/or prolonged appearance of a helpful 'other,'" he
cautions, "is not clear."

The Third Man is nothing if not helpful. In his fascinating
compilation of accounts, *The Third Man Factor*, journalist John
Geiger is perhaps the first to have explored this uncharted realm
of human experience, establishing how extraordinarily preva-
lent the Third Man is across different landscapes and predica-
ments. Geiger first noticed the phenomenon when writing about
historic polar expeditions. When he extended his gaze, he found
dozens and dozens of references in memoirs and diaries and
letters and interviews with explorers and adventurers. Nobody
individually realized how widely shared the experience was,
which accounts for why the scientific theorists were acting like
the proverbial blind men and the elephant, chalking things up
to oxygen deprivation here and sunstroke there. Geiger's book
is a must-read for anyone who wants to contemplate this subject
in depth.

A second book, which describes a wider range of mysterious
and transcendent experiences by endurance athletes, is journalist Maria Coffey's *Explorers of the Infinite*. Coffey—as surprised as
Geiger by what she found—encountered a number of typically
hard-headed pragmatists who had experienced precognitive

dreams about their coming struggles, telepathic access to distress messages from partners, or guiding sensed companions. She wondered if these were common to this group of people because of the intense focus and heightened awareness they entered into as athletes, which might enable them to tune in to fields of perception that we are ordinarily oblivious to.

But what is a sensed presence? What is the nature of the experience, whether in the mountains or in no man's land, in the rubble of earthquakes and broken towers or the dark and quiet of my sister Katharine's bedroom? It isn't the shivery sensation you get that you're being stared at, or a momentary apprehension caused by stirrings of shadow and light. It isn't a fun-sized belief, like thinking someone's there when the wind whispers through a candle. There is nothing faint about the experience. Those who encounter the Third Man describe having a sudden, vivid and indisputable awareness that *someone is with them*, sometimes for hours and even for days.

Nor is the presence indifferently with them, the way pop culture depicts forlorn and sulking ghosts who pass us by in haunted houses. These sensed presences are relational: they are purposefully and supportively with the people who sense them, which is what Peter Suedfeld, one of the few experts on sensed presence in extreme environments, points to as the most difficult part to explain.

Sometimes the presence acts merely as a quiet friend. Geiger reports cases when a climber has offered the sensed presence a snack before realizing no one is there, or has already divided the dinner ration in two. Sometimes people pause on the trail, waiting for the presence to catch up, before remembering with a start that no one is physically there. At other times the presence actively guides people out of danger. In 1983, twenty-year-old American climber James Sevigny was so severely injured by an avalanche in Banff National Park that he could barely move. His back was broken, as were his arms, his nose and some ribs. He was bleeding internally. He lost consciousness for an hour. When he attempted to stand, he collapsed. He assumed he would die, and he was yielding to shock and hypothermia when a sensed presence materialized. "It was something I couldn't see, but it was a physical presence," he told Geiger.

The presence more or less bullied Sevigny to get up and move, prodding him through deep-crusted snow every raw inch of the one and a half kilometres back to his camp. "All decisions made," he said, "were made by the presence. I was merely taking instructions." As soon as he reached his tent, his bossy companion disappeared. Moments later, Sevigny was found by some cross-country skiers and helicoptered to hospital.

Joshua Slocum, the first man to sail solo around the world, reported that, in the midst of a battering storm, he had fallen ill with food poisoning and couldn't attend to the helm of his boat. To his bewilderment, a tall man appeared and said that he would handle the tiller so that Slocum could recover. Slocum had the impression that this man was "a friend and a seaman of vast experience." The man kept the vessel on course for 145 kilometres, until Slocum could resume control. He then dematerialized.

Several other sailors have witnessed this startling turn of events in moments of danger, finding themselves assisted by a mysterious other when their own strength was failing, and so have pilots. Edith Stearns, a contemporary of the more famous female flyer Amelia Earhart, came to expect a sensed presence on her flights in the 1930s and '40s, as if she'd conjured an imaginary friend. "I never fly alone," she told a journalist for *Life* magazine. "Some 'presence' sits beside me, my copilot as I have come to think of it."

These sensed presences meddle. On one occasion the presence actively warned Stearns, shouting "No! No, Edie, don't!" when she began attempting an emergency landing on railway tracks, unaware that a safe airfield runway lay a few miles ahead. Pilot Brian Shoemaker, disoriented in his H-34 helicopter during an Antarctic storm, was accompanied by a presence that told him to "turn 20 degrees to the right." He obeyed because, he admits, "I had nothing else to go by." That steering adjustment got him safely out of trouble.

The presence seems to vanish moments after the danger is resolved, even if that resolution isn't yet clear to the person at risk—which is one of the most striking mysteries about the longer-lingering hallucinations. Shipwreck survivor Ensio Tiira had been adrift on a raft for thirty days. "I'd lost all sense of a second person being in the raft. The guardian angel who kept me company . . . left the raft with my own sense of hope." But the day the "angel" vanished turned out, in fact, to be the day of his rescue.

The same steadfast accompaniment and sudden vanishing act happened to an American climber named Rob Taylor, who broke his ankle on Mount Kilimanjaro in 1978. He was left to wait, propped against a boulder, at the base of the mountain while his climbing partner struck off in search of medical assistance. Taylor's envisioned overnight stay turned into a much longer ordeal. He ran out of water and his ankle became badly infected. On the third day he grew aware of a man sitting on a boulder nearby. He assumed at first that the figure was a member of the rescue party, but when calls and then yells failed to elicit a response, he got angry, throwing rocks at the figure, to no avail. He settled down to being entirely mystified. At length he concluded that the man was there simply to keep him company.

"Hours upon hour this companion watcher, as I call him, peers out at me through the curtain of snow," he later wrote. As Taylor's health deteriorated, the figure quietly drew closer, until after a few days it was "right at the foot of the sleeping bag." Then this benevolent and reassuring presence, who Taylor says "took up absolutely solid space like a stone or anything else," suddenly left him. Minutes later, a rescue group arrived.

For Taylor, as for Shackleton and many others who have encountered such protective presences in times of peril, the world's subsequent cheerful dismissal proved to be painful. "I don't often talk about my companion watcher these days," Taylor writes.

> He is a creature out of place here, misunderstood. After the [rescue], when I first spoke of him to people, they reacted quite predictably: "What an imagination!" "Your fever had you hallucinating." At first I persisted in my stand: "He was real. There in the flesh or at least in some concrete form I could see." Later, I left him out altogether. It was easier than trying to define or defend him to people who could not understand. Now I know this and say this

to you: He was there and as real as you or I. I do not know
to this day his purpose, but I sense that it was good.

Taylor is making a plea to respect the power of a phenomenon that is best known and keenly observed by the people who
actually encounter it. It puts me in mind of a poem by the
American poet Mary Oliver about the dying visions of William
Blake: "When a man says he hears angels singing / he hears angels
singing. / *When a man says he hears angels singing, / he hears angels
singing.*" It's impossible to objectively measure subjective perception. In the study of consciousness, subjective perceptions are
sometimes referred to as *qualia.* "Something beyond our understanding occurs in the genesis of qualia," neurologist Oliver
Sacks has written; it is "the transformation of an objective cerebral computation to a subjective experience."

What is the quality of redness? How do we invest red with a
different feeling than yellow? What is loveable and meaningful
about a red rose? What makes the scent of jasmine transporting?
What is beautiful about a snowy field? Why are we awed by a
sunset? Why is the Third Man so comforting and so real? *We are
not in a position to answer objectively.* This is where the conversation about brain-based "hallucinations" gets tricky.

"There is a fundamental explanatory gap between brain
activation and conscious experience," psychologist Alexander
Morelos said at a University of Arizona conference on the science
of consciousness that I attended to get a better handle on the subject. The "explanatory gap" is widely referred to amongst scholars
who study consciousness. Most academics are respectful of this
gap, but those who are impatient to stride over it tend to engage

in what their critics, such as Morelos, call promissory materialism. To wit, they take it on faith that everything we experience is generated by the brain. They figure that, sooner or later, the brain will reveal its secrets. We might not yet understand why brains project the image of a consoling, guiding presence such as the Third Man, but we can assume that the brain is doing it somehow. "But that is a hope," Morelos argued. "It is not a scientific fact."

Part of the problem with that hope, interestingly, is that it has a slightly fantastical quality about it. As psychologist Julio Peres asked at the same conference,

> What kind of empirical evidence would we need to prove that "the brain believes" or "the brain interprets"? These are enchanted metaphors. How does it make sense to assign a psychological trait to an organic brain part? What materialists are actually engaging in is animism. This represents a return to a much less critical and more naive metaphysics than what they were hoping to overturn. We are not explaining anything. We have not progressed beyond the *assumption* that all will be explained by the brain.

In the meantime, neuroscientists are trying to identify, if not the causes of qualia, then their neural correlates. This refers to the parts of the brain that turn on or "light up" in relation to certain activities. Brain regions correlate different activities such as listening to music or processing a visual image. Particular groups of neurons switch on when we listen to music—it does not follow that music is hallucinated by the brain. The music is out there, and it is being received and interpreted via particular neural pathways. What's so challenging about qualia is figuring out how the brain imbues certain bits of visual or auditory or olfactory information with emotional significance.

Wrote Sacks: "Philosophers argue endlessly over how these transformations [from computation to qualia] occur, and whether we will ever be capable of understanding them. Neuroscientists, by, and large, are content for the moment to accept that they do occur," and to seek out correlates. For instance, for several years now neurophysiologist Richard J. Davidson, at the University of Wisconsin–Madison, has been studying the brainwaves of meditating monks (in close cooperation with the Dalai Lama) without presuming to overturn the Buddhist view that consciousness originates not in the brain itself, but in what Buddhists call the "ground of being."

Efforts are being made to chase down the neural correlates of pathological hallucinations, as in schizophrenia, but there tends to be a circumspect silence surrounding the cause or correlation of hallucinations in mentally healthy people at times of peril and sorrow. What would prompt normal, functioning brains in roughly half the grieving population, for example, to suddenly see or hear things that aren't there? It turns out that we don't know. Not yet, at least. As neurobiologist Patricia Boksa notes, "It is unknown at present whether hallucinations are generated by similar mechanisms in patients and in healthy people."

Surprisingly, it turns out that we also don't know what the mechanism is that creates hallucinations in mentally ill patients. "Neuroimaging data have confirmed the expectation that hallucinations involve altered activity in the neural circuitry known to be involved in normal audition and language," Boksa writes. In other words, unlike imaginings, auditory hallucinations can be shown to *physically* involve our hearing. "However, the major question of how this altered activity arises is still unanswered . . . . In studies with human participants, neural processes can only be shown to correlate with, not to definitively cause, hallucinations."

The brain remains as mysterious as the deeper fathoms of our oceans and the unutterable vastness of dark matter. Saying that hallucinations in healthy brains are caused by this thing or that is the equivalent of medieval cartographers filling in uncharted corners of the world with the inky statement *Here be dragons.* What we're actually talking about is an assumption: *We will, at some point, find dragons in this quadrant of the globe.*

Britain's National Health Service gave King's College, London, research funds in 2012 to orchestrate collaborative research between experts in psychiatry, neurology and ophthalmology, "to better understand what causes" visual hallucinations. That is an open concession of the current limits of brain science, such as careful and disinterested scientists make. They *don't know* precisely the nature of complex auditory and visual hallucinations. They can map bits and pieces, and they are curious and eager to figure out the whole picture. But in the meantime, describing a sensed presence as a hallucination is no more or less presumptive than describing it as a deathbed companion come to guide us away, or as a guardian angel. As physicist Harold Puthoff said, it isn't what we know that gets in our way, it's what we believe.

I belabour this point on behalf of Rob Taylor and everyone else whose story I am telling you, but Martha Farah, director of the Center for Neuroscience and Society at the University of Pennsylvania, has said it best. "We should cultivate a certain epistemological modesty," she warned her colleagues in a 2009 lecture, "and not assume that we can explain everything that matters—or even what it means to matter—in terms of chemistry, biology and physics. And certainly, we should not infer that whatever cannot be explained in those terms does not matter."

✳

People who experience the Third Man draw strength and guidance from the mystery; they have a sense of being cared for and watched over. This is not dissimilar to people who sense the presence of the dead. Indeed, sometimes the two phenomena overlap, as in William Bird's story from the First World War, suggesting that the category distinctions are superficial—even if one experience is scientifically attributed to oxygen deprivation, say, and the other to loneliness and grief.

American adventurer Ann Bancroft was completing the first all-female land crossing of Antarctica in 2000, lagging behind her travel mate as she tired, when she encountered "an abrupt sense of being in very close company with another person." She soon realized this companion was her deceased grandmother. It wasn't the grandmother she had been close to in life—not the one she might have expected, insofar as she had anticipated anything beyond the rhythmic crunching of her boots on snow. Nevertheless, she was all at once "infused with a sense of comfort, warmth and strength." Later, in an interview with John Geiger, Bancroft said: "It startled me because there was a flood of emotion with it, because it was so strong, and it was good medicine, it was what I needed."

Astronaut Jerry Linenger was working on the space station *Mir* in 1997 when he became aware of the presence of his father, who had died in 1990. Linenger spoke to him and felt uplifted and moved by the "visit." His father conveyed his pride that his son had realized his dream of travelling into space. Later, Linenger chose to interpret the presence as a projection of his imagination, nothing more. And yet, at the time, he derived great consolation from the encounter.

In the grief literature, sensing the presence of someone deceased has been defined as "clearly seeing a figure of a human form, someone who was not physically present at that moment," or "vivid sensations of some presence, as if someone or something touched or pressed on all or some part of the body." Visual perception of the presence seems to be the rarest. Only about 5 percent in one study actually saw the deceased; auditory perception makes up about 15 percent, and the rest are partial impressions, such as my sister feeling hands on the back of her head and noticing a distinct presence in the room.

The New Mexican writer Nancy Coggeshall told me about feeling the presence of her deceased partner, rancher Quentin Hulse, five months after he died in 2002. "I feel pressure on the mattress beside me in bed. The second time the pressure is so great I roll over to see who is there." Hulse, locally celebrated as one of Gila County's last true cowboys, returned to her four years later. "So strong I woke up and asked who's there? I swept my hand over Quentin's side of the bed to see. This was the second visit. So strong was the sense of his being there I felt someone lying down beside me. FELT the impact of weight on the mattress. (Both times.)"

The prevalence of this experience ranges across cultures; it seems to touch, on average, about half the bereaved population. In a 2006 study it was found that in 86 percent of cases the sensed presence was the first revelation that a death had even occurred. Eighty-four percent of those interviewed were in good mental health at the time of the encounter. The time of day and the level of light made no difference. Only 5 percent found the encounter to be negative or distressing. For the majority, it was profoundly comforting.

For most of the twentieth century, the model for grief therapy was to encourage people to let go, to seek closure, to give up their neurotic attachment to the dead. It was in the context of this "breaking bonds" approach that sensed presences were first characterized as pathological hallucinations. Sigmund Freud's 1917 essay "Mourning and Melancholia" described healthy recovery from loss as the successful severing of ties. Loved one—exit stage right. Those who sensed presences were, in Freud's view, "clinging to the object through the medium of a hallucinatory wishful psychosis." Not only were the presences and voices and touches not real, they were *unhealthy.* It was a sign of therapeutic progress when patients "gained insight" into the fact that they were imagining things.

Freud was able to theorize freely about wishful hallucinations because there was as yet no neuroscience to test his claim that the brain is capable of conjuring such visions at will. What is fascinating here is that, now that we have a better-developed neuroscience, we haven't proceeded to test his claim; instead we use his claim to validate current psychiatric thinking about grief. It is also striking to think that Freud was writing his essay while young soldiers were experiencing guiding and helpful presences on the front. Even while they were coping and surviving with the aid of what they felt were deceased loved ones and guardian angels, their mental state was effectively being stigmatized by the armchair analysts of Europe.

With Freud in the background and no neuroscience to go on, here is what medical students typically learn about grief hallucinations in their textbooks: "The hearing or seeing of a close, recently deceased friend or relative is not a mental disorder," explains one introductory psychiatry book I perused. (Well, that's a relief.) "Usually these hallucinations become less frequent and cease over weeks or months." (Actually, according to bereavement counsellors, they can go on for years, or appear after many years. In a study of surviving AIDS partners in San Francisco, 22 percent were still sensing or seeing their beloved three and four years later, and the majority of these reported a deepened sense of spirituality as a result.) Continues the textbook: "They are comforting and benign. Perhaps they have a role in helping the individual adjust to the loss. While there is no clear evidence that persons with limited social supports experience more hallucinations during bereavement than those people with extensive social supports, such a finding would not be unexpected."

People held in solitary confinement have been found to hallucinate. Random, often paranoid imagery accompanies agitation, panic attacks and general mental disintegration after days upon days in total isolation. But this is not what is happening to widows and widowers. They haven't been left alone in tiny, windowless cells as their psyches disintegrate. It remains totally unclear how the act of longing could cause a hallucination. Why don't we hallucinate long-time lovers and partners who have left us heartbroken but don't die—people who just went off to forge new romances? Do those kinds of sorrowing visions exist?

In 2008, psychiatry professor Vaughan Bell wrote an article about grief hallucinations for *Scientific American,* pointing out how common they are. He ended by saying:

> We often fall back on the cultural catch all of the "ghost" when the reality is, in many ways, more profound. Our perception is so tuned to [our loved ones'] presence that when they are not there to fill that gap, we unconsciously try to mold the world into what we have lived with for so long and so badly long for.

That's gracefully worded but is it based on any evidence? It is an unkempt tangle of assumptions about what causes what.

Research has shown no consistent connection between levels of social support, levels of education or even religious belief systems when it comes to who perceives the dead. Here is an account from a lawyer interviewed by psychologist Erlendur Haraldsson in 2006, which shows why a longing for the lost one isn't in itself the cause of what we see. "I was coming home from a dance. I had not tasted a drop of alcohol," the lawyer recalled.

> It was about four o'clock in the morning and full light as we were in the middle of summer. I was walking over a

bare hill on my way home from town. Then there comes a woman towards me, kind of stooping, with a shawl over her head. I do not pay any attention to her but as she passes me I say "Good morning" or something like that. She did not say anything. Then I notice that she has changed her course and follows me a bit behind. I got slightly uneasy about this and found it odd. When I stopped, she stopped also. I started saying my prayers in my mind to calm myself. When I came close to home she disappeared. I lived in a house on the compound of a psychiatric hospital where my father worked. I go up to my room. My brother wakes up and says half asleep, "What is this old woman doing here? Why is this old woman with you?" And I tell him not to speak such nonsense and to continue sleeping, although I knew what he meant.

The next day, their father told them that one of his patients had died at three that morning. "What I had seen," the lawyer—well familiar with the challenges of eyewitness testimony—told Haraldsson, "fitted her description perfectly."

Whatever drove this man's encounter, it wasn't the poetry of longing and it wasn't the crisis of isolation.

In 1994 advertising professional Karen Simons lost her father unexpectedly to a heart attack. The events surrounding his death show again the fluid overlap in experiences that theorists keep trying to box up and separate. It took me a couple of years to get her to talk about it after she'd conveyed it to me in passing one day—she is busy, and it is difficult. Hard to explain. A tall woman with striking green eyes, she sat in her spacious office with her elbows on the desk, company key lanyard around her neck, paper and books in piles all around her. Her laptop pinged almost continuously as new emails arrived. But she ignored them, wanting to focus on the events surrounding the death of her father.

He was a farmer who had just turned eighty, and although he had had heart problems, he was still hale, with many plans. In the autumn he flew out to the west coast to visit his grandchildren, and there one of them had a dream.

> I had a dream where he asked me to take him home, that
> he couldn't die here, that he needed to get back to the
> farm. I remember the dream being outside, with miles of
> hills and forests and roads around, and he was very weak
> looking. He kept asking me to take him home but I couldn't
> figure out how to get him there. I asked him how and he said
> I could carry him, but I wasn't strong enough and I told him
> so. He told me that he really needed to get home and knew
> I could carry him there if I really tried. So I boosted him and
> started to walk.

It's a lovely image. It reminds me of something a palliative care counsellor once said about what we fear most: "Who's going to carry us when we die?" Who is going to remember us, to know we're still there, to keep us from feeling alone?

"Dad arrived back east on a Saturday," says Karen. "On Sunday night he insisted on cooking dinner for us"—Karen and her husband and sons—"and the next day he was going to a farmers' convention. The last sight of him I had was early in the morning; he waved at me and whoofed our newspaper close to our door with an overhead throw." She mimics the gesture. "That night, on the way to the convention banquet, he had a massive heart attack and died."

Karen continues: "After Dad died, I began driving his big old Ford Taurus. It was comforting, in a way, the way you hang on to people's shirts. But that's all it was. Until about six weeks after he died." She tilts her head and gazes past me, furrowing her brows as she tries to recall the exact timing.

It was a very cold night in January. I'm driving on the highway, and into the passenger seat comes Dad. I could feel him settle in. He had a very distinctive lean to the left, because of the way his back was. Also, you know how you know the sound of people's breathing? How you can tell whether it's your son or your daughter in the room? There was Dad. He rode with me from about Kennedy Road to Pickering [sixteen kilometres]. It was incredibly real, and it was completely transforming. I was almost giddy. I was hoping he would stay.

She never sensed him again, and decided that he had, in effect, been taking his leave. She remembered speaking with a Buddhist friend, who explained their view that the soul lingers for forty-nine days—roughly six weeks—before departing. That, however, wouldn't account for her aunt, whose son died thirty-five years ago.

He was a heavy-equipment operator who went through river ice into a deep and fast current. They never found him, or his machine. On a very regular basis her son comes and sits on the end of her bed, and they have a conversation. "And don't tell me I'm crazy!" my aunt always says.

Simons folds her hands beneath her chin, gazes at me and laughs. *This is just the way life is,* she is saying. *Our families are full of ghosts.* (Interestingly, Simons comes from Norwegian and Scottish ancestors. A study of sensed-presence experiences in Norwegian widows and widowers found that an unusually high number—75 percent—reported having them. This again raises the tantalizing possibility that there may be a genetic basis for the gift of a sixth sense.)

Surveys of people's reactions to grief counselling show, unsurprisingly, that they often feel "unaccepted, abnormal, not understood" when they relay these encounters to health-care professionals who aren't comfortable with the spiritual implications. Australian palliative care physician Michael Barbato, moved and astonished by the uncanny experiences he repeatedly encountered in his patients, writes: "Only after being informed about the commonness and normality of post-bereavement hallucinations did most other widows and widowers speak freely, expressing relief from thoughts that they might be considered insane."

Why should you be considered insane for experiencing something so lovely? Here is an account from the Scandinavian writer Johan Kuld, about an experience he had shortly after the death of his wife. It is a tale that surely one can only envy:

One day in January about three in the afternoon I was sitting on a bench in my room. Suddenly I saw the door to the room open and my wife came through. She was smiling and walked right up to me where I was sitting. I stared at her as if I was hypnotized and could not say anything. When she came close to me she put out her hand and said: "Do not be scared, I am alive." I took her hand and felt that she was not cold, she felt normal to the touch. Then I dared to ask: "Where have you been, what has happened?"

His wife replied, "Soon after I died in the hospital they let me stay there to look after a woman who was very ill. Since then I have been many places. Now this time is over, I am leaving. I have come to say goodbye." Then she said: "Take off your shoes and lie in the bed. I am going to lie down in front of you."

I did as she asked. She stroked my cheek and whispered beautiful things to me. And I was filled with a feeling of joy. Then I was filled with calm and I was surrounded with a sense of peace that cannot be described with words. I could feel that she still held my hand and stroked my cheek and I fell asleep. When I awoke a few minutes later I was alone. The space in the bed where she had been was empty. She was gone but I knew she had been there, spoken to me, had stroked my cheek and my skin. In that way she said goodbye and thanked me for our time together.

This incident is still so vivid in my mind. It does not get old or fade with the years that have passed since then. I have often asked myself: "Could I have dreamt it all?"

But my answer to that is definite: "No." This was reality as far as there is a reality, unusual and unforgettable at the same time.

✳

That a large percentage of people sense, see or hear from the deceased would not have surprised most humans throughout history. They lived out their lives with the bedrock assumption that the dead continued watching, consoling, guiding and even meddling in their affairs. From Rome through to nineteenth-century Iceland, the living shared their pastures and roads with those who'd predeceased them (they still do in parts of Indonesia, Thailand and Japan, among other places). Everybody could potentially see the dead, and communities invested a huge amount of effort in preventing some of those spirits from wandering or getting lost on their way to their appropriate destination in the afterlife. Certain spirits were at risk of haunting the living because of the tragic or violent nature of their demise. To keep them at bay, in some societies bodies were decapitated before burial or tied firmly to the ground. Suicides and criminals were secured beneath boulders or burned. Some were thrown into bogs and rivers. It wasn't only Bram Stoker's Dracula who had to be mutilated before his undeath became a more reassuring true death.

As the French medievalist Claude Lecouteux notes,

> The world was haunted, by the dead transformed into spirits passed on to another state, living another life in permanent conjunction with "contemporary" humans and

always capable of either giving them information or ceding to their imperious requests. The people of the Middle Ages had no fear of death: they dreaded the dead—some of the dead, in any case.

English historian William of Newburgh wrote in the 1190s, "one would not easily believe that corpses come out of their graves and wander around, animated by some evil spirit, to terrorize or harm the living, *unless there were many cases in our times,* supported by ample testimony [italics mine]." Given what we know now about the prevalence of deathbed visions, grief hallucinations and Third Man appearances, you can't accuse our ancestors of being unenlightened. They saw what they saw, and it was no different from what some of us see.

In Europe, the Church was uncomfortable with this lived reality of sensed presences, because it didn't dovetail properly with Christian doctrine. "Augustine posed the problem of perception," writes Lecouteux, referring to the influential fifth-century theologian. "Are these apparitions the creations of slumbering, somnolent or feverish men?" Upon reflection, Augustine decided that the apparitions were illusions or messages projected into the psyche by God: "It communicates to the dreamer that these dead bodies require burial," for instance, "and all without the knowledge of the former owners of these bodies." God acting as a ventriloquist? Fifteen hundred years later, scholars interested in the subject continue to speculate that a combination of things may be going on here: spirit, imagination, dream, source signal. The mystery continues.

Chaz Ebert, a Chicago lawyer and the widow of film critic

Roger Ebert, awoke the night that her first husband's father died to an almost cartoonish encounter with the Grim Reaper, as if her response to the faint signal she was picking up was to engage in a childish dream. "This sounds really crazy, I know," she told the historian Studs Terkel.

> I never believed in the grim reaper, I thought it was just some mythological thing . . . In the middle of the night, something woke me up. I opened the door of the bedroom, and there was this figure, about seven feet tall. It had the monk's robe and the whole thing, like the grim reaper. I looked into the face but it was not a face—it was just all dark. There were kind of lit orbs where the eyes should be. He communicated to me telepathically. He said, "Don't be afraid, I didn't come for you." He said, "Go over to the bed." I look in the bed where my husband was asleep, but it wasn't my husband anymore. This coffin appeared, and my father-in-law was in it. This lasted for a few seconds, then it all disappeared. Then my husband was there again and I woke him up and I told him that the grim reaper was there and about his father. He said, "I think you were dreaming." I said, "No, I wasn't dreaming, I'm awake!" So we go to sleep, and the next morning we call and they say his father died. His father died at the same time that the grim reaper came to my house.

Did the Grim Reaper literally go to her house? No, but the news of her father-in-law's death did.

Of such phenomena the scientist Dean Radin writes: "That vision is a construction from your memory and imagination, similar to a waking dream, except that the stimulus for the image is occurring somewhere, or some-when, else." Perhaps, speculates psychologist Erlendur Haraldsson, "The deceased moulds the perception in the mind of the living person." Again, like the ringing alarm clock piercing your sleep and becoming a telephone or a church bell in your dream, there is an instantaneous collaboration between world and mind.

Pope Gregory the Great (540–604) pursued the quandary of apparitions down a path that would ultimately contribute a little to the establishment of Purgatory as a distinct location between Heaven and Hell where restless souls awaited assignation. "Henceforth these individuals were regarded as imprisoned souls, or the damned. It was believed that the elect show themselves at times, but they are easily identified because they are radiant with happiness and beauty, and the clerics were incapable of confusing them with the sinners suffering the punishments of purgatory."

Eventually, what seems to have happened is that the Christian Church reshaped revenants from guiding ancestors and the disoriented or vengeful dead into spiritually suspended beings who depended upon the living to pray for their passage to heaven. This reshaping enabled the Church to take control of pagan ancestor worship and bend its purposes to Christianity. Hence the monks of Cluny established November 1 as All Souls' Day, to incorporate the pagan feast of the dead. The irony of what the Church accomplished, though, is that it managed to take common and powerful experiences, each of which has its own context—the Third Man in times of peril, the deathbed apparition and the beloved deceased in our ongoing lives—and turn them into church-related set pieces that nobody believed. In other words, when belief in Church doctrine in general declined in the West, so did belief in experiences that were never inherently connected to a particular religion in the first place. This distortion never happened in Asia, where the dead are still freely interacted with and honoured.

There is a kind of sensed presence that is not helpful or beloved but instead is completely unnerving. It's worth digressing into this territory because it may explain why people throughout history have gone to so much trouble to quiet the troubled dead. This is the terrifying spectre that assaults some of us during episodes of what has come to be called, in medical language, sleep paralysis.

David J. Hufford, professor emeritus at the University of Pennsylvania's medical school, is the world's leading expert on this phenomenon. Hufford discovered it through his own, out-of-the-blue experience in the 1960s. "I was a sophomore in college," he says.

> I'd gone to bed early after my last final exam. I was very tired. Being sleep deprived makes this more likely. I woke up hearing the door of my apartment open, and I thought it's probably somebody coming to see if I want to go for dinner. I heard footsteps coming across the room. And then I found I couldn't move, and that was very frightening. Then I felt the bed press down as if somebody was

climbing up on it; then I felt what felt like someone kneeling on my chest, and then I felt hands on my throat. I thought I was being killed. It was horrible. I had a feeling of revulsion and terror about this thing on my chest, not just because it was trying to kill me, but also because it seemed evil. I struggled to move, and when I did move it was gone. I leaped out of bed and nothing was there. That is a very typical sleep paralysis experience.

Approximately 30 percent of the population has experienced a simple episode of waking up and briefly feeling paralyzed, but encounters with the malignant sensed presence happen to 3 to 6 percent, according to psychologist J. Allan Cheyne, of the University of Waterloo. It was initially assumed that episodes of sleep paralysis were coloured by cultural expectation, that if you roused in this peculiar halfway state between sleep and wakefulness and expected to be visited by a werewolf, a witch or whatever your culture believed in, then you would be. But people like Hufford, who had no prior knowledge of the phenomenon, can experience it out of the blue. Another such person is the novelist Barbara Gowdy.

"It began in my early twenties," she told me. Gowdy is a beautiful woman: physically graceful, with rich brown eyes and a fierce intelligence. She questions everything, holds every object up to the light and examines every facet. This experience was no exception.

It only happened when I took naps, and if I was lying on my back. The first time it happened, the room got very cold, and very dark. I could hear my husband in the kitchen [but] I was suddenly aware of a hideous, unspeakable evil in the room. And then I was aware that it was on my chest. It was so real, and concrete. And I couldn't move or call out. Suddenly, as if waking up, it would be gone.

Twelve or fifteen years later it started again, also during a nap.

I had my eyes open. I hadn't gone to sleep yet, and the temperature changed again, and the evil presence was back. It's the complete opposite of bliss, or of the feeling you have with a newborn baby. This evil was deeply old. It wasn't the evil of a brand-new psychopath. It was evil that had been in the world since time immemorial—a wise, experienced evil. It gave me access to an idea of evil that I hadn't had before. It was dirty . . . and old . . . and sexual. [Experiencing] it was a fate worse than death.

Gowdy went to the public library to research what was happening to her, but there was scarcely any information available. Until the late 1970s, the sensed presence in sleep paralysis was considered to be a rare side effect of narcolepsy. "I saw artists trying to capture the evilness, but no one could quite capture it. Until you've had the experience, you can't know it."

Desperate to avoid her tormentor, Gowdy stopped having naps. For years she managed to evade the ineffable terror. "But then it started happening again. This time it whispered, low and growling, in my right ear: 'I am the wolf.'" Fed up with being terrorized, Gowdy abruptly and angrily surrendered. "Well," she replied, "do your worst." At this, "the hallucination popped and disappeared and never came back. That suggests to me that I actually took on my own subconscious and, by fearlessness, I beat it." She also wonders whether it wasn't a deeper, collective unconscious she was tapping, or, as she put it, "the memory of pain, the memory of evil."

Gowdy's reflection reminded me of a time—about a week after I interviewed Audrey Scott, the woman who died in her home—when I woke up at 3:30 a.m. beset by troubled thoughts. I was haunted by a book I'd just been reading called *The Tiger*, by the journalist John Vaillant. A man in some hellishly barren and isolated town in far eastern Russia had hanged himself with his belt after his only son was eaten—nothing left but his boots— by a solitary Amur tiger. For some reason I awoke feeling intense empathy for this father, fully inhabiting the horror of living with his knowledge that his child had become meat and that there was nothing else—no job, no love, no prospects—to ameliorate that soul-destroying truth. I tossed and turned in the airless bedroom, drifting along the shoreline of sleep. And then all of a sudden I was in . . . a lucid dream? A night terror? I felt as if I'd fallen into a force field, like a wind or electricity, or at any rate a realm—a *living* realm—of dread.

Maybe I was simply feeling intense dread in response to the unfamiliar sensation; I'm not sure. But I'm certain that, within it, I was powerless; I was trying to hold on to myself, talking to myself in my head, saying something along the lines of "Stay strong, you can survive this," although I can't remember now exactly what I was saying. I think I was trying to separate myself—the backbone or essence of myself—from this force. It wasn't dissimilar to the effect that Tolkien describes when the hobbits foolishly gaze into Saruman's crystal and behold the eye of Mordor.

I've never experienced anything else like it. There were no physical effects, the way there is with a panic attack; my heart wasn't racing. I just wanted to avoid the experience like the plague. At last I was able to turn on the light, and I listened to a talking book for an hour until I felt it was safe to try falling asleep again. Whether that could be considered an episode of sleep paralysis, I can't say.

"We have been especially struck with the frequency that the specific term 'evil' is applied to this presence," writes Allan Cheyne about such episodes, "even by people to whom this term does not readily spring to mind." As one of his study subjects said, "I literally fear for my soul."

What does that mean? How does it feel different than the perception of threat, as in a feared attack by a wild animal or a hurtling car or an impending tornado? In order to explain the terror of sleep paralysis in persuasive terms, we may first have to understand how consciousness discerns a difference between imaginary threats of one kind—impersonal, animal, weather-driven or even from a palpably insecure and jittery assailant—and a threat that is *powerfully evil*. There has to be a quality to that perception that extends beyond what is generally perceived by the threat-scanning function of the amygdala in the brain. But no one seems to know what it is.

Why do these terrifying presences materialize only when people are dozing off? It is argued that they inhabit the realm of hypnagogia—*hypnos* is "sleep" and *agogos* is "leading in"—that strange level of consciousness between sleeping and waking that often features whacky thoughts and images. Research at Fukushima University in Japan has established that people experiencing sleep paralysis show an EEG signature that mixes wakefulness with REM sleep. So we are speaking of dream physiology but not of typical (which is to say wildly idiosyncratic) dream content.

"Hypnagogic experiences are a bit of a mystery in the sense that scientists don't know exactly how to classify them," writes Jeff Warren in *The Head Trip: Adventures on the Wheel of Consciousness.* "Are they dreams, or thoughts, or something else entirely? Where exactly do they come from? Is there any logic to their appearance?" Those are important questions, particularly in light of the research suggesting we are more susceptible to "telepathic impressions" and other uncanny perceptions when we have dimmed down the other noise in our conscious awareness.

Most dreams and hypnagogic images are entirely unique to the dreamer, but the more consistent experience of hearing a door open and footsteps and sensing or seeing a deeply evil creature that crushes or even sexually assaults you is what makes sleep paralysis so puzzling. Why not react to the sound of crickets outside your window or distant sirens on a city street? Why not incorporate the sensory input that is a houseguest flushing the toilet or a neighbour having a party? Why does the door open? Why do the footsteps come? In a medieval account from Sweden, the presence is said to sound like a cloth sack dragging across the floor. The Navaho have heard moccasins shuffling; patients have heard stockinged feet on hospital carpets.

Then there is the dread beyond words. "The greatest primal terrors that I have ever witnessed: character-forming stuff," says one person. "These attacks leave me shuddering and crying," says another. "Sometimes I'm so scared I get sick to my stomach." Very commonly, there are also auditory hallucinations. For one man, these included a growl that was hellish beyond reckoning: "To describe the demonic growl as the epitome of evil would be an understatement. It was pure, unadulterated malevolence. It struck fear into the very core of my being, almost shattering my soul. I hope to God that I never hear it, or anything like it, ever again."

"The complex pattern of sleep paralysis, including the evil presence, the shuffling footsteps and a host of other details, does not arise from culture," David Hufford has argued. "Rather, in cultures around the world, traditions of spiritual assault arise from this experience." Thus we have the succubus and incubus of medieval Europe and the "sitting ghost" of China. The experience is the origin of the word *haggard*, which began as *hag-rid*—being ridden by the hag. Similarly, *nightmare* comes from the Anglo-Saxon word *mare*, or "crusher." Nightmare: someone who crushes you in the night.

There are occasions when the experience is intersubjective, meaning that it happens to a number of people in, say, a village during the course of one week, or to two people in the same room. I spoke to a friend who recalls waking up in an English country house in the early 1970s. She had a sensation of being paralyzed, an apprehension of pure dread. She heard a baby crying and crying—a desperate, needful sound in the hollow dark. Her lover, lying beside her, had the exact same experience at the same time. He was also paralyzed; he also heard the wailing child.

"The neurophysiology of the paralysis is very well understood; we know the biochemistry and we know the pathways," says Hufford.

> But we don't know any pathway that produces *all* of this. We can say that in the sleep paralysis state, with that physiological trigger, you're in an altered state of consciousness. So far so good, but that's as far as the conventional explanation takes you . . . . I don't know any explanations that fit the data, other than the traditional ones, which is that it's a spiritual experience.

Hufford notes that when a group of psychiatrists were presented with a sleep paralysis case study and asked to diagnose the patient, more than half labelled the anonymous subject psychotic. As with other sensed-presence encounters by the grieving, by the lost or stranded, this is the label they receive—and fear. "When I interview people, they often tell me I'm the first person they told," Hufford says. "I ask them why that is, and they say, 'Because I didn't want people to think I was crazy.'"

"One of the most fascinating social issues here," Hufford continues, "is that all of these kinds of experiences were well known in Western tradition up to three or four hundred years ago. It's not simply that Western culture never had a clue about these things. We erased knowledge of these experiences from the cultural repertoire while the experiences were continuing to happen. That's a level of social control that's very impressive." Perceiving a spiritual being, whether loving or cruel, has become, he says, "an illegal experience."

✳

This prejudice is beginning to change, particularly in the area of grief therapy, as counsellors start to take note of other cultural approaches. There continue to be societies throughout the world that sense or see the spirits of the dead and accept them for what they appear to be. One influential study of Japanese widows found that their continuing bond with the presence of their deceased spouse in the context of Japanese ancestor worship—setting up altars in the home, leaving food, treats and incense—made them much more psychologically resilient than their American counterparts. The people they loved brush their shoulders, their cheeks, remain among them and are nourished in turn. I remember this from the country of my birth, Mexico, where All Soul's Day remains Día de los Muertos, or the Day of the Dead, and families picnic in the graveyard. They lay out favourite foods and drink and festoon the tombs with marigolds, while shopkeepers sell skulls and prancing skeletons. Death is in life—it is part of life.

London neuropsychiatrist Peter Fenwick has commented on this:

> Often—and for the people concerned this is the most significant aspect of the experience—its emotional impact is so great that it remains a lasting source of comfort to the recipient and often has the power to alter their own perception of what death means. For them, whether what

happens is dismissed by others as "simply coincidence" is irrelevant: the fact that it happened is enough.

Sometimes it's enough, but often it is not. We are held back from embracing the comfort and reassurance of spirits by a society that belittles the experience, that says "show me the money," which is to say, "the proof." There is no proof. Neuroscience simply cannot tell us, at this juncture, why people have sense-of-presence experiences. What used to be thought of as guardian angels, succubi or ancestors are now simply called hallucinations. The shift in semantics is fine for some people, such as the astronaut Jerry Linenger, who figured his visiting father was an illusion but felt consoled nonetheless. For others, however, it creates an enormous loss of meaning. "There is a danger that in objectifying or analyzing an experience we may lose sight of its significance for the bereaved or the dying," palliative care doctor Michael Barbato has ventured. The best thing that ever happened to you becomes a thing that others want to deem unreal. *I don't mean to be unkind, but your sister was clearly imagining things.*

"Where is the wisdom we have lost in knowledge?" T. S. Eliot asked in his poetry, almost a hundred years ago now. "Where is the knowledge we have lost in information?" We need to be far more careful about tossing around assumptions about what the bereaved—and the terrorized and the stranded—do or don't see, because we don't know. Until we do, they are entitled to forge their own meanings.

BE STILL

How the Dying Attain Peace

leak midwinter in northern Ontario: a frozen forest, hushed and empty, with scarcely a road cutting through the miles of trees. People for the most part traverse it high above, in jetliners or, if they are making their way from one regional spot to another, shakily in twin-propeller planes. In January 1979 a young doctor named Yvonne Kason was travelling in this regional fashion, evacuating a critically ill Ojibwe woman with measles encephalitis from a tiny fly-in reserve to the nearest hospital, a few hundred miles away. Travelling with Kason was a nurse, Sally Irwin, and the pilot, Gerald Kruschenske, who was confident he could keep his twin-engine Piper Aztec on course even as the wind began to rise and snow swirled in from the west. The passengers hunkered down, tense and cold, as the weather intensified into a blizzard.

Over the course of some horrifying moments, ice began to film the plane and the right propeller blade faltered. Then the left propeller sputtered and stopped. The Piper started to lose altitude, and when it became apparent to the pilot that he couldn't clear a looming hilltop, he had no choice but to try to glide in for a crash landing.

"I felt intense panic, intense fear," Kason told me thirty years later. "I thought, 'Oh my God, I'm going to die.' But it came out fast; it was like a death prayer—*omygodImgonnadie*—this call from my soul for help." Immediately, to her immense and lasting surprise, she felt a wave of tranquility descending, washing out the terror, which receded to leave only peace. "My mind became calm and I was no longer afraid, and I was alert and conscious, like I am right now." Perhaps a second or two had elapsed, no more. Then, again to her astonishment, she heard a voice. *Be still,* it said, *and know that I am God.* Born into a Christian family, Kason hadn't been to church since she sang in a United Church choir during adolescence, but she was clearly remembering—or somehow hallucinating—a verse from the Old Testament's Psalm 46. "God is our refuge and our strength, a very present help in trouble," the psalm begins. Relax, fear not, be still. "I am with you, now and always."

"What do you mean by a voice?" I asked her, pen in hand as we sat catty-corner at her dining room table drinking coffee. I had sought her out after hearing about her experience from a psychologist at the University of Toronto. I wanted to know why my sister had seemed so serene and unafraid at the end of her life, as if she were surrounded by or encountering an invisible source of joy. In Karlis Osis and Erlendur Haraldsson's deathbed research, they found that 753 of the dying in their American and Indian surveys experienced an "elevation in mood" right before they passed away. Eighty-seven percent of those who saw visions with a "take away" purpose—someone beckoning, for example—died within sixty minutes.

While most of the patients who saw the "take away" visions reacted by becoming elated or serene, only 7 percent responded to other kinds of hallucinations with a mood change. If some biochemical process was involved, it was oddly selective.

> Some patients in our sample received injections of morphine and other substances closely resembling endorphins, yet afterlife-related experiences were not increased in that group. If these medically administered substances did not induce the phenomena, why should they be the cause when internally secreted by the body?

So, what would be another way to get at this mystery? Could someone who hadn't died, yet who'd come to that very edge, shed light on why the dying might become radiantly peaceful regardless of drug or endorphin levels?

For Kason it was the experience of the unexpected voice that began to calm her. "How was it not your own voice or thought?" I pressed. She considered the question, pushing a pale strand of hair behind her ear. Kason is in her mid-fifties now, an elegant woman whose high intelligence is warm and engaged. She understood why I was pushing her for more detail. In medical circles you don't get to simply claim that you held yourself together during a plane crash because a voice commanded you to calm down. "Okay, it's like you're walking down a hall and someone comes on a loudspeaker and tells you to stop. You *know* it's not you." She studied me to see if that analogy worked. "I mean, it was that clear. I was being instructed."

By whom? A man, a woman?

"If I were to put a gender on it, I would say it was more masculine than feminine. It was a low voice, a deep tone. It was *profoundly* comforting." She spoke confidingly, as if all these years later she still couldn't believe this crazy thing had happened.

Listening to her, I mused. Here we have the Third Man in an emergency, what the soldiers experienced at the front. Only, instead of providing guidance, the presence or voice offers strength, calm. In a rushing matter of seconds, wind howling and plane tumbling, Kason felt herself to be in an altered state of consciousness. "I was not thinking or judging or analyzing, the way one normally does." Nor was she numb or in denial; it was "the sort of peace one gets in meditation," she explained.

> You're in what they call a "higher mind" state, which is intuitive and receptive. I was watching the plane crash, and the nurse and I were bracing the patient, and I felt profoundly peaceful and calm. I knew there was nothing to be afraid of. I just knew it in my soul. *Even if we were going to die.* And I started comforting the patient, 'cause she had woken up and her eyes were looking at me, as the doctor, and I was able to now speak to her and transmit the sense of comfort. I just kept saying, "It will be okay, it's going to be okay."

That was a lightning-quick uptake of certainty for a twenty-six-year-old woman who hadn't pondered the afterlife much. "I knew with absolute certainty something I had never known before: that there is absolutely nothing to fear in death."

I ran my hand absently along the back of her cat and remembered what Katharine had whispered to our sister Anne in the hospice, that she was no longer afraid. In a recurring dream that Katharine had for years, she found herself in a slowly crashing plane, skimming the tops of trees. Always it was a nightmare. Always she was afraid. In the hospice I hadn't been able to understand why she no longer was, and she was too short of speech to elaborate. Was it denial? Evasion? Morphine? An endorphin rush? Or had a mysterious, loving voice commanded her to "be still"?

Kason resumed her recollection of descending to a partially frozen bay on the Lake of the Woods, just north of the U.S. border. "The pilot, really heroically, tried to do a guided crash landing on the ice," she said. "He almost did it, but the ice was so thin that as soon as the plane stopped, it broke through and sank. We had to quickly try and get out, and I was trying to get the patient out, but I couldn't [undo the straps]." The cargo door, through which the stretcher had entered the plane, was soon submerged. Unable to extricate it, the surviving three soon fell into the water themselves, weighted down by winter gear, and gazed helplessly as the stretcher-bound patient was lost with the Piper.

The Third Man—not a seen presence, mind you, just a voice—took charge of Kason once more.

This voice started repeating, "Swim to shore." I actually argued with it, because I had taken lifeguarding, and they always tell you, in a boating accident, don't try to head for the shore. It will be farther away than it looks. I tried to ignore the voice and get on the ice. But every time we put any weight on it, the ice would break off. And when you're cold and wet, you get tired *really* fast. My parka and boots were like lead, dragging me into the lake. So I surrendered to the voice because what I was doing wasn't working, and I started swimming to shore. It was really, really difficult. I didn't think I was going to make it. I kept going under and the water filled my lungs.

"Somewhere in that life-and-death struggle is when my consciousness suddenly *whooshed*"–she gestured with her hands, sweeping them up to either side of her head–"and it was like I was no longer looking out of my eyes. I was twenty or thirty feet up, and I could *see* myself swimming." She gazed down at her dining room table as if still amazed. "This, to me, was very bizarre, because I'd heard descriptions of people going out of body when they were lying down, but not when they were swimming!" She looked up at me and laughed. "I puzzled over it for years."

To this point in her story, what Dr. Kason experienced remains within the realm of what psychologists are comfortable explaining, or at least theorizing about. A body of research shows that when people are confronted with their own demise— in plane crashes, car accidents, falls from cliffs, even jumps from bridges (as later reflected upon by the few who survived)—they enter a state of dissociation. It is a defensive stance, essentially, triggered by anticipating trauma and psychologically fleeing from it, making it seem as if it is happening to somebody else. Different researchers put different spins on this theory, but all agree that certain elements are common.

In Atlanta-based cardiologist Michael Sabom's 2004 study of accident survivors, forty-three of fifty-two people experienced dissociation during the event, suggesting that it is a typical, rather than unusual, reaction to the prospect of death. A flight attendant, Jan Brown-Lohr, who survived a United Airlines crash in 1989, told Sabom: "I felt, this is . . . this is it, this is how I'm going to go, this is how I'm going to die, and it was the most incredibly peaceful moment I've ever known, that I was in no pain, I had no fear anymore, it was total peace." This occurred even though she never physically came close to death, or even serious injury. Sabom decided to dub this extraordinary psychological state the "acute dying experience," or ADE, which is not to be confused with actually, acutely dying. (Nor, as my cousin briefly thought I'd said when I was talking about my research, a cute dying experience. No, not accidentally smothered by puppies, but equally pleasant perhaps.)

"Peace and painlessness commonly occur," Sabom notes, "followed by overwhelming emotion and pain after the threat has passed . . . thus, the ADE is a subjective response to threat of death, including dissociation and hyperarousal that, with the removal of the threat, is replaced by delayed emotional and cognitive response." For example, a soldier might rouse herself to heights of calm and clarity in the midst of a firefight and then only afterwards succumb to all the emotional and autonomic

nervous system responses you'd expect to see in someone feeling terrified.

Sabom argues that his concept of ADE "mirrors the three-
stage response of perception, defense, and recuperation observed
during predator–prey interaction in animals. It appears to be an
adaptive response promoting survival in the acute situation." He
points to research on mice. They appear to have a two-tier fear
response, depending upon how extreme a threat is. A sudden
banging sound in the kitchen where they've been scarfing down
crumbs will put them in flight mode. But "threats perceived to
be life-threatening, such as mammalian odors or calls of night-
hunting aerial predators, elicit a higher, second-tier response in
mice associated with . . . an instant release of endorphins."

If the predator attacks, the mouse needs to concentrate on
survival strategies and not be distracted by anxiety and pain.
Hence the endorphin flood, which would make them feel pain-
free and calm. If the mouse manages to scoot away, it can enter
the "recuperation" stage, in which pain floods in and commands
attention to whatever wounds it has received. Following this
animal model, Sabom and other researchers argue that the
perceived severity of the threat determines whether we shriek,
freeze, cower or . . . go into Zen mode. The horror movies have
it all wrong. Anthony Perkins attacking Janet Leigh in the
shower would not necessarily have made her scream. Instead,
she would have stood frozen and silent. But is dissociation all
there is to it?

In 1893 the Swiss geologist Albert Heim published his
exploration of the emotional state of mountain climbers who
had fallen in the Alps. Heim himself had taken such a plunge,

and he had been astonished by his radical transformation from terror to "a divine calm [which] swept through my soul." The other climbers he interviewed had similar experiences of transcendent peacefulness. As death appeared imminent, his collection of tumbling men "often heard beautiful music and fell in a superbly blue heaven containing roseate cloudlets."

Here is a woman describing being trapped beneath a waterfall in an interview with Sabom:

> The very first reaction was [that] I was terrified for about 2 seconds. Complete terror and panic. After the 2 seconds, I just gave up. I remember consciously thinking "there is nothing I can do, just give up." That's when I started breathing water. I remember the water going down my lungs. There was no pain. I just started breathing water realizing that I was going to die. And [then] this extraordinary feeling of total peace. I have never experienced that before—extreme peacefulness. It was just this overwhelming feeling." [Others were able to extricate her before she drowned.]

Some, like Kason, have the bizarre perception of leaving their bodies. A U.S. marine experienced a fifteen-thousand-foot free fall into the Pacific Ocean caused by a failed parachute. He recalled this startling shift in his perspective:

> I was falling and working with the chute and just like that [snap of the fingers] I was 15 or 20 feet away watching me struggling. I can remember vividly my orange flight suit, my helmet was yellow and had three big blue diamonds

stenciled on it. I can remember vividly seeing my boots. I had thought that I had boondockers on, low boots that we normally wore, and was surprised that I had on these brown high-topped boots . . . I have never experienced [anything like] it before or since.

A flight attendant on a Pan Am plane that was set on fire during a terrorist attack in 1973 provided this account. Suddenly,

it was just all light. It was just incredible happiness and joy! It was indescribable. I saw myself. I was lying there in my uniform. I could see myself clearly through the smoke and I thought "why aren't I moving?" But I really didn't care because I was so happy where I was.

A second tale from the Alps was written by the amateur Swiss climber J. L. Bertrand, who got caught on a ledge so narrow that if he moved he would fall to his death, but if he didn't move he would freeze. He chose the latter course, and as he got colder, at some point he began floating above himself. "'Well,' thought I, 'at last I am what they call a dead man, and here I am, a ball of air in the air, a captive balloon still attached to earth by a kind of elastic string, and going up and always up.'" From his newly expanded vantage point, Bertrand spied his climbing guide farther down the mountain, drinking Bertrand's Madeira wine and eating his chicken lunch, about which he teased the guide later. He also saw his wife, hundreds of miles away, travelling to the village of Lucerne.

"My only regret," he wrote, "was that I could not cut the string. In vain I traveled through such beautiful worlds that earth became insignificant." When he "returned" to his body after being found and revived by the lunch-thieving guide, "my grief was measureless. I felt disdain for the guide who, expecting a good reward, tried to make me understand that he had done wonders. I never felt a more violent irritation."

Psychoanalyst Oskar Pfister, a contemporary of Freud's, read some of these mountaineering accounts and called the experiences of Heim's climbers "shock thoughts." This idea would lay the groundwork for what later became known as "peritraumatic dissociation." Psychiatrist Russell Noyes, of the University of Iowa, researched such experiences in the 1970s and concluded that "depersonalization as a defense against the threat of extreme danger or its associated anxiety" was the best available explanation. But in Noyes's research, the most common features of peritraumatic dissociation are distorted time perception, a sense of surreality, a sense of being on automatic pilot, and confusion or disorientation.

What this describes actually happened to me once, when I was a novice driver who accidentally (and idiotically) turned left into a phalanx of fast-moving taxis on Broadway at Columbus Circle in New York City. I promptly got hit broadside, and I remember that sense of time slowing, of becoming preternaturally calm; when my crushed Toyota finally stopped spinning, I primly shifted into Park. About half an hour later, after the police and paramedics had come and gone, taking my passenger and the cab driver who'd hit me to hospital with them, I began sobbing, and for several hours I could not get a grip on myself. This was the delayed emotional and physiological response that is said to occur with peritraumatic dissociation.

In Sabom's accident study, however, there was a difference between how people reacted when they were suddenly embroiled in uncertain danger—like me in my careening car—versus how they reacted when they recognized the almost certain prospect of dying. The first group "frequently described an acceleration and sharpening of physical, mental, and visual perceptions consistent with the psychological state of hyperarousal." The accelerated perception, for instance, is what causes time distortion. For Sabom, this feature distinguished his concept of ADE from Noyes's idea of peritraumatic dissociation. He argued that the reactions worked along a continuum, like the first-tier and second-tier responses of mice. Some people merely felt depersonalization, as I did, but "when fear and horror were present, these were always the initial emotions, were short-lived, and were followed by a feeling of peace of equal or greater intensity."

"Considered together," Sabom wrote, "these findings present an interesting paradox: the more terrifying and traumatic an accident may appear, the more peaceful[ly] and painless[ly] the accident may be experienced." And witnesses take heart: it is apparently more upsetting for the bystander than for the person undergoing the accident, a fact often lost in depictions presented by novelists and moviemakers.

But if we, like mice, are capable of tailoring our responses to the severity of the danger we're in, does that account for the entirety of these experiences? Perhaps we are both mice and men. We are capable of having both a psychological and a spiritually transcendent reaction to danger at the same time. There is no other way, at least for Yvonne Kason, to account for what happened to her next.

✳

For about an hour after the plane went down in the Lake of the Woods, Kason found herself suspended between the earthbound and the ethereal, with part of her awareness engaged in the effort to keep swimming in the iron grip of icewater while the blizzard blurred her sight, and part of her awareness shifting to what seemed to her an infinitely beguiling light. It was as if the day were morphing in some impossible way, at once storm and radiant sun. She found herself encompassed by and somehow absorbed into the light. This was no longer about endorphins, if it ever had been. For one thing, she could feel the pain being inflicted by the cold, which an endorphin rush would have blocked. For another, the light was well beyond anything she had ever encountered.

"The experience of . . . it was formless," she said in her airy dining room in the house she shares with her teen son. "It was like dissolving into the light." She considered that description for a moment. "Yes, that's it. It was like dissolving. I was like a drop of water which had now merged into the sea of light. I still existed, it was still me, but I was in this incredible ocean of light and love." It wasn't just a visual perception of light; it was an experience of full immersion in a sentient, emotional atmosphere. "The strongest aspect for me was the love. Perfect love. It's impossible to describe."

Ineffable, calming love. Erotic love? Platonic love? Something you love, or that loves you? People who take heroin or opium will describe an impersonal sense of bliss, as if they didn't have a worry in the world. They don't remark upon a relational dynamic—an active love. But people who witness this light are veritably shattered by the emotional quality it somehow seems to have. Kason closed her eyes and smiled, assuming the expression you see when people are recalling the most exalted moment of a love affair. She even unconsciously hugged herself in her white sweater as she spoke: "It was a maternal love. Like I was a newborn baby on my mother's shoulder, utterly safe." Then she added more shading: it was not only an infant bliss but also a revelatory discovery. "It was like I'd been lost for centuries and I'd found my way home."

Was that what my sister was immersed in as she lay so peacefully on her bed in the West Island Palliative Care Residence? Is that why she wasn't afraid?

Light is the core, the essence of experiences that are mystical in nature. "In accounts of the light, contemporary testimony bears a striking resemblance to medieval narratives," writes Smith College religious studies scholar Carol Zaleski. "Both medieval and modern descriptions of otherworld light blend visual qualities such as splendor, clarity and transparency with sensory/emotional effects such as warmth and energy." There seems to be something wildly synesthetic going on in how people encounter this light. Its strange beauty is "one of the few truly 'core' experiences," notes Zaleski, "that cut across cultural and historical boundaries."

It is also a central experience in every religious tradition:

Spoke Zoroster: "Righteous souls will enter heaven, and there they will have a vision of God who is depicted as pure light."
"The Lord," says Isaiah in the Torah, "will be your everlasting light."
In Hinduism: "Place me in that deathless, undecaying world / Wherein the light of heaven is set."
Jesus: "I am the light of the world."
In Buddhism: Clear Light, Infinite Light
Said the Baha'i prophet Abdu'l-Baha in nineteenth-century Persia: "That divine world is manifestly a world of lights."

The sixth-century pope Gregory, who was obsessed with collecting first-hand accounts of spiritual encounters, reported what he'd heard from witnesses of the light in a series of manuscripts he called his *Dialogues*.

Anyone who has seen a little of the light of the creator finds all of creation small, because the innermost hidden place of the mind is opened up by that light, and it is so much expanded in God that it stands above the world. In fact, the soul that sees this is even raised above itself. Rapt above itself in the light of God.

Here is a description from about a thousand years later, by the accomplished and respected sixteenth-century Spanish abbess and mystic Teresa of Avila:

The splendor is not one that dazzles; it has a soft white-
ness, is infused, gives the most intense delight to the sight,
and doesn't tire it; neither does the brilliance. It is a light
so different from earthly light that the sun's brightness
that we see appears very tarnished in comparison with that
brightness and light represented to the sight, and so different that afterward you wouldn't want to open your eyes.
It's like the difference between a sparkling clear water that
flows over crystal and on which the sun is reflecting and a
very cloudy, muddy water flowing along the ground.

Six hundred years after that, hospital patient Monique
Hennequin described the light to her cardiologist, Dr. Pim van
Lommel: "This luminescence consisted of a kind of infinite river
of brilliance, like the brilliance of a setting sun reflected in rip-
pling water with little pinpricks of light like small stars. The brilliance was made up of beautiful little globules of light, extremely
bright and quite unlike anything on earth." Another patient of
Lommel's exclaimed, "Too much! It's simply too much for human
words. The other dimension, I call it now, where there's no dis-
tinction between good and evil, and time and place don't exist.
And an immense, intense pure love compared to which love in
our human dimensions pales into insignificance, a mere shadow
of what it could be."

It is perhaps, then, in response to similar perceptions that
the dying murmur "wow, oh wow," or "I am melting into all this
beauty." As palliative psychologist Kathleen Dowling Singh has
noted, "the dying become radiant, and speak of 'walking through
a room lit by a lantern,' or of their body 'filling with sunlight.'

They share these experiences with a quiet, thankful awe. There is something about the quality of their demeanour and expression at these times that has a feeling of purity, like a world wiped clean by new snow or as seen through the eyes of an infant. Ego is not in these expressions. . . . It would appear that we move into a sacred realm of Being that we recognise with faith, confidence and gratitude to be our own. One woman kept returning from this depth of being to let those of us around her know: 'I cannot tell you how beautiful this is.'"

Rene Jorgensen, a Danish NGO worker who encountered this light during an adverse drug reaction in India, tried to get across to me the sheer power of its sentient luminescence. He was in his scantily furnished apartment in Montreal. The main visual draw in the living room was an enormous framed print of a lighthouse surrounded by raging ocean waves. "If you stand on that ledge behind Niagara Falls—you know, where tourists can be sort of underneath or behind the water," he said, "imagine that the incredible roar and volume and energy of that water is love. It's something like that." His heightened sense of awareness, he added, was also beyond compare. "The experience is so powerful that it doesn't leave any room for doubt."

When scientists and journalists describe the "white light" that people see during near-death experiences as if they were talking about fleeting quirks in visual perception related to oxygen deprivation, they are misunderstanding the phenomenon. Yvonne Kason, for one thing, wasn't having an NDE—there was no oxygen deprivation in play. She hadn't even lost consciousness. In fact, the through line with experiences of this light is not our physical state when we encounter it but our emotional response. "When you look at the essence of what people are going through," Kason says, referring to the variety of spiritual experiences she later dealt with as an open-minded physician, "that essence is getting closer and closer to the same thing. So if you had your experience because you're a mystic spending hours and hours in prayer, that is very similar to the yogi who is meditating, and the near-death experiencer, and the dying person having a deathbed vision. To me, these are all glimpses of the same spiritual reality."

People have encountered this light in moments of extreme depression as well as at times of acute terror. When Beverly Brodsky was twenty, the young Jewish American from Philadelphia lost half the skin on her face in a traumatizing motorcycle accident. Deeply despondent, and still grieving the death of her father as well, she offered up a bitter prayer to a God she didn't believe in, to just let her life end. "The pain was unbearable," she wrote. "No man would ever love me; there was, for me, no reason to continue living." As she lay face down on her bed in a rented apartment in Los Angeles, "somehow, an unexpected peace descended upon me. I found myself floating on the ceiling over the bed . . . I barely had time to realize the glorious strangeness of the situation—that I was me but not in my body—when I was joined by a radiant being bathed in a shimmering white glow." She accompanied this being,

> traveling a long distance upward toward the light . . .
> Within it I sensed an all-pervading intelligence, wisdom,
> compassion, love and truth; there was neither form nor sex
> to this perfect Being. It, which I shall in the future call He,

in keeping with our commonly accepted syntax, contained everything, as white light contains all the colors of a rainbow when penetrating a prism. And deep within me came an instant and wondrous recognition: I was facing God.

"I've spoken with people who have had full-blown spiritual experiences with all the characteristics of near-death experiences," Kason told me, "yet nothing happened to them. Men who fought in the wars: A grenade drops in front of them. They're absolutely certain they're going to die. 'There's a live grenade just dropped in front of me,' and *boom*, they go into the light. And then by some freak thing the grenade didn't go off. Or another man told me about fighting in World War II and his plane got shot down. He goes into the light, and then somehow the pilot managed to pull the plane out of spin and they never crashed. In 1979 I didn't even know what to call what had happened to me."

Whatever the phenomenon is, it is extraordinary and transformative, and it propels human beings far beyond what endorphin rushes or tricks of the optic nerve could ever achieve. It has likely driven religious conviction since the onset of human consciousness.

In the 1920s, the German theologian Rudolf Otto tried to grapple with the impossibility of understanding how, at the same time, light could be love, could be knowledge, could swallow you—and your ego—whole. He argued that religious orthodoxy had almost fatally committed itself to defining the religious experience in rational terms. By doing so, it had abandoned the very essence of spiritual experience, which is that it is ineffable, indescribable. It is like a culture lacking a concept for *palm tree* or another society having no word for snow. Until you have experienced it yourself, the experience is totally untranslatable. That is not the same thing as saying "You have got to have faith because we say so." It is the opposite of that statement. Mystical light is a powerfully evident experience when you have it; you're taking nothing on faith—you are bowled over sideways. But when you have not had the experience, you are left with unconvincing words lying flat on a page.

The word *holy* denotes moral or ethical goodness. A holy man. Or just "holy cow." The word has deteriorated in meaning to the point of sheer ridiculousness, the way the word *awesome* has. ("Do you want me to put your receipt in the bag?" "Yes, please." "Okay, awesome.") For mystics and shamans, *holiness* refers to a radically deeper meaningfulness that rests at the very centre of all religions. Otto chose to call it the numinous experience, borrowing from the Latin word *numen*, which roughly translates as "divine power" or "God's majesty."

The numinous, Otto wrote, "is beyond our apprehension because, in it, we come upon something 'wholly other.'" The numinous contains an element of fascination, of "strange ravishment." It contains energy, "vitality, passion, emotional temper, will, force, movement." It isn't what you saw (if you saw it) in Clint Eastwood's movie *Hereafter*, in which a woman caught in the Thailand tsunami perceives vague and flickering figures in a watery white light. That doesn't even begin to convey the dynamic complexity and force.

"Oh that I could tell you what the heart feels, how it burns and is consumed inwardly!" said the sixteenth-century Italian mystic Catherine of Genoa. "Only, I find no words to express it. I can but say: Might but one drop of what I feel fall into Hell, Hell would be transformed into a paradise." Try as they might, the language of mystics always comes across as weirdly ornate, as if they are being decorative rather than desperately at a loss for the right, sufficient words. In his recent book on hallucinations, neurologist Oliver Sacks writes that people can hallucinate only images, sounds and odours that they are already familiar with. Yet according to people who encounter it, the numinous is as unprecedented an experience as it gets. People devote years of their life to finding something in human society that replicates the enthrallment of their encounter with this light; they leaf through art books, visit libraries, search for the music they heard, scour art galleries. But the only place they find it, ultimately, is in how it reverberates in their souls. *I felt like I'd been lost for centuries and I found my way home.*

This, then, is what we hear from the sensed presences and the dying. "I'm going home now." "I have to go home." One woman described the day after her mother died: she saw a vision of her mother leaning against a wall in a hallway, saying, "I am back home." Could it be that the dying and the dead are trying to tell us something that is difficult to convey? We're so busy defending the fact that we saw or heard them at all, we can't even arrive at the point of wondering what they mean.

"Everything turns upon the character of this overpowering might," Otto wrote of the numinous experience, "which can only be suggested indirectly through the tone and content of a man's feeling-response to it." He described having a conversation with a Buddhist monk and asking him to describe nirvana. "After a long pause came the single answer, low and restrained, 'bliss . . . unspeakable.' And the hushed restraint of that answer, the solemnity of his voice, demeanor and gesture made more clear what was meant than the words themselves." So it is with the radiant transformations we witness in the dying. There is nothing they could say that would be any more moving to us than what we see. When psychologists Osis and Haraldsson did their deathbed-vision research in the 1970s, the witnessing doctors and family members told them this repeatedly. "Patients reacted to otherworldly visions with otherworldly feelings," they wrote. "A coal miner's wife was dying of a very painful cancer. Her consciousness was clear when she said to the nurse: 'Virgin Mary! How beautiful!' The nurse said, 'She seemed to be in ecstasy—very happy.'"

When we speak of feeling peaceful, we can mean many things. When we speak of contentment or happiness, many things. To say unequivocally that an endorphin cascade in the bloodstream in response to terror is the same as spiritual bliss is to say that Romeo's love for Juliet is the same as his love for his uncle, or for Verona. Lost in translation, the emotional concepts become cruder, simpler, easier to misidentify. We have no model to help us think. Or rather we do, in writing such as Otto's, but the scientists who tell the journalists how to think about this elusive yet powerful experience are specialists in their own language, not in spiritual texts. Only a few have tried to bridge that divide.

Andrew Newberg, a neuroscientist and professor of radiology at the University of Pennsylvania, collaborated with psychiatrist

Eugene d'Aquili in the late 1990s to study peak spiritual experiences in Buddhist meditators and Franciscan nuns at prayer. The two men were curious to see if there was a neural signature to spiritual experiences, something that would distinguish them from other emotional states. When the meditators and nuns reached a point in their meditation or prayer where they felt they were attaining mystical consciousness, they were instructed (beforehand) to tug on a string, which signalled the researchers to initiate an intravenous injection of radioactive material that would show up in the brain during a SPECT scan. After the injection, the subjects where wheeled from the room in which they had been praying or meditating to an examination room with a SPECT scanner, which whirled around them, scanning for the radioactive tracer while they lay prone on a table. (Was this distracting? Yes, it surely was, but the tracer had locked on to the peak experience, so however the poor subjects felt immediately afterwards was irrelevant in terms of the science.)

The scans revealed a "sharp reduction" in blood flow to the posterior superior parietal lobe, which is the part of the brain that orients us in space. When it is damaged by a stroke, for example, it becomes impossible for people to tell where they end and the room around them begins. This was the subject of neurologist Jill Bolte Taylor's autobiography, *My Stroke of Insight*. When a sudden, unexpected stroke in her thirties damaged that part of her brain, Bolte Taylor couldn't tell her fingers from the phone as she tried to dial 911; everything rapidly became boundary-less. We need this function of our brain to, quite literally, put one foot in front of the other when we walk down the street.

Somehow the nuns and meditators were able to temporarily quiet or disable this brain region, preventing sensory data from reaching it and enabling them to experience what has been called the *unio mystica*, the sense that Yvonne Kason had of being merged into a sea. As described by the fourteenth-century German mystic Johannes Tauler, the soul becomes

> sunk and lost in the abyss of the Deity, and loses the consciousness of all creature distinctions. All things are gathered together in one with the divine sweetness, and the man's being is so penetrated with the divine substance that he loses himself therein, as a drop of water is lost in a cask of strong wine.

As with descriptions of sentient light, this sense of dissolution into a universal whole is referenced in every spiritual tradition, from Sufism to Taoism to Christianity. "Thou shalt not love him as he is: not as a God, not as a spirit, not as a person, not as an image, but as sheer, pure One. And into this One we are to sink from nothing to nothing," said Tauler's contemporary, the mystic Meister Eckhart.

"We saw evidence of a neurological process," wrote Newberg and d'Aquili, "that has evolved to allow us humans to transcend material existence and acknowledge and connect with a deeper, more spiritual part of ourselves." Whether that part of ourselves is within or beyond the brain, they couldn't say. "At this point in our research," Newberg wrote,

> science had brought us as far as it could, and we were left with two mutually exclusive possibilities: either spiritual

experience is nothing more than a neurological construct created by and contained within the brain, or the state of absolute union that the mystics describe does in fact exist and the mind has developed the capability to perceive it. Science offers no clear way to resolve this question.

.Subsequent research by Montreal neuroscientist Mario Beauregard imaged the brains of Carmelite nuns with an fMRI machine. He found distinct patterns of activation in several parts of the brain, repudiating any notion of a "God spot" but otherwise confirming Newberg's discovery that the brain is doing something quite different during a mystical experience than what it does when we remember, dream or imagine. This is really the key point here. Whatever is going on, it is not akin to other emotional or psychological states, and it isn't simply a by-product of random neural malfunction. Put another way, it could well be an injury that facilitates the experience, the way a tear in the hull of the *Titanic* facilitated the pouring in of sea-water. But the sea is not therefore a delusion.

From the point of view of the person encountering the numinous, a word such as *hallucination* isn't quite up to the job of describing the sensory, emotional, moral and psychological complexity of what is going on. "It's like the first time you jump in an ocean," Kason said.

> You experience a lot of things at once. You experience that it's wet, you experience that it's cold, you experience that there are currents. Maybe you experience weeds, maybe you experience the salt. I mean you experience a lot of things at

once that maybe later you can put words to. It was like that; there were many facets to it. The light, the love, the higher power. There was no *question* that I was . . . sort of *embraced* by a higher power. How do you know these things? I don't know; you just knew. In that love and in that light and in that intelligence, I just knew that what was meant to be was meant to be, down there, and it really didn't matter. I was in complete joy, complete love, complete contentment.

Like the meditators who remained oriented enough in this world that they were able to tug on the string and initiate the SPECT scan injection, Kason was at one and the same time oriented to the light and to the lake, the blizzard, the pilot and nurse also swimming, and her physical peril. "I would say part of my mind was still in the body, but most of my consciousness was not. It would shift back and forth. It's sort of like you're cooking dinner, your kid's watching TV and you're talking on the phone, and you remain aware of all three things throughout." This description of being mindful of two worlds corresponds with what nurses and family members sometimes observe with the dying in hospice care. Nurse Maggie Callanan commented on this recently in a radio interview:

> They, on some level, understand that it's odd, that they have one foot in two worlds. Do you remember the old Brownie Hawkeye cameras where, if you didn't advance the film, you'd get two pictures on one negative? Two images on one film—I think—is what the experience is like. I have sat for hours and hours and watched this, and I

think it's like two images on one negative. Some of what they're saying belongs to this world, and some of it belongs to a world we cannot see.

"Sort of like a split-screen TV is the best I can describe it," Kason said. "The big picture was the light and the little tiny picture was the body swimming to shore, and the light was *far* more interesting." She laughed. "I still knew my body was there, but my awareness shifted to the light. At a certain point, as my body was sinking, I shifted more of my attention to it. I remember, because I was so calm, thinking, 'Oh yes, so you do drown the third time you go down.'" Switching back to the perspective of her floundering physical form, Kason saw at lake level that the current was carrying her swiftly towards a fallen pine tree by the shore. If she could angle herself with two more swim strokes, the current would—and did—deliver her to the tree. "And that's how I survived, because I did not have the strength to swim the last few feet to shore."

For another thirty minutes Kason and her pilot, Gerry Kruschenske, languished on the edge of the lake at Devil's Elbow, while nurse Sally Irwin remained in the water, clinging improbably to some driftwood. Their mayday had been caught by an overhead jet, whose pilots relayed it to the nearby town of Kenora. A complicated and heroic helicopter rescue ensued; it won the two helicopter pilots awards for valour and became the focus of media coverage, while Kason's private spiritual experience remained out of view.

By the time they reached the hospital, the young doctor was slipping in and out of consciousness, continuing to hover above her body. She was now severely hypothermic. The emergency room nurses at first covered her with a light blanket. Abruptly, Kason told me, "My body spoke—this is without me planning to speak. It said, 'Boy, could I use a hot bath.' Clearly it was something higher speaking through my mouth, telling them what to do. How did my body speak this when I was not even thinking it?" Kason had no training in the treatment of hypothermia.

The nurses said, "Gee, maybe that would help. Let's take them to the whirlpool in physio." When they put me in the bath, I felt like a genie being sucked back into a bottle. Suddenly I'm fully back. It was like finding out the end of the story, because I didn't know how it would end until then.

It ended with life, enlightened.

DEEPER

What NDEs Tell Us About Where the Dying Go

am wary of the sea. My sister and I once spent Christmas in a cabin on the westernmost edge of Vancouver Island, near Tofino. The power of the roaring Pacific during a winter storm, tossing fifty-foot deadheads onto the beach like so many twigs, seemed tornadic to me. This is the ocean that David Bennett once drowned in.

In 1983 Bennett was a twenty-seven-year-old native of Syracuse, New York, working as chief naval engineer on the research vessel *Aloha*, which was owned by International Underwater Contractors in California. One evening in early March, the weather grew stormy and the sea became restive. The crew of *Aloha* had just spent the day testing a remote-operated submersible in the company of its manufacturer, and now they found it too rough to bring the ship safely back into port at Ventura. Bennett was asked to ferry the manufacturer and a few crewmen back to shore in a rubber Zodiac, which was flexible enough to take a pounding in the waves.

It was very dark. From the bow, Bennett scouted for the harbour, but the wind was blowing salt water directly into his face while huge Pacific swells nudged the Zodiac off course, towards a sandbar a mile or so south of Ventura that was creating massive twenty-five-foot breakers. Before they could retreat out to sea and skirt the sandbar, a wave rose up, curled and crashed on top of them, folding the Zodiac in half and shattering its fibreglass floor. Bennett was thrown into the gargantuan surf. "It was the most raging, violent force that had ever attacked my body," he said later.

Bennett was submerged in the ocean with no sense of which way was up, wearing an old canvas life jacket that was soaking up water like a sponge and preventing him from floating to the surface.

> My years of experience as a diver had taught me not to panic, because if you panic you will surely die. I'd [also] learned that a strange thing happens to me in dangerous situations. A clear, calm sense comes over me, allowing me to work through the danger. So I knew not to try to swim for the surface, because I could be swimming the wrong way. I could tell by the pressure of my ears that I was in deep water, past the sandbar.

He began feeling starved for oxygen. "In dive school I had been forced to experience oxygen deprivation in a safe and controlled environment. The instructor slowly decreases the oxygen going into your dive helmet, so that as you breathe, you build up carbon dioxide." Remembering what that felt like from his training, Bennett began to realize he might die. "I couldn't hold my breath any longer, and I couldn't find my way to the surface. I clearly remember the burning, choking and pain in my lungs as I breathed in the salt water and went through the agony of dying. [But] the agony quickly melted away into darkness."

With the darkness came silence, or what Bennett more aptly described as "a shocking absence of noise." Given what he'd just been going through—the almost deafening roar of the breakers, the frantic thrumming of his pulse—this soundlessness must have been remarkable. He noticed that he no longer felt as cold. He wondered if this was yet another stage in the experience of oxygen deprivation, one he hadn't encountered in his training. Was it a dream? It couldn't be; he knew he hadn't lost consciousness.

All at once Bennett began to sense a "connectedness" in the dark. It was, somehow, more than mere darkness and silence; it had an emotional quality to it. How could that be? "Although I could not quite grasp the meaning of this perception, I sensed there was something going on around me." He began to become aware of a field of light, growing brighter and beginning to surround him, although he couldn't tell if he'd moved towards it or if it had moved towards him.

"As I got closer, I started *feeling* the light." This utterly unexpected sensation intensified as the luminescence grew all the more radiant.

The light was brighter than any light I had ever experienced. As a chief engineer on a ship, I had many occasions to use an arc welder. The light emitted from the arc is so bright you have to wear protective eye gear to look at it without burning your eyes. This light was brighter than that, yet I could still view it comfortably. [This is a common remark from people who have had these experiences. Light that ought to make them squint or flinch, like sunlight on snow, is painless to gaze at.]

At this stage in Bennett's undersea adventure, having run out of air and swallowed ocean, he should have blacked out, died or—at the very least—lapsed into an acute state of confusion. Instead he discovered that he could see more clearly than he ever had before (he doesn't see well without his glasses) and that further, he could see in multiple directions simultaneously, which he found fascinating. At some point he realized that he was merging with the light—had become light himself. He accepted the transformation, feeling overwhelmed and awed. "Every time I explain my experience in the light, I feel a touch of the love that accompanied it. It is still incredibly emotional for me even many years later."

Bennett has reflected on the difference between this numinous experience of love and what we more typically feel:

In the light, without a body, I could handle that level of love because I had left the physical side of emotion behind . . . in our physical body we feel excitement in our stomach, and love can make us light-headed. In the light

I felt love, joy, passion and excitement without the physical sensations. I had no physical reaction that might cause one to say, "This is something I want to distance myself from," "I am not ready," or "I am not worthy."

The other reaction one might have, of course, is terror at losing oneself, at surrendering autonomy and identity in this merging. There's a reason that most dystopic fiction, from Orwell to Koestler to Madeline L'Engle, frightens by dwelling upon the prospect of forced conformity and groupthink. To become ants in a colony, fish in the sea, drops in an ocean of light—those fates are alarming to highly individualistic Westerners. Yet in the *unio mystica* the loss of self isn't experienced as frightening. On the contrary, separateness is suddenly understood to be the illusion that we have been living with our whole lives.

In his survey of afterlife beliefs, *The Modern Book of the Dead,* journalist Ptolemy Tompkins describes this from the Buddhist perspective:

> Whether we are currently in a physical body (be it human or animal or supernatural) or in the forty-nine-day period that separates [for Buddhists] one incarnation from the next, all of us suffer from having forgotten one absolutely crucial piece of information: neither we, nor anyone else, nor any single thing or quality or situation in the entire universe, has any underlying *separate* existence whatsoever.

Tompkins likens this existential amnesia to his own recurring dream in which he finds himself back in high school, appalled that he faces a test and hasn't studied for it. The emotion is appropriate to the situation, the classroom is ordered and it all makes sense as a scenario, but for the fact that he hasn't been in high school for thirty years. That is the key missing piece of information. We can completely buy into a reality without ever realizing that we are missing one totally obvious fact, whatever that fact may be. In this case, the missing fact is that we are inseparably connected. As Sogyal Rinpoche writes in *The Tibetan Book of Living and Dying*, "the memory of your inner nature, with all its splendor and confidence, begins to return to you when you are dying."

Alan Ross Hugenot, a San Francisco engineer who had an NDE during a motorcycle accident, found that the experience lent him insight into why those who are dying more slowly in a hospice might seem to "know" when they were going to die. It isn't a premonition, in his opinion. "It's your decision," he says, referring to the dying drifting back and forth between worlds. "You begin to be at peace, knowing that you're going home, and aware of that peace to come, you cease the tiring effort of holding the illusion [of separateness] together." An interesting thought. If we want to understand what the dying are demonstrating or conveying to us, it certainly doesn't harm the inquiry to listen to those who've had NDEs.

Near-death experiences have been reported by 12 to 18 percent of the American population. They differ from what happened to Yvonne Kason insofar as they occur during periods of physical near-death, which is to say during incidents of drowning, car accident, coma. It's important to note that, because of brain trauma, over 90 percent of cardiac-arrest survivors have no memory of what happened before and after their resuscitation, so the true incidence of NDEs remains unknown.

An interesting example of this is what happened to forty-two-year-old Vancouver realtor Tony Cikes, who doesn't remember that his heart stopped for two minutes during a routine operation in 2011. But when he was roused to consciousness, "I knew that something had saved my life. It was a bizarre feeling. I felt off and I couldn't quite explain it. I felt that someone had saved my life even though I didn't know what had happened. I had no idea that my heart stopped." Upon awakening, he discovered a surge of compassion that he could only describe as "an energy." The nurse who was attending him in recovery was the first recipient. "I wanted to help her. It was an awakening to being compassionate. I felt this love inside me. The doctors were surprised."

Psychiatrist Carlos Alvarado, who has written extensively on the subject of NDEs, fixes the known incidence rate at 17 percent. To decide what to recognize as a bona fide NDE, he uses the Near-Death Experience Scale, developed by University of Virginia psychiatrist Bruce Greyson, head of the university's Division of Perceptual Studies and long-time editor of the *Journal of Near-Death Studies*. This scale comprises sixteen items, including feelings of peace, being surrounded by light, experiencing cosmic unity, seeming to enter another world or landscape, encountering other beings, undergoing a life review, and receiving new insight or knowledge. A classic NDE is considered to have occurred when more than seven of the sixteen items are involved. The greater the number of items, the deeper the NDE. David Bennett, submerged in the ocean, experienced all of them.

After Bennett merged with the light, he encountered what he could only roughly describe as silhouettes or presences that projected "waves of love and compassion." Although he didn't recognize anyone in particular, he experienced these presences as family, or as more familiar to him on some level than the people he was related to in his day-to-day life—a soul family. "I just knew unequivocally that I was home," he said, echoing others, "and it felt so exceptionally magnificent." In the company of these presences, Bennett proceeded to review his life. "Did it take twenty-seven years?" I asked him in a phone interview, entirely unable to imagine what this would entail. In the experience, "time doesn't exist," he said. "It's one of the things I have a hard time grasping. I haven't come across anything [in literature] that adequately describes the sense of timelessness. The detail [of my life] was richer and more vivid than in this life. It was my interactions, and others' as well. We're unbounded. I could envision multiple streams of experience."

Bennett was at times embarrassed by what the presences who encircled him were witnessing in his life review—the toes he had stepped on to become a chief engineer at such a young age, the way he'd treated certain people, his rough upbringing in foster care—but they exuded no judgment. "Their form of communication involved projecting a knowing and comforting energy that contained more information in a millisecond than our [typical] thoughts could assemble in a day." The most captivating part of his life review, he said, was gaining the perspective of those whom his actions had affected. He gave me the example of being in a bar he scarcely remembered and picking a fight with an unwilling foe, goading and taunting the man—he'd been in his fair share of brawls—but now he observed and felt the emotional energy his aggression had generated, the sourness, like an acrid smell.

Bennett was lucky, in a sense, that all he'd done wrong by the age of twenty-seven was throw some punches, steam ahead in his career and occasionally behave like an asshole. One man, a California arms dealer who had sold weapons in Latin America, had a near-death experience when he was struck by lightning in 1984. He underwent a life review in which he felt the ripples of pain in every family who'd lost someone murdered by one of his weapons. After his NDE, he became a hospice volunteer.

Small kindnesses also appear in the life-review experience, driving home the point that love and compassion are what neurosurgeon Eben Alexander, who had an NDE in 2008, calls "the absolute coin of the realm." Bennett didn't even remember his interactions with one woman who showed up in his life review. "When I was young," he says, "I was brash. At one point I was working in a butcher shop and I took a liking to this lady, and she was the grumpiest lady around. But for some reason I took a shine to her. For months I did special things for her." Mostly he was trying to coax a smile out of the woman, just to see if he could—a little game. "But I got to re-envision it and see how all those small efforts I made affected her."

After a million years or none, twenty-seven years or five seconds—who knows?—Bennett suddenly "heard a clear, distinct voice that didn't emanate from my [presences]. I sensed it came from the light itself. I stopped paying attention to my life experiences and the group. I listened carefully to an incredibly loving voice, which told me, 'This is not your time. You have to return.'"

He had by now been deep underwater for several minutes. Bennett's arm had got entangled in a bowline dangling from the broken Zodiac on the sea's roiling surface. As a wave shoved the boat across the water, the still-attached line jerked him upwards, dislocating his shoulder and thumb but dragging him to the water's surface. He watched this from an out-of-body perspective, observing as another wave flung him against the boat with such force that it expelled the water from his lungs, much the way you might get the wind knocked out of you. At this point he experienced a "rushing, buzzing vibration" and found himself roused to consciousness within his cold, dense-feeling, injured and gasping body. The shock was equally an emotional one. "Separating from the light and rejoining my body was the hardest thing I had ever been asked to do. It was more painful than drowning."

Bennett's fellow travellers regrouped with him around the shattered vessel—all had survived—and now they collectively began to kick-swim to shore. When they got there, they were too shocked and exhausted to talk to each other, first lying on the sand, drained of strength, then walking to the highway to flag down a lift back to the marina and to Bennett's van (one crew member had popped Bennett's shoulder back in). Speechless, they drove back to Santa Barbara.

By this time it was after midnight. Bennett's wife, unbeknownst to him, had just woken from a nightmare in which he had died. When he arrived at their apartment bedraggled and covered in sand, she roughly deduced what must have happened—a man overboard or the ship capsizing. "She was trying to question me, get a reaction. I wasn't responsive because I couldn't stop thinking about my experience. Eventually I said, 'Hon, I think I died tonight.' This confession so frightened her that she started slapping me. Afterward she told me that she hit me because she thought I was in shock."

But Bennett received the gesture as an act of immediate and absolute censure, like Pandora trying to slam down the box lid. "I shut up for eleven years," he says. "It was too much for me, it was overwhelming, I couldn't face it." This statement brought to my mind another bit of T. S. Eliot's poetry: "We have lingered in the chambers of the sea / By sea-girls wreathed in seaweed red and brown / Till human voices wake us, and we drown."

Those human voices are clamorous in their attempts to find a purely scientific explanation for NDEs. A number of theories have been offered since the experience was first formally described by psychologist Raymond Moody in his 1975 book *Life after Life*, just as multiple explanations have been proposed for the Third Man since Shackleton wrote of his Antarctic sojourn in the early twentieth century. The NDE has been attributed to psychopathology, altered blood gases, sleep disorders, and changes in brain activity around death. Every theory, no matter how tentative, invariably gets headlined in the media as "NDEs Explained." As I write this, the *Guardian* newspaper arrives in my mail, featuring the headline "Near-Death Experience: The Brain's Last Hurrah" and citing a new study done at the University of Michigan, where induced heart attacks in rats demonstrated continuing electrical activity in the rodent brain for thirty seconds post mortem.

The small number of scientists who engage in NDE research in depth and personally interview those who have had the experience tend to be uncomfortable with sweeping conclusions. The power and complexity of NDEs have not been explained to their satisfaction, they say. Mysteries about human consciousness abound. "The most important objection to the adequacy of all [these] hypotheses," writes psychiatrist Bruce Greyson, "is that mental clarity, vivid sensory imagery, a memory of the experience, and a conviction that the experience seemed more real than ordinary consciousness are the norm for NDEs." Yet they occur in brain states that should not be conducive to any coherent thought process at all, regardless of whether you want to call that process a dream, a memory or an elaborate hallucination. Science has yet to be persuasive about how that could be. Severe brain impairment due to oxygen deprivation or powerful sedation doesn't set up the right conditions for incisive thought.

Jayne Smith, a retired teacher from Pennsylvania, had an NDE before they had a name, in 1952. "I thought I was the only person in the entire world that this had ever happened to," she said. "I couldn't imagine why." An attractive, crisply dressed woman, she spoke very matter-of-factly at a conference I attended in Raleigh, North Carolina, put on by the International Association of Near-Death Studies. She was on a panel of "experiencers," which is the awkward label that people who have had NDEs seem to have agreed to use. Maybe we should call them accidental mystics.

In any event, the NDE took place during the birth of her second child. "They used, back in those ancient days, a device called a Trilene mask, which was a bracelet on the wrist with a nose cone. When your labour pains became more than you wanted to cope with, you would put it to your nose, breathe in, and for a few seconds lose consciousness. I remember, after a particularly disastrous pain, putting that nose cone up to my nose and inhaling as deeply as I possibly could." When she finished that inhalation, she had overdosed on general anesthetic, not unlike Michael Jackson. She went into cardiac arrest and the doctors began emergency resuscitation.

But that's not what she experienced.

I felt . . . I felt myself rising up out of my body, up through the top of my head, and was in total blackness. I didn't see a tunnel. I thought, *This is not right, I should be unconscious, but I'm still awake. Something is a little bit off; I don't know what it is.* And then, as quickly as that, I found myself standing in a kind of grey mist, and I knew right away what had happened.

Here Smith's voice took on a musical sense of wonder as she recalled the moment: "I remember distinctly thinking, *I know what it is,* I've died. *I've died.* And I was so overcome with joy, because I had not been annihilated. I thought, *I am still me, I am still here,* and I felt so grateful."

What is striking about NDEs is that they are narratively coherent through consciousness and into what ought to be blackout. Smith knew that she was in labour in a delivery room, self-administering gas; and then she questioned why she no longer felt pain but wasn't unconscious; and from there the thread of awareness continued, the way it had for David Bennett. "I remember joy pouring out of my being," she said. "And as I did that, the grey mist dissipated and everything became brilliant white light."

At the time of her experience, in the early 1950s, doctors would have assumed that she was having a hallucination brought on by the anesthetic—had she told them about what happened, which she didn't. As it stands, about 2 percent of patients hallucinate briefly before surfacing from general anesthetic, but the content of their hallucinations is disjointed and random. Unconsciousness during anesthesia, as measured by EEG, is associated with an immense quieting of brain activity.

Smith's rapturous response to the love surrounding her grew so intense that she worried she would shatter. As if sensing this, the light dimmed a little, and then it revealed or unveiled an exquisite meadow, featuring colours she had never seen before. "The colours were extraordinary," she said. On a ridge above the meadow she saw some figures, to whom she went and wordlessly communicated. "There was a block of knowledge," she continued, touching again on an element that seems to feature in deeper NDEs, "or what I later suspected was a *field* of some kind, that came in and settled on me all of a piece, and I suddenly knew that I was eternal, that I was indestructible, that I always existed and I always would exist. There was no *end.* There was no end."

Smith recovered, delivered a healthy daughter and said nothing about her NDE for twenty-five years. By the time I heard her speak about it, more than fifty years had passed, but her facial expression during the telling was gradually transfigured by joy. Hers was the first story I heard after my father and sister died, and I felt so consoled that when I later met her in an elevator, I actually hugged her (she reciprocated in amused surprise). I was disappointed only that she could say nothing of meeting a sister who'd gone into death before her.

The closer that NDEers are to actual death—such as being clinically brain-dead or in cardiac arrest—the more likely they are to encounter deceased people in the NDE, according to research by University of Virginia psychiatrist Emily Williams Kelly. This is reminiscent of the take-away role that the deceased seem to play in deathbed visions. In fact, both phenomena can occur to dying people, as the terminally ill may have NDEs in palliative care days or weeks before they actually die.

In some cases the person perceived is not yet known to be dead by the person who has the NDE. Thus it isn't merely a matter of expectation. A nine-year-old boy with meningitis awoke from a coma and told his parents that he had seen his teenaged sister—who had in fact just died in a car accident, unbeknownst to the boy and his parents. Children in particular will sometimes spontaneously recognize photographs of dead relatives in the family album after their NDE, as detailed in several studies. "Another striking finding," says Dutch cardiologist Pim van Lommel, "was that people with a deep NDE, and especially those with a very deep NDE, were significantly more likely to die within thirty days of their cardiac arrest, although medically they were no different from the other patients. I cannot offer an adequate explanation for this." (Oddly enough, I was going to interview someone in Vancouver who had had a deep NDE on a cardiac ward, and although he was young, with a good recovery projected, he died suddenly.)

About 56 percent of Westerners who have NDEs experience themselves going out of the body. A child who sustained a major head injury in a car accident spent months in a coma before returning to waking consciousness with slurred speech and a permanent mental disability. Nonetheless, he recalled his time in the hospital this way:

> I felt like the inner part of me, I felt like my inner part in me was up like a ghost and I felt like my inner body was taken out of me. I felt like I was going out, like my inner body was going out of me and I felt like, I felt like a dummy almost, that my body was like a dummy and I was outside it.

Two years after the accident, when the boy visited the ICU he'd originally been treated in before being wheeled elsewhere for the sojourn of his coma, he went straight to the correct section and the specific bed.

Other features of the near-death experience are more varied. People in indigenous cultures, for instance, never report going through anything resembling a tunnel. Instead they journey across otherworldly landscapes, much the way their shamans do. Here is a Maori account:

> I became so ill that my spirit actually passed out of my body. My family believed I was dead because my breathing stopped. They took me to the *marae*, laid out my body and began to call people for the *tangi*. Meanwhile, in my spirit, I had hovered over my head, then left the room and travelled northwards, towards the Tail of the Fish.

She sailed over rivers and mountains, "until at last I came to Te Rerenga Wairua, the leaping off place of spirits." There are accounts in Hawaii of walking towards Pele's Pit, a volcano into which dead souls hurl themselves. An Australian Aborigine, meanwhile, described an NDE in which he set off by canoe until he reached an island, where he met traditional spirits and dead relations. Journeys on land and by water are likewise taken in Africa and South America. While they differ in terms of cultural contour, what they seem to have in common is the person being brought to a halt at some point by some relative or spirit, and then being told to go back, that it isn't their time.

Beyond that, the indigenous accounts are uniform in what they lack. No account collected from a hunter-gatherer, "primitive cultivator" or someone from a "herder culture" features the kind of life review that David Bennett described. Because they inhabit cosmological worlds in which a sense of unity and interconnectedness is already fully expressed in day-to-day life, the idea of individual fate (and personal accountability) is perhaps less relevant. As sociologist Allan Kellehear notes, "Individuals are no more responsible than the world."

Accounts from India, China, Thailand, Tibet, North America and Europe do feature the experience that Bennett had, of reliving and learning from some (or all) of their actions. A 2013 study of severely brain-injured patients suffering post-traumatic amnesia in Guangzhou, China, uncovered three NDEs out of eighty-six patients. One experienced a life review that involved a "structure of many animals" in which the impossible creature "reminded him of the wrong deeds he had done in his life" by "sending him light rays that pierced his chest region and created huge waves of negative feelings like fear, sadness and anger." In India, people often encounter the spiritual equivalent of irritated bureaucrats, telling them they're the wrong one, that Yamdoot (the death messenger) has brought the wrong person. This would be the same Yamdoot that shows up in the hospital room in deathbed visions in India.

"Clearly, NDEers meet an assortment of social beings, and their previous experiences shape their interpretation of the identity, function and meaning of these beings," Kellehear wrote. Perhaps an analogy could be made to Dr. Ellie Arroway, a character in Carl Sagan's sci-fi novel *Contact*. Travelling to meet some unknown alien intelligence that has broadcast a signal to earth, she finds herself on a beach that resembles one from her Florida childhood and then encounters the alien, projecting itself as her beloved deceased father so as not to frighten her.

Do we encounter what we can emotionally and conceptually relate to? That doesn't seem to work for hellish and distressing NDEs, though, which make up a small percentage of those reported. When Nancy Evans Bush, a young Protestant American in Connecticut, had an NDE during childbirth, she found herself confronted by black-and-white circles that flickered back and forth, *clickety-clack, clickety-clack*, and told her maliciously that she didn't exist and had never existed, that her baby didn't exist and had never existed. It would be years before Bush came across an illustration of these circles, in Carl Jung's book *Man and His Symbols*, and realized that they were the Taoist symbols for yin and yang. "I got a feeling of just sheer horror, because my immediate thought was 'My God! Somebody else knows about this!' I was so horrified that I simply threw the book and ran." It took her several more years to feel ready to learn the meaning of the symbols, that they are a representation of interconnectedness in the universe: light exists in relation to dark, high in relation to low, death in relation to life. She was being presented with a kind of spiritual teaching, but because she didn't recognize what it was, it had terrified her.

There is no question that people remember the emotional content of an NDE with extreme clarity, regardless of its symbolic or cultural content. Neurologist Steven Laureys, of the Coma Science Group at the University Hospital of Liège, Belgium, recently tested the hypothesis that people who have NDEs merely imagine them. The researchers compared the memories of three groups of coma survivors: those who had had NDEs; those with memories of their coma without NDEs, such as recalling being talked to by a family member; patients with no memories of their coma; and a control group who had never been in a coma. Each group was asked to recall five types of past events: recent and old memories, such as a first kiss; recent and old imagined event memories, such as a daydream; and one target memory—the NDE, for those who had one; the memories of being talked to during a coma, for those who had that experience; and, for the control group, a memory from childhood.

The researchers discovered that memories of a near-death experience were by far the sharpest, most detailed and clearest. NDEs "seem to be unique, unrivalled memories." Intense emotion has been shown to sear memories into our brains. Heartbreak, the birth of a child, being caught in a hurricane—people recall these in greater detail than the boring plod to work. Neurologists call them "flashbulb memories," in that a "highly emotional, personally important and surprising event can benefit from a preferential encoding that makes them more detailed and longer-lasting." NDEs appear to trigger the most preferential coding of all.

There is no evidence that NDEs become confabulated over time. Even children who have experienced them carry forward precise recollections across the years. "Interestingly," the Belgian researchers noted, "NDE memories in this study [also] contained more characteristics than coma memories, suggesting that what makes the NDEs 'unique' is not being 'near-death' but rather the perception of the experience itself." This was Rudolf Otto's point about encountering the holy. God, spiritual majesty, the Ground of Being—whatever you choose to call it—uniquely elicits this emotional response.

The researchers concluded that the only explanation, at least from a materialist point of view, is that NDEs are elaborate hallucinations, because hallucinations can be perceived—and responded to—as if they are real. However, while working on her doctorate from the University of Cardiff, Wales, critical-care nurse Penny Sartori compared NDE narratives with medication-related hallucinations and found distinctive differences, as has also been noted with deathbed visions. Hallucinations related to morphine and other palliative drugs "tended to be random and non-specific," she said. (Sartori also measured blood gases during her five-year study of NDEs and did not find any correlation between reduced oxygen levels and which patient had the experience.)

As Andrew Newberg and Eugene d'Aquili have pointed out, "when hallucinating individuals return to normal consciousness, they immediately recognize the fragmented and dreamlike nature of their hallucinatory interlude, and understand it was all a mistake of the mind." This is not the case for those who encounter the numinous. Wrote Teresa of Avila in sixteenth-century Spain: "God visits the soul in a way that prevents it doubting when it comes to itself that it has been in God and God in it, and so firmly is it convinced of this truth that, though years may pass before the state recurs, the soul can never forget it, never doubt its reality."

It's hard to understand what that means in experiential terms. It is perhaps a question of contrast: this world begins to feel less real, the way a dream feels less real to us than waking consciousness, but only after we wake up. Here is what the psychologist Carl Jung wrote after his near-death experience during a heart attack in Switzerland in 1944:

> The view of city and mountains from my sickbed seemed to me like a painted curtain with black holes in it, or a tattered sheet of newspaper full of photographs that meant nothing. Disappointed, I thought, "Now I must return to the 'box system' again." For it seemed to me as if behind the horizon of the cosmos a three-dimensional world had been artificially built up, in which each person sat by himself in a little box. And now I should have to convince myself all over again that this was important!

In the aftermath of their NDEs, people describe the world around them as flat, dull, two-dimensional, filled with stick figures and "paper cut-out dolls." Asked simple "agree or disagree" questions, 56 percent agree that the NDE realms were "1,000 times stronger" as a reality than their everyday reality. Even people who have had frightening NDEs accept them as real. Nancy Evans Bush could have written off her encounter with the heartless yin/yang circles telling her she didn't exist by dismissing the vision as an unsettling dream; instead, she was devastated for years.

While the grieving populace may feel abashed and self-doubting about their telepathic impressions and encounters with sensed presences, people who have NDEs are often driven by the overwhelming intensity of such experiences to break with their churches, their professions and sometimes their spouses. Their lives have been turned absolutely upside down, and society doesn't know how to respond. Here they were, perfectly ordinary people who'd been going about their business, whatever the business of their lives happened to be. A chemist working in a lab, a teenager on a road trip, a Vietnam vet being treated for lung cancer: all of them as unsuspecting as the innocents in horror films. Life going just tickety-boo, and then *bam!*—their world radically and irrevocably altered. Only it wasn't a monster who'd assaulted them, but an intimation of God.

For several days after his near drowning, David Bennett went about in total disarray. He had developed a kind of synesthesia, that unusual perceptual condition a small number of people have in which one's senses are crossed, such that you can "see" music or hear words as colours. For Bennett, the effect was completely confusing.

I could see the life energy in my surroundings. There was an aura of light around all the plants and rocks in the planting beds. I could feel and touch them without physically touching them with my hands. My engineer brain kept trying to figure it out. *How is this possible?* I could hear rhythms, notes.

The experience of heightened perception and blended senses is a common one for people who have had NDEs and other numinous experiences. New York journalist Maureen Seaberg, who has had synesthesia all her life, experiencing the alphabet as a sequence of luminescent colours, calls it a "God hangover." Although Seaberg was born with synesthesia, as was violinist Itzhak Perlman and possibly the novelist Vladimir Nabokov, she senses something transcendent in the capacity. She has found references to it in ancient religious texts; there are allusions to crossed sensory perceptions in the Old Testament, for example. When Moses ascended Mount Sinai to receive the Ten Commandments, according to Exodus 20:18, the presence of God affected the crowd below. "All the people saw the voices, and all the people heard the visions." It is a curious bit of scripture if it is not intended to literally describe a collective state of synesthesia.

There is also a description in the Old Testament of the spiritual conferring of instantaneous knowledge that Jayne Smith described in her NDE. Here comes a bit from the Book of Acts:

When the day of Pentecost had come, they were all together in one place. And suddenly from heaven there came a sound like the rush of violent wind, and it filled the entire house where they were sitting. Divided tongues, as of fire, appeared among them and a tongue rested on each of them. All of them were filled with the Holy Spirit and began to speak in other languages, as the spirit gave them ability . . . All were amazed and perplexed, saying to one another "What does this mean?"

Journalist Maria Coffey unearthed an intriguing account of people understanding languages they didn't actually know. In 1985 the Mexican mountaineer Carlos Carsolio

was climbing Nanga Parbat with a Polish team, attempting the south spur of the Rupal Face, the biggest mountain wall in the world. Conditions were dreadful, with blizzards so dense that often the men lost sight of each other. Through the ascent they communicated by two-way radio, and their conversations were recorded by people at Base Camp. Before they reached the top of the face, their food and fuel ran out. During their desperate descent, they all felt very close to death.

Back at base camp, as they recovered from the ordeal, they listened to the recordings of their conversations. They were shocked. The Polish climbers spoke no Spanish and Carsolio spoke no Polish, so normally they conversed in English. During the final part of their ascent, however, and on the way down the mountain, they had all been speaking in their native languages. Listening to the tapes, the Poles couldn't understand Carsolio and he couldn't understand them. "But when we were up there we had understood each other perfectly," says Carsolio. "We had opened some channels, to another level of communication."

The thirteenth-century Jewish mystic Abraham Abulafia engaged in prayers that caused the letters of the alphabet to come across to him as musical notes, a practice of enhancing and blending perceptual awareness that he called "breaking the seal of the soul." Research at the University of California, Irvine, by psychiatrist Roger Walsh determined that 86 percent of advanced meditation practitioners experienced synesthesia, whereas only 35 percent of the less experienced meditators did. A very small percentage of the general population experience it. Said David Bennett of his time beneath the sea: "My perceptions were unbounded." Can something about the numinous experience itself, whether cultivated by prayer and meditation or abruptly imposed by terror and peril, break the seal of the bounded embodied senses?

A study by Australian sociologist Cherie Sutherland of people who had had near-death experiences found that 83 percent had these kinds of synesthetic after-effects, including enhanced or extrasensory perception such as telepathy and clairvoyance. Meanwhile, Brown University's Willoughby Britton discovered that people showed differences in left temporal lobe activity after an NDE, suggesting that the experience had somehow altered their neural circuitry. What's interesting about this is that synesthesia has been associated with increased neural "hyper-connectivity" in the temporal lobe. So here we have hints of how the brain may be accommodating—or generating, depending on your point of view—an experience of expanded consciousness.

Most people were "surprised and disrupted" by these changes in their perception of the world. A Toronto architect who experienced going out-of-body when she almost hemorrhaged to death after the birth of her son in 1990 told me that, in the aftermath, humanity felt to her like a clanging bell. "I would walk down the street and be hit by all these emotions, how everyone passing me was feeling, I could feel it—*wham, wham, wham*. It was so difficult that I avoided being in social gatherings. Six months later, I remember being in a crowded room for a business function and it was almost *annihilating*." She didn't connect it to her out-of-body experience; she thought it had to do with some kind of postpartum crisis. A Japanese-American businessman who had an NDE during a motorcycle crash became able to empathetically sense others' emotional pain, which would overwhelm him in the middle of sales meetings.

Alan Ross Hugenot, who had an NDE during a motorcycle accident, told me, "We become outsized when our consciousness leaves our body during the NDE, and then I don't think it entirely fits back in when we return." I think I understand what he means. It's as if all the filters that the brain has evolved to screen out distracting or irrelevant signals in the world around us no longer suffice. "I've had to develop strategies to guard myself against other peoples' emotions." To demonstrate, he raised his bent arm at me like someone fending off a vampire. I suddenly felt guilty for sitting in front of him with God knows what psychological baggage. I wondered (but didn't want to know) what he was picking up, or trying not to pick up.

Yvonne Kason discovered that she knew a friend had meningitis before the friend was aware of it, because it flared up as a vision in front of her while she was driving over to the friend's house. The perception—an anatomical image of an inflamed brain—was utterly disconcerting. When Kason arrived, her friend had a headache, and Kason, feeling a bit crazy, warned her to monitor it closely and pay attention if her neck felt stiff. Within a day, the friend was admitted to hospital for treatment.

Occasionally someone returns from a near-death experience with a hitherto unknown talent. In the early nineties, an orthopedic surgeon in New York State, Tony Cicoria, suddenly gained an obsession with learning to play and compose for the piano, after he was struck by lightning while standing in a phone booth and went into cardiac arrest. He would go on to give several concerts. When I met him in 2013, he said that he was still trying to understand what his musical gift was intended for, in terms of healing others. He had no sense that the music was for him alone to practise and enjoy; that didn't seem to have even crossed his mind.

Learning to live with a reversal of perspective about what matters can be extremely challenging for some NDEers. In one study, more than half were found to have "moderate to major" problems taking up the reins of their lives in the aftermath. Seventeen percent had considered suicide in order to return, and one actually bit through her breathing tube moments after her NDE in a Dutch hospital, plunging herself back into cardiac arrest. Seventy percent felt isolated and depressed because of not being able to share what they felt they now knew about a parallel or higher reality. "It's sad that you can't talk freely about it," one woman said. "I feel penned in. I have so much exuberance and no one to hear me." Like the dying and the dead, they have something to say—but who is listening?

They are also caught, in a sense, between worlds. David Bennett told me, without the faintest trace of uncertainty, "When life is over, you know you're going home. And that creates a longing. It's emotionally difficult." What an extraordinary statement for a non-depressed person to make! An optimistic yearning for the grave? People who have experienced it become, in effect, homesick for that numinous reality they have glimpsed. Lamented the Spanish mystic Saint John of the Cross,

> I no longer live within myself
> and I cannot live without God
> for having neither him nor myself
> what will life be?
> It will be a thousand deaths
> longing for my true life
> and dying because I do not die.

Military veterans who have survived blast injuries—increasingly common in the era of Iraq and Afghanistan—are radically challenged by the contrast between their NDE and their ordinary reality. They find themselves going from the hunkered-down hell of battle to a realm of joy and peace, then abruptly back again into the military conflict. One platoon commander described being unable to discipline his troops after his NDE. "All I wanted to do is put my arm around them and say: 'It'll be okay.' The army's not big on hugging for discipline. Trust me." He had to resign.

Many vets can't talk about their experiences at all, according to retired colonel Diane Corcoran, who began counselling soldiers with NDEs when she was a young nurse in Vietnam, because they will be assessed as psychiatric risks. Admit that you've spoken with a being of light and you will instantly be diagnosed as psychotic and either heavily sedated or discharged. After the world wars, a great and probing literature emerged about what men weren't allowed to say of their horror. How they couldn't express terror and guilt and anxiety, how their experiences were carefully mediated in the sanatoria and presented to the public as "shell shock." A commensurate literature has yet to arise around the modern experience of the spiritual in circumstances of combat. If soldiers have psychic intuitions, if they sense presences, if they have NDEs, then they are understood to be suffering from "post-traumatic stress disorder."

An unexpected aspect of combat NDEs is that, because several soldiers are often injured in one blast, they will sometimes go out-of-body *together* and witness one another in their astral states, Corcoran has learned. There is a variation of this phenomenon called the "shared death experience," which is not unlike the shared illness experience in telepathic impression cases. Those researching it are not talking about literally shared experiences but rather some sort of sharing or entangling of perceptions between people. It has become a new focus of Raymond Moody's research. The psychiatrist who kick-started the whole near-death experience field feels that it may one day cast the conversation about what NDEs are in a different light. In the meantime, it goes largely undiscussed.

I first heard of this phenomenon from the psychologist Joan Borysenko, who described having such an experience when her eighty-one-year-old mother died in the Beth Israel Deaconess Medical Center in Boston while Borysenko was on faculty at

Harvard. The room seemed to fill with a brilliant light, and both she and her teenaged son witnessed her mother rise spectrally out of her body. Needless to say, this was beyond unexpected. Raymond Moody had rarely heard of such cases when he first began collecting stories of NDEs. For decades, doctors and nurses were more likely than family members to be present at the moment of death, so it wasn't until that custom shifted in favour of family vigils that he began to hear about these curious experiences from ordinary people. Here is an example: "When my fifteen-year-old son died," an unidentified woman told him,

> I was there in the room. He had diabetes from a very young age and, of course, that greatly complicated his life. I was holding his hand when he died and I felt the life force surge from him, somewhat like an electric current, although vibration might be a more appropriate term. The shape of the room changed all at once and instead of the hospital room there was a field of intense light, far and away brighter than anything anyone can imagine who has not seen it for themselves. In place of the hospital room and the medical equipment a vision appeared of every-thing my son had ever done in his brief life. He was there right in the middle of it, beaming a bright smile of joy. I know that this is inconceivable for others, but as sad as I was to lose him, I felt the joy of his release from the con-stant discomfort and concern of the diabetes. It was just his time, is the best way I can describe what I understood at that moment.

In the course of his research, Moody noticed several common elements to the shared death experience, although not all of them feature in every case. They include a perception of changed geometry, which is bizarre. "This trait is difficult to describe," Moody writes,

> because it takes so many different shapes. It is also one that is not found in near-death experiences. A woman who was at the bedside of her dying brother said it was as though the square room she was in shifted into another shape. As one man, a math teacher, described it, "it was as though the room collapsed and expanded at the same time."

A frequent perception in the shared death experience is the sound of music. Reported one woman who experienced it with her dying husband, "This was the most beautiful and intricate music I had ever heard." Some, like the soldiers who spoke to Colonel Corcoran, share an out-of-body perception. For example, this account from a woman in Virginia: "The night Jim died, I was sitting next to him, holding his hand, when we both left our bodies and began to fly through the air. It was amazing, frightening and puzzling. Above us was a bright light, and we were headed directly for it. The light was beautiful and vibrant and powerful." At this point the woman was "sucked back" into her body and found that her husband was dead.

About 50 percent of people who have NDEs move beyond an encounter with light to also perceive places, such as cities or gardens. Sometimes, Moody has discovered, this also happens in a shared death experience. Here is an account from a woman whose close friend had just died as she sat with her:

> I was suddenly walking up a hill with Martha and we were surrounded by light. Not an ordinary light, but everything around us—plants, the ground, even the sky, glowed with its own light. It was unbelievably beautiful. I am sure this place was heaven or some place like it, because there was a feeling that was wonderful. I honestly felt fifty years younger.

Also present in the shared death experience, according to Moody, is a border of some kind beyond which the living cannot follow their beloved. It has been experienced as a bridge, a river, a tree or a verbal command to go back.

Writes Moody,

> Since I first began to study death, I have [also] heard people tell of a mist that is emitted from the body of those who die. People attending the deathbed ... describe it variously as white smoke, steam, or as assuming a shape, like the spiritual body of the deceased. Whatever the case, it usually drifts upward and always disappears fairly quickly.

He offers one account from a physician:

> I have seen mist coming up from deceased patients twice in a six-month period. As the patients died they lit up with a bright glow—eyes shining with a silvery light. A mist formed over the chest area and hovered there. Time stood

still for me as I watched this happen. I watched very closely, focusing as intently as I could. The mist had a depth and complex structure. It seemed to have layers with energetic motion in it, which is a poor description, I know, but just think of something as subtle as water moving within water. During the second occurrence, I felt an unseen presence, as though someone was standing beside me and waiting for the patient to die. I have no idea who or what the presence was, but if I had to guess I would say that it was someone who loved the patient. That is the feeling I got.

These experiences, whatever causes them, require a totally different set of scientific explanations than what gets put forward to account for NDEs. It may be that in the highly charged atmosphere of the dying person's room, our empathy and yearning lead us into a form of shared consciousness. In 2013 the late film critic Roger Ebert wrote about his wife's intimation that he was still vital and present during an episode of cardiac arrest. I mentioned earlier that Chaz Ebert saw the Grim Reaper in her bedroom when her first father-in-law died. She appears to be one of those people who has a talent or capacity for these heightened intuitions. In an article on *Salon*, Ebert wrote,

After the first ruptured artery, the doctors thought I was finished. My wife, Chaz, said she sensed that I was still alive and was communicating to her that I wasn't finished yet. She said our hearts were beating in unison, although my heartbeat couldn't be discovered. She told the doctors I was alive, they did what doctors do, and here I am, alive.

Do I believe her? Absolutely. I believe her literally—not symbolically, figuratively or spiritually. I believe she was actually aware of my call and that she sensed my heart-beat. I believe she did it in the real, physical world I have described, the one that I share with my wristwatch. I see no reason why such communication could not take place. I'm not talking about telepathy, psychic phenomenon or a miracle. The only miracle is that she was there when it happened, as she was for many long days and nights. I'm talking about her standing there and knowing something. Haven't many of us experienced that? Come on, haven't you? What goes on happens at a level not accessible to scientists, theologians, mystics, physicists, philosophers or psychiatrists. It's a human kind of a thing.

There have been NDEs that can be directly connected to a period of flatlined brain activity from the observations made by patients. Cardiologist Pim van Lommel describes a case based on his Dutch study in which a cardiac-arrest victim was found lying comatose and cyanotic in a field thirty minutes before his arrival at the ER, yet after his recovery he was able to describe accurately the circumstances of his resuscitation. Skeptics have argued that these observations are false memories, conjured out of medical dramas such as *House* or *Grey's Anatomy*. To test this hypothesis, American cardiologist Michael Sabom interviewed patients who had reported NDEs and also interviewed cardiac patients who had *not* had NDEs, asking each group to describe their cardiac resuscitation procedure as if they'd been watching it. Eighty percent of those who had no memory of an NDE, Sabom found, made at least one major error in their description, whereas none of the NDE patients made errors. This comparative study was replicated by doctoral researcher Penny Sartori in 2008, with a study of hospitalized intensive-care patients: those who reported leaving their body during cardiac arrest described their resuscitation accurately, whereas every cardiac-arrest survivor who had not reported an out-of-body experience described incorrect equipment or procedures.

In addition, Sabom found that the NDE group "related accurate details of idiosyncratic or unexpected events during their resuscitations." Said one:

> I was above myself looking down. They was [*sic*] working on me trying to bring me back. Cause I didn't realize at first that it was my body. I didn't think I was dead. It was an unusual feeling. I could see them working on me and then I realized it was me they were working on. I felt no pain whatsoever and it was a most peaceful feeling. Death is nothing to be afraid of. I didn't feel nothing. They gave me a shot in the groin.

The "shot" was a hypodermic drawing blood from his left femoral artery to test his oxygen levels—which were above normal.

In another example, from research by University of Virginia psychiatrist Bruce Greyson, a patient described leaving his body and watching the cardiac surgeon "flapping his arms as if trying to fly." The surgeon verified this detail by explaining that, after scrubbing, to keep his hands from becoming contaminated before beginning surgery, he had developed the unusual habit of flattening his hands against his chest while giving instructions by pointing with his elbows.

In a recent review of ninety-three published reports of potentially verifiable out-of-body (OBE) perceptions, 43 percent were found to have been corroborated to the investigator by an independent informant (usually nurses and doctors). Of these, 88 percent were completely accurate. "The OBE phenomenon is interesting," says science journalist Jeff Warren, "because you get these incredibly detailed perceptions happening in people with apparently no brain activity. I wouldn't say this is conclusive proof of the existence of mind beyond body—it's foolish to conclude anything about reality—but if you *are* in the game of proving and disproving, it's definitely a piece of evidence worth taking seriously."

The people who come across NDEs most often are, of course, medical professionals, which is why so much of the near-death research has been initiated by cardiologists, anesthesiologists, critical-care nurses and surgeons confounded and intrigued by what they see in their operating rooms and wards. Sam Parnia, director of clinical care at Stony Brook University's school of medicine in New York, began investigating NDEs in the context of cardiac resuscitation and soon heard accounts from his own colleagues. Here is British cardiologist Richard Mansfield, from the very early days of improved resuscitation methods in the 1960s, recalling to Parnia a patient who had died and whose body had been left on the table. Mansfield went back into the room after fifteen minutes to check how many vials of adrenaline he'd administered in his futile resuscitation effort, so he could finish writing up the death report. He discovered that the man had spontaneously revived and could describe details of what had just happened.

> He told me everything that I had said and done, such as checking the pulse, deciding to stop resuscitation, going out of the room, coming back later, looking across at him, going over and rechecking his pulse and then restarting resuscitation. He got all the details right, which was impossible because not only had he been asystole and had no pulse throughout the arrest, but he wasn't even being resuscitated for about fifteen minutes afterwards. What he told me really freaked me out.

Parnia, in turn, also felt something along the lines of being freaked out. Since then he has heard numerous first-hand accounts of this kind from startled physicians. Dr. Tom Aufderheide, for instance, told Parnia and other attendees at a 2012 conference on cardiovascular care that he had had a patient in cardiac arrest—actually, as a brand-new doctor, his first patient in cardiac arrest—who kept being revived and then re-arresting over the course of eight hours. After an initial flurry of Code Blue attention, the more senior doctors eventually left the continuous resuscitation efforts to Aufderheide, who thought furiously at them, *How could you do this to me?*

"At [some] point the housekeeping staff came into his room to serve his lunch. I was hungry. So I ate his lunch. I certainly couldn't leave his room, and he wasn't going to eat it." The patient finally stabilized several hours later and remained in hospital for a month. Before he left for home, he spoke to young Dr. Aufderheide about having had an NDE—the light, the tunnel, all the shattering extraordinariness of it—and then he added teasingly, "You know, I thought it was awfully funny . . . here I was dying in front of you, and you were thinking to yourself, *How could you do this to me?*' And then you ate my lunch." (Shades of the nineteenth-century Alpine climber who remonstrated with his guide for drinking his Madeira and eating his chicken.)

"The one common feature among all these accounts," Parnia later wrote, "was that patients with cardiac arrests had come back and recalled incredibly detailed accounts of conversations and events relating to the period when they were seemingly dead to their physicians. Specifically, they all claimed to have been able to see the events relating to their own cardiac arrests while watching from a point above at the ceiling."

None of this would surprise Tibetan monks, who sit beside the deceased and read aloud from the *Book of the Dead* because they assume the words can be heard. Nor would it have shocked our ancient kin, who dreamed up ways to assist revenants in finding their way from this realm to another. But two things happened in the interim. First, death was medicalized and secularized, removed from a sacred context, and then—a subsequent and unexpected development—patients began returning from it. Dr. Richard Mansfield's exchange happened at the dawn of the era of modern medical resuscitation, before which there would have been far fewer NDEs to report in the medical setting. Since then, playing God by raising Lazarus has become an increasingly widespread and effective medical intervention, and one result is this increase in NDEs. So we have managed to lose the language and ritual around spiritual experiences of death even as we have managed to increase the likelihood of hearing back from the near-dead about their spiritual encounters. This is the paradox that creates so much astonished unease.

One of the most intriguing cases for the medical staff involved occurred in the Netherlands. A critical-care nurse was working the night shift when paramedics brought in a forty-four-year-old man in a coma. He had been found an hour earlier in a park, where a couple of good Samaritans had tried to resuscitate him after a heart attack by pounding and massaging his chest. Once in hospital, still without a pulse, he was attached to an artificial respirator and subjected to defibrillation procedures.

"When I want to intubate the patient," the nurse reported, "the patient turns out to have dentures in his mouth. Before intubating him, I remove the upper set of dentures and put it on the crash cart. Meanwhile, we continue extensive resuscitation." It took another hour and a half to stabilize the man's heartbeat and blood pressure. He remained comatose and was transferred to the intensive care unit. "After more than a week in a coma," continued the nurse,

the patient returns to the coronary care unit, and I see him when I distribute the medication. As soon as he sees me he says, "Oh, yes, you, you know where my dentures are." I'm flabbergasted. Then he tells me, "Yes, you were there when they brought me into the hospital, and you took the dentures out of my mouth and put them on that cart; it had all these bottles on it, and there was a sliding drawer underneath, and you put my teeth there." I was all the more amazed because I remembered this happening when the man was in a deep coma and undergoing resuscitation. After further questioning, it turned out that the patient had seen himself lying in bed and that he had watched from above how nursing staff and doctors had been busy resuscitating him. He was also able to give an accurate and detailed description of the small room where he had been resuscitated and of the appearance of those present.

This has become known as the "dentures case" and is often discussed by those now debating what near-death experiences mean. The other poster child for the debate is the Reynolds case. In 1991 musician Pam Reynolds underwent surgery in Atlanta, Georgia, to remove a brain aneurysm that risked bursting and killing her at any time. Because of its location, surgery would have been fatal forty or fifty years earlier. Now, however, she could be put into hypothermic cardiac arrest, with her core temperature dropped to sixty degrees, so that the aneurysm wouldn't hemorrhage while the surgery proceeded. Once she was cooled, all the blood was drained from her brain. Somehow, in the midst of her induced clinical brain death, Reynolds experienced herself as awake and out of her body. Not only did she not feel groggy, she felt sharper and more alert than she ever had in her life. (One analysis of the medical records of people reporting NDEs found that they described enhanced mental functioning significantly more often when they were actually physiologically close to death than when they were not—make of that what you will.)

From her out-of-body location, Reynolds observed the unusual cranial saw that the neurosurgeons were using to cut her skull (this was above the level of her eyes, which were at any rate taped shut); she later reported that the saw emitted a natural D tone. She noted the unexpected pattern they'd shaved into her blonde hair, and heard the voice of a woman commenting that her femoral vessels were too small for the cardiopulmonary bypass shunt. She also reported—after "returning" from an extraordinary encounter with light and deceased relatives—that she saw her body "jump" twice; she had gone into cardiac arrest post-surgery and was being defibrillated. Re-entering her body "felt like diving into a pool of ice water." (If people are feeling a euphoria related to endorphin release, as is sometimes proposed as the explanation for NDE, the chemical effect shouldn't end abruptly and coincidentally at the exact moment when they have the psychological experience of returning to their body. Endorphins have been shown to circulate for hours.) She also heard the doctors playing "Hotel California" and joked that the line "You can check out anytime you like, but you can never leave" was "incredibly insensitive," given her distress at having to return to her prone form from the marvellous peace of the NDE.

Everything she saw and heard proved true. Reynolds's neurosurgeon, Robert Spetzler, would later say to the BBC:

I don't think the observations she made were based on what she experienced as she went into the operating theater. They were just not available to her. For example, the drill and so on, those things were all covered up. They aren't visible; they were inside their packages. You really don't begin to open until the patient is completely asleep so that you maintain a sterile environment.

Keith Augustine, a young philosopher and avowed skeptic, reviewed the Reynolds case and argued that she could have seen things later and retroactively described them. She could have heard the music, the sawing and the conversation through ordinary means, somehow rousing from the anesthetic while eluding the monitors that were tracking her brainwaves. To this the psychologist Janice Miner Holden responded:

> Ms. Reynolds' brain was being monitored three different ways to ensure that she was deeply and consistently anesthetized. One of these ways was the monitoring of her most basic level of brain function by stimulating her hearing with ear speakers. Augustine did not report that the ear speakers molded into Reynolds' ears emitted clicks throughout her entire period of general anesthesia at a loudness of 90 to 100 decibels and a rate of 11 to 33 clicks per second. That volume has been described as [being] as loud as a lawn mower.

It took that level of noise just to ensure that the patient was deeply unconscious.

Imagine being profoundly sedated by general anesthetic, with your ears sealed and filled with lawn-mower sounds that you were too unconscious to register, and still managing to hear doctors mutter about an arterial vein. It's not completely impossible. After all, as my musician husband points out to me, deaf people can play music by sensing vibration. But it's safe to say that the Eagles weren't playing live in the operating theatre that day, so the vibrations would have to have been coming from the radio, and from the muttering surgeons. The only alternative explanation is that Reynolds heard about her procedure in great detail after the fact and decided, for some reason, to weave a false memory into an imagined encounter with the divine.

British psychologist Susan Blackmore, who believes that mind is explained by brain, has circulated the most well-known theory about what happens in NDEs, which she called the "dying brain hypothesis." The perception of going out of your body, she argues, "is the brain's way of dealing with a breakdown in the body image and model of reality" when near death. This may be due to pain or injury, or "it may be that the brain is no longer capable of building a good body image even if it had the information, because it is ceasing to function properly." To construct a body image in this state, Blackmore argued, we draw on memory and situate ourselves with a bird's-eye view. "Memory can supply all the information about your body, what it looks like, how it feels and so on. It can also supply a good picture of the world. 'Where was I? Oh, yes. I was lying in the road after that car hit me.'"

To make the case that memory would act in this manner, Blackmore reportedly drew on two experimental studies, one on drug-induced hallucination and the other on how undergraduates construct their memories—neither of which definitively or specifically concluded that most people take a bird's-eye view of their remembered experiences. The research is exploratory, experimental, and raises several different possibilities. For example, for immediate or recent experiences with strong emotional resonance, some of the data suggested that people are more likely to remember from their current vantage point, such as lying on their back in the road. Try it yourself. When do you ever remember a particularly charged episode of your life from the vantage point of a ceiling? Her critics contend that she builds a speculative argument on an insufficient ground of evidence. She is, they complain, being far too declarative. "At last we have a simple theory of the OBE," Blackmore has contended. "The normal model of reality breaks down and the system tries to get back to normal by building a new model from memory and imagination. If this model is in a bird's eye view, then an OBE takes place."

A lightly stated dismissal of any remaining mystery around the OBE simply doesn't sit well with other investigators. There is still no consensus as to what happens to people who experience themselves as being out of their bodies, or even whether they are all experiencing the same thing. Swiss neuroscientist Olaf Blanke, who has studied the sensed-presence phenomenon, suggests that OBEs are the result of "paroxysmal cerebral dysfunction of the temporo-parietal junction (TPJ)." Other scientists, however, have been critical of Blanke's work. "The interpretation of the empirical findings of Blanke and his colleagues is controversial," writes neuropsychiatrist Michael Kelly. The main objection, apparently, is that most people who have spontaneous OBEs haven't been shown to manifest this particular brain dysfunction. "The generalization from these few patients with identified neurological problems to all persons experiencing OBE, most of whom have no known neurological problem, is purely conjectural," Kelly and his colleagues at the University of Virginia have cautioned. So it's a long way yet from being fully and definitively explanatory. The same objection is made about OBEs as a symptom of seizures. The Austrian neurologist Ernst Rodin, who specialized in epilepsy before his retirement, has said, "In spite of having seen hundreds of patients with temporal lobe seizures during three decades of professional life, I have never come across that symptomology [of NDEs] as part of a seizure."

What the arguments amount to is a lack of clarity about what may be going on. "People are pushing the boundaries to extremes to try to put a label on this," Dr. Sam Parnia wrote in his 2013 book, *Erasing Death*. He offers the example of a study done with student volunteers, who were outfitted with special goggles that showed them an image projected by a camera stationed behind them. They were staring, in other words, at a picture of their own back inside the goggles. "After a while they became so used to that image that it felt like they were looking at themselves from behind. Then the researchers pretended to attack the camera with a hammer. The people were startled because for an instant they felt like someone was attacking them." From this, Parnia complains,

> the researchers concluded that they had reproduced an out-of-body experience in the laboratory. Of course, this is not even close to what someone who is critically ill, suffers

a cardiac arrest, is resuscitated, and then describes hearing conversations or seeing events in an out-of-body experience would go through . . . I even wondered whether [the researchers] had actually ever met and interviewed people with out-of-body experiences.

Parnia has found in his own, ongoing research with several collaborating hospitals in the U.S. and Europe that OBEs are being reported by around 2 percent of the cardiac arrest survivors now being resuscitated. In other words, of every one hundred patients successfully brought back from flat line in these ER and cardiac wards, two patients will have recall of exiting their bodies and observing details of what is transpiring. (More than that will experience NDEs generally, without the OBE feature. Important to note that this is different than the overall prevalence rate of Americans having NDEs, which is calculated over time, and includes people like David Bennett who weren't medically resuscitated.)

Who reports an OBE in Parnia's research and who does not may be the result of brain trauma in relation to the cardiac arrest itself. Cells in the hippocampus, the area of the brain considered crucial for the formation of memories, are particularly sensitive to damage. Both head injuries and oxygen deprivation (known as anoxia) usually feature amnesia around the incident. *I don't remember falling . . . The last thing I recall . . .*

Parnia is wary of chalking up near-death experiences to oxygen deprivation for this reason. Before he moved to the United States to work at Cornell University, he did a one-year study of cardiac-arrest survivors at Southampton Hospital in England.

Those who had NDEs showed slightly elevated levels of oxygen relative to the patients who reported no memory of an NDE. "Our sample didn't seem to support the concept that NDEs were being caused by a lack of oxygen to the brain," he wrote.

> From a medical point of view, lack of oxygen is a very common problem in a hospital. Most doctors working with emergencies come across it regularly, particularly in patients whose lungs or hearts aren't working very well—for example, in cases of severe asthma or heart failure . . . . When oxygen levels fall, patients become agitated and acutely confused. This "acute confusional state," as it is known medically, is very different from the near-death experience. During it, people develop "clouding of consciousness" together with highly confused thought processes with little or no memory recall. . . . If the dying brain theory were correct, then I would expect that as the oxygen levels in patients' blood dropped, they would gradually develop the illusion of seeing a tunnel and/or a light. In practice, patients with low oxygen levels don't report seeing a light, a tunnel, or any of the typical features of an NDE.

In 2005, University of Kentucky neurologist Kevin Nelson proposed that a near-death experience is more akin to a waking dream. Specifically, people who had NDEs seemed more susceptible to REM intrusion when their fight-or-flight system was aroused, which is the kind of sleep disorder proposed for people experiencing the terror of night paralysis: you have the impression of being awake and observant when you are actually in the dream state known as "rapid eye movement" (REM). This idea garnered lots of media attention, and I remember listening to Nelson explain it on my local radio station when he brought out a book on his findings. Two NDEers were interviewed for comment on the show, and they said, basically, *Back off from my NDE.* Nelson has shown sympathy for that sentiment and has publicly described NDEs as "spiritual experiences." He just thinks they can be scientifically accounted for.

Radiologist Jeffrey Long and psychologist Janice Holden responded to Nelson, pointing out that 40 percent of the NDEers in his survey had actually said no to his questions about whether they'd experienced REM intrusion. "If 40 percent of NDEers deny ever having experienced a single episode of REM intrusion in their entire lives, the idea that REM intrusion 'underlies' and 'predisposes' a person to have an NDE when encountering a life threatening event seems questionable at best," they cautioned. Brown University researcher Willoughby Britton found (in an unrelated study) that after their NDE, people entered REM sleep almost sixty minutes later, on average, than other sleepers. When you're a journalist trying to sort through all this, your hands just go up in the air.

We are brought back around to the meaning of the experience. It is as profound and as resonant as a hero's journey, as complex and instructive as myth—and it feels epically real. Why would the realm of the numinous be more real than this reality, more real by a thousand times? Because all the senses are sharpened, the emotions are heightened and somehow the awareness of truth is radically enlarged? We don't know. It just is.

"I make my living as a clinical psychiatrist dealing with people who have trouble dealing with what's real and what's not real, what's not delusional," says psychiatrist Bruce Greyson.

> And I've also spent thirty years dealing with people who've had near-death experiences, who have told me that this world may be real, but *that* world is more real. So I've done a lot of thinking about "What is reality?" We don't use, as our criterion, what's going on in our brains. People say, Is it subjective or is it objective? But in fact that's not how we talk about reality. We all talk about emotions being "real" or being feigned. Is that a real pain or is that a fake pain? That's not an objective thing. Pain, love, hatred, arrogance—these are subjective things, but we call them real or not real.

When Nancy Bush, the woman who had the frightening NDE, was asked what question she found most irritating to be asked, she said,

> Probably the one I dislike the most is "Do you believe these NDEs? Are they really true? Do you really believe near-death experiences?" It's such an annoying little mosquito of a question because it indicates just such a lack of thought. They are experiences! You can't ask people "Is your experience true?" any more than you can ask someone with an abscessed tooth if their experience of pain is true. You're

having the experience; of course it's true—as a genuine experience. Now, what does it mean? That is something different. Do I believe these experiences? Of course I believe them. Do I believe they are literally true? That is a different question with a far more complex answer.

The uniqueness and power of the spiritual experience is ultimately what we are left with. As Bruce Greyson said in New York in 2008, at the U.N.-sponsored meeting on the mind–body problem where he mused about the nature of reality, "We have no blood levels for enlightenment, but we can study its after effects." It is consistently found, for instance, that people who have NDEs are measurably changed by them, just as people who encounter the presence of their deceased loved ones are measurably consoled and lightened.

NDEers become less dogmatically religious—if they were religious to begin with—yet more actively spiritual. The proportion of Australians in Cherie Sutherland's study who claimed to have no religious affiliation prior to their NDE was 46 percent; that number jumped to 84 percent afterwards. In other words, their NDEs convinced the majority of people who had one that the doctrine they had been accustomed to, whatever it was, was off base. Pim van Lommel's Dutch research showed that church attendance declined by 42 percent in his NDE group, while spirituality nearly doubled. By contrast, his control group of cardiac-arrest survivors who did not have an NDE showed a 42 percent decrease in interest in spirituality after eight years. (There may be no atheists in foxholes, as the saying goes, but many may revert to that philosophy once out of danger—unless they've encountered the numinous. And then they don't.)

So what does an active spirituality look like? Compassion and empathy for others increased by 73 percent at the eight-year mark, versus 50 percent for the control group in Lommel's study. Interest in material status decreased by 50 percent, whereas that same interest—the pursuit of money, the quest for accomplishment—*increased* by 33 percent in the controls. Spirituality is the cultivation of love, the knowledge that you have a purpose and the acceptance that ego is nothing if not entirely irrelevant.

In May 2013 I caught up with David Bennett in Syracuse, where he had arranged for neurosurgeon Eben Alexander to give a talk about his own NDE. In person, Bennett, with his white-grey hair in a military cut and frameless glasses, has a pugnacious look that reminds me faintly of the late actor James Gandolfini—a working-class New York State guy, but with a faintly haunted look about him. It takes someone who has had a deep NDE an average of twelve years to integrate the "radical shift in reality" into their life, according to psychologist Yolaine Stout, who has studied the impact of the experience. That was certainly the case for Bennett. It wasn't until he was invited by friends to meditate in the Arizona desert in 1994 that he faced what had happened to him. In fact, he relived the entire NDE in the midst of meditation and was left sobbing and shaking on the edge of a mesa. "It was like being hit by a two-by-four," he told me. "And I was like, okay, *okay*, I get it. Now I'm going to have to start living my life knowing what I know." When an acquaintance came across him weeping, Bennett told his story for the first time. Ultimately he began running a support group in upstate New York.

In Syracuse, Bennett, wearing a blazer without a tie, seemed a bit overwhelmed by the number of people in attendance. Ordinarily his group gets a dozen or two people out to their events, but Alexander had been on the bestseller lists for months. Hundreds of people filled the place to bursting. My sister Anne had ordered Alexander's book after I told her about how he was calling for a reckoning between science and spirituality. I'm not sure what it was that caught her attention specifically, since I've been reading NDE books for the past few years, but there was something about Alexander that inspired her to drive with me, down along the I-90 East above the Finger Lakes, to hear him speak.

Like most people I've met who have had a spiritually trans-formative experience, Alexander had an air of calm about him when he took the podium. Calm, but with a self-effacing humour. I suppose when you've been told that you're loved by God and will always be loved, you lose that edge of performance anxiety that tends to plague the rest of us.

Not that Alexander is unselfconscious. He sports a signa-ture bow tie and comports himself with the assured air you'd expect to see in a surgeon who has been financially and intel-lectually powerful for years. This isn't Francis of Assisi discov-ering God and throwing away all his worldly possessions. Instead, Alexander threw away his world view, or at any rate his prestige as a medical rationalist. (As one surgeon said after his NDE, "walking around saying that you'd seen and heard things that weren't there wouldn't bode well with the Department of Health. Telling my colleagues was low on my to-do list.")

Alexander was a busy neurosurgeon in Virginia when, in the fall of 2008, he came down with a rare bacterial meningitis so extreme that he lapsed into a seven-day coma. He had a roughly 3 percent chance of surviving, much less emerging without brain damage. But he did survive and emerged completely intact, and, like Saint Paul on the road to Damascus, he was thunderstruck by a spiritual revelation. His experience began with what he chose to call the "earthworm view."

"Time flow in that realm is very different, so I don't know how long I was in a murky underground place," he said, "like being in dirty Jell-O, listening to a pounding, smashing sound. It sounds foreboding, but since I remembered nothing of my life, I accepted it." This description brings to mind the Egyptian *Book of the Dead*, where the afterlife begins with a plunge into the murky and disorienting realm of Duat before ascending to the higher realms. The "book" is actually a papyrus scroll that was tucked in with the mummy, like a travel guide or road map for afterlife use. This similarity in the descriptions doubtless also occurred to Alexander's ghostwriter, Ptolemy Tompkins, who has written about ancient afterlife beliefs. But to me it also sounded like how consciousness might seem when you're catastrophically ill with meningitis.

Alexander's NDE was unusual insofar as he cycled repeatedly between three different realms: the murky place, a beautiful valley and some sort of higher God realm. Maybe he was drifting between being in his diseased body and outside of it, the way dying people sometimes do, but who can say? Of the valley, he said—with a slight wobble in his voice that has become familiar to me in people giving such testimonials—"It was *lovely*. It's very hard to put words on this." And of the more infinite God realm and the experience in general, he said, "I cannot tell you how *totally* reassuring that unconditional love is. It was absolutely pure and perfect . . . even when I was just research-ing this as a neuroscientific experience, I remained haunted by the power of that love."

Reading for the first time the prevailing theories about what goes on in an NDE, Alexander was "astonished by how flimsy they were." He clarified to the Syracuse audience that he hadn't planned to call his book *Proof of Heaven.* "No one will ever have scientific proof of that realm," he said, "so my title is misleading. That realm is beyond our understanding. *God* is a teeny little human word. There's no way that a creation can ever fully under-stand the creator." He also wanted to be clear that he didn't think of the realm as Heaven in the Christian sense. Although he had a Christian upbringing, his NDE did nothing to convince him that Jesus Christ was the only prophet or saviour.

"In the four-and-a-half years since my NDE," said Alexander, "I have been trying to come up with a world view that makes sense. We need to take down the artificial boundaries between religions, and between religion and science." My sister was nod-ding in agreement. She is a professor of religious studies and a Baha'i. Baha'i followers believe that all prophets are from the same god, and that humanity will prevail if religions and the sciences come together. *Unio mystica.*

The next morning, we sisters and Anne's daughter went for a walk alongside a little lake. The new spring green and the sunny blue sky reminded me of the weather in children's books—smoothly benign, lovely and perfect blue and green. Everyone was cheery. We headed off to a massive factory outlet mall so Anne and my niece could hunt around for cheap purses and sunglasses. I love the way my sister balances her fierce spiritual commitment with a fondness for bargains. At my father's memorial service, she recalled for the mourners how he used to tease her: "After enlightenment, the laundry."

On the way home, my niece was worrying about finding her place in the world, in this economy, in this time, even with a master's degree in science; youth unemployment was so high. She also felt anxious about Eben Alexander's reference to life reviews, to being made to feel the pain you have inflicted on others. This scared her, even though she is one of the sweetest young women I know; at this juncture she's probably harmed only a few ants . . . well, and the mice in her research lab. She was overwhelmed just thinking about it, though, and Anne, as indulgent and protective as any mom, reassured her, told her not to concern herself—not for now. Anne won't impose her personal faith on her daughter; it is actually a tenet of the Baha'i faith not to do so.

It occurred to me, though, that such postponement is also the essential quandary of our culture in how we approach a larger spiritual reality, especially around death. We're not ready to think about it. Life is complicated enough without all the uncertain complexity of what might ensue. We want either a quick reassurance that it's heavenly or a declaration that it's swift execution—lights out, brain gone. It's just simpler that way. I remember driving with my mother about ten years ago, and. for some reason getting onto the subject of the afterlife. Confidently Mum quoted some ancient Greek thinker: "Where death is, I am not; where I am, death is not." It sounded good.

That was before Katharine and Dad died, and the unravelling of everything we knew. Now, after interviewing people like Yvonne Kason and David Bennett, after pushing my way through the thorny thickets of scientific debate, confronting my own prejudices and anxieties, and basically doing all the complicated shit people don't want to do because it's *too complicated*, I am fonder of this quotation, which is frequently attributed to the Indian Nobel laureate for literature in 1924, Rabindranath Tagore: "Death is not extinguishing the light; it is only putting out the lamp because the dawn has come." There is nothing that we know scientifically in 2013 that says that he was wrong.

WALKING THE ENCHANTED BOUNDARY

*The more that critical reason dominates, the more impoverished
life becomes; but the more of the unconscious and the more of myth
we are capable of making conscious, the more of life we integrate.
Overvalued reason has this in common with political absolutism:
under its dominion the individual is pauperized.*

—CARL JUNG

t is nearing Halloween in Rhinebeck, New York, about an
hour and a half's drive north of New York City. It's a place
of perfect American autumn, like something out of a Martha
Stewart pictorial: white picket fences, neat sidewalks featuring
artfully decorated pumpkins, the air spiced by blazing oak and
maple trees. Well-groomed horses graze on hobby-farm grass.
At Halloween the dead are welcome here, in tidy costume or as

expensively spooky lawn ornaments, but this year they have been summoned in earnest to the Omega Institute, a retreat complex in the forest near Rhinebeck that holds weekend workshops on the art of meditation, reiki, sound healing. This weekend is all about "soul survival," and it's a sellout event.

In the main hall, surrounded by piney woods and organic gardens in late harvest, Raymond Moody sits in a winged armchair on a wooden dais backed by red drapes, one leg crossed over the other, lightly bouncing a foot clad in a black-and-white sneaker with neon green laces. The footwear is somewhat incongruous for this aging Southern gentleman. Is he aiming for ultimate comfort, like the three hundred people who have strolled from their spartan cabins in this converted old summer camp to hear him, many of them shell-shocked by recent deaths? There is a young woman who lost her fiancé two weeks earlier in a motorcycle accident in Brooklyn and feels driven to despair because she didn't somehow know he had died and carried on working her restaurant job for three more hours. There is a woman, neatly attired in a cashmere sweater set, who saw her father rise up in his bed upon death, as if his body were being animated by a mysterious force. A Russian who devoured Moody's first book when he came across an illicit copy in the officially atheist USSR is in attendance. There is a man of evident wealth who had a near-death experience during a skiing accident in Aspen and now feels lost, with "one foot in both worlds." In short, the attendees are pretty much anyone who feels stranded with their spiritual questions. Turned away by the scientific, medical and media establishments, as well as by the many churches that frown upon spontaneous spiritual encounters with the dead, they wind up congregating at events like this.

"What the universe is interested in is how you have learned to love," Moody assures the audience, who sit on cushions and chairs with notebooks and cups of coffee. With his Southern lilt and high-pitched voice, he sounds a bit like the novelist Truman Capote–diminutive, an outsider, smart. After describing what he's heard from thousands of people over thirty years of probing the NDE, he's like a sage. "Whatever people were chasing before–fame, power, money–they come back knowing that what matters is love," he explains. He talks about the struggle to live with what you know, how elusive the path can be. They "know what the goal is" but not necessarily how to achieve it. "It's very hard to get through the average day without wanting to choke at least one person." The audience chuckles ruefully.

Everyone has difficulty reaching the goal of being perfectly loving, but one thing NDEers do achieve is a certain fearlessness, Moody says. He has seen NDEers die years later, still retaining their "absolute lack of fear of death." He muses over other characteristics he's seen, citing unusual cases of "swan song," in which people sing or recite poetry at the time of their dying. "Her face was going grey," he recalls of one patient he was trying to resuscitate in medical school. "My resuscitation didn't work, and [yet] she was reciting poetry." (This sounds to me like terminal lucidity, which in turn mirrors the enhanced sensations and perceptions experienced during mystical encounters and NDEs. As the brain dies, the senses become unbounded.)

Although he is a psychiatrist, Moody is now acting–not unlike Eben Alexander–as a kind of priest. Where Alexander is a charismatic preacher, Moody is a gregarious village friar, providing the counsel and reassurance that people who have encountered the numinous are hungry for, offering the research wisdom that leaves them feeling less stigmatized, less credulous, less psycho. "In my experience as a psychiatrist, everyone is crazy," Moody says soothingly. "When people who've had NDEs ask me if they're normal, I say, 'What's normal? Normal is somebody you don't know very well.'" The audience's rueful chuckles turn into a belly laugh. "Some of the people who have NDEs are the least neurotic people I know."

Moody asks the audience members to raise their hand if they have had a shared death experience. Twenty-three hands waver in the air, about a tenth of the people there. "Why would the people at the bedside have the same experiences? It doesn't make sense," Moody says. One woman in the audience describes being six months pregnant when her mother was in grave condition in the ICU. She lay curled up with her on the hospital bed all night long, and at some point she began sharing a panoramic review of her mother's life. She thought she was hallucinating, but when her mother emerged from her coma some days later, she described the same experience, the same witnessed details. "We're into things here that are very difficult to explain away. When this comes to public consciousness," Moody declares, "it will change the format of the debate. In another five years it will be an entirely different field."

Perhaps. It isn't easy to change the debate, and you need to be mindful of walking along what has been called the "enchanted boundary." It is difficult to navigate along the edges of what's true and not true, what's possible and what's not possible, as the edges blur and shimmer along this boundary between skepticism and belief. There was a medium at Omega, an affable Bostonian named John Holland. He is quick-witted and self-deprecating, telling us stories of his awkward childhood when he saw things he shouldn't have been able to see, that weren't supposed to be possible, and was belittled and shunned by other kids. He ignored his capacity for years, he explained, because it brought him nothing but derision. He was working in Los Angeles as a bartender and periodically venting his bitterness at how the world had made fun of him by abruptly reading people sitting at his bar, knocking them off their stools with unbidden secrets such as "Your aunt just died." It was a kind of psychic vandalism. A friend persuaded him to cut it out, grow up and train his gift. So he attended a school for mediumship in England.

At Omega, Holland began preparing for a group reading. First he bade us go for a walk in the woods and ask our loved ones to come if they wanted, to speak if they needed to; he cautioned us not to approach our dead with need but rather with love. Out in the autumn sunlight, I walked the enchanted boundary, asking my sister to come if she wanted. I asked her if she wished me to write this book, or should I quit it, just get on with my life, "break the bonds," as grief therapists used to implore. Should I stay or should I go? I had no confidence that what I was doing was real. It felt pretend; the Enlightenment Scot in me was fully armed. And yet, at the same time, this was about my own, dear sister, one of my best friends. What if she *was* there, somewhere, and I was too proud to listen?

Back with the group, Holland explained that he would be drawn to various places in the room. At some point in the reading he came over to my area and said, "For someone here, in this section, I'm seeing an old-fashioned radio." Immediately, behind me, a middle-aged woman with shaggy dark hair cried out that she volunteered for a radio station. He began offering her images, which seemed, impossibly, to relate to me. These are the ones I remember:

"Okay," Holland said. "The left side of me is sagging. I'm seeing a breast cancer, left side, a mastectomy."

"I had a breast cancer scare!" the woman cried.

"This wasn't a scare," Holland said. "This was fatal."

The room was silent. I could not raise my hand.

"Okay, I'm getting Paris," Holland said, and although Katharine had been born in Paris and I'd just been there for this book, I stayed quiet.

The woman behind me called out, "I'm thinking of going to France next summer, to the south."

"It's not southern France," argued Holland. "It's Paris." He paused, seeming to listen to a disembodied voice. "I'm seeing a thyroid condition."

Just before Katharine died, I was diagnosed with hypothyroidism. In essence, it was one of the last things she knew about me. I remained silent.

"Okay," Holland said, clearly frustrated but giving it one last go. "When is the book coming out?"

"My uncle is publishing a vanity memoir," said the woman, but Holland had decided that this message wasn't for her, and moved on.

I sat there with my head thrumming, suddenly remembering my last conversation with Katharine before she went to the hospice. We had talked about a book we'd both read by the fantasy novelist Connie Willis, called *Passage*. The main characters are scientists investigating near-death experiences by inducing the state in one another and monitoring the results. One of them crosses the threshold and dies. She finds herself on the deck of the *Titanic*, a metaphoric construct for where she actually is—like Ellie Arroway's Florida beach in *Contact*—and she tries desperately to signal her fellow research scientists by using the ship's radio. An old-fashioned radio.

Adrenaline rushed through me. I waited in line to talk to Holland, who was now signing books. "I just wanted to check with you," I said when I finally got to the front of the line. "You had a message from someone who died of breast cancer after a left breast mastectomy, associated with Paris and a radio and thyroid. My sister was born in Paris and died of that cancer, and I have a thyroid condition and am writing a book about her, and we promised to communicate through an old wireless radio. Could the message have been for me?"

He stared at me, his bushy eyebrows arched in gobsmacked amusement. "Why didn't you *raise your hand*?"

"I'm shy," I joked. But the truth was that I hadn't been able to. And now I was left with this insane ambiguity that was making my blood sing.

"Come on," said my friend who'd driven down with me for the weekend. "Let's go get a drink." But I couldn't just drop this and shrug—*Oh well, mighta been Katharine, mighta not been.* It would be like thinking that your fiercely adored sister has just banged on your front door when she's lost and you have been longing to hear from her and help her . . . but on the other hand it was probably the wind banging the door, so just go out the back way and attend that cocktail party you've been invited to. *Like that.* If you take this thing a little bit seriously, you have to take it all the way seriously or it messes with your head.

Carl Jung wrote about this dilemma in his book *Memories, Dreams, Reflections*:

> One night I lay awake thinking of the sudden death of a friend whose funeral had taken place the day before. I was deeply concerned. Suddenly I felt that he was in the room. It seemed to me that he stood at the foot of my bed and was asking me to go with him. I did not have the feeling of an apparition; rather, it was an inner visual image of him, which I explained to myself as a fantasy. But in all honesty I had to ask myself, "Do I have any proof that this is a fantasy? Suppose it is not a fantasy, suppose my friend is really here and I decided he was only a fantasy—would that not be abominable of me?" Yet I had equally little proof that he stood before me as an apparition. Then I said to myself, "Proof is neither here nor there! Instead of explaining him away as a fantasy, I might just as well give him the benefit of the doubt and for experiment's sake credit him with reality." The moment I had that thought, he went to the door and beckoned me to follow him. . . . That was something I hadn't bargained for. I had to repeat my argument to myself once more. Only then did I follow him in my imagination.

Jung envisioned himself following his friend, newly deceased physicist Wolfgang Pauli, to his nearby house and into his study, where Pauli climbed onto a stool and pointed to "the second of five books with red bindings which stood on the second shelf from the top." Having made this gesture, Pauli—and his study—vanished. The next day Jung asked Pauli's widow if he could look in his friend's library.

> Sure enough, there was a stool standing under the bookcase I had seen in my vision, and even before I came closer I could see the five books with red bindings. I stepped up on the stool so as to be able to read the titles. They were translations of the novels of Émile Zola. The title of the second volume read: "The Legacy of the Dead."

When I was travelling back to Toronto from the Omega Institute, the train I was riding in collided with a car. It was 10:30 a.m. on a Monday. I was transcribing notes into my laptop about Moody's comments on shared death experiences. Suddenly I registered a muffled bang or thump. I was in the back of the train, so the sound was remote. Had we hit a deer? We came screeching to a halt; I looked up from my computer and gazed out the window at a harvested cornfield in silvery light. This would, as it turned out, be my view for the next five hours.

Moments after the train stopped, I smelled smoke and burning rubber. I wondered if I would actually have to act on the emergency instructions I'd received from the steward that morning, to break the glass at my designated exit window with a ball-peen hammer. Was the train on fire? Wow, an adventure! But no.

Unbeknownst to us passengers, a black Ford Escape was in full meltdown behind us on the tracks, accordioned and spun. A twelve-year-old boy lay dead in the cornfield while his mother struggled for breath through fractured ribs.

The train-crossing gate hadn't worked properly, hadn't lowered; she had noticed our approach and slammed on the brakes a fraction too late. These details I learned by searching the local news on my laptop. All that we passengers officially knew was that we'd come to a stop and could smell smoke. A train official crackled on the loudspeakers, warning us to expect a delay.

Oh crap, a delay. Cellphones were flipped open and meetings in Toronto were postponed or put on notice. The woman across the aisle from me phoned her trip-cancellation insurance provider to clarify her options in case she missed the afternoon charter flight to her all-inclusive hotel in Punta Cana. People sighed, joked about the train service, rolled their eyes.

A steward came through with a trolley of coffee and snacks, looking haunted and acting irrationally. To some he sold sandwiches and to others he said, "We're just doing juice here, just drinks. We'll deal with food later." Had he been up at the front, yakking with the train conductor, when together they saw the car approaching, pressed an urgent, useless bell and then watched a child fly through a windshield? Likely yes, for the French-Canadian steward sought out anyone in my car with a passable knowledge of French and proceeded to rant to them about what he'd seen on the job—the suicides, the accidents, the reckless attempts to rush the crossing. "*C'est fou,*" he declared. Crazy.

No, what was crazy was that a child who had been alive

when we boarded that train was now lying mangled and life-less fifty yards behind us near the tracks, and we couldn't manage a collective moment of silence or a brief ecumenical prayer for the family or for his soul. There we sat for five hours, first waiting for the paramedics and police and then for the coroner, and in all those hours no one proposed getting off the train to pay our respects or to acknowledge in any way that this death had happened, other than referring to our interrupted schedules.

When we got moving again, the man across the aisle said, "You know, people have been surprisingly patient about this delay." And I said, "Well, maybe that's because they realize that the delay is trivial compared to being killed by a train." He gave me an apologetic smile. "Oh, that's probably right."

We finally arrived in Toronto at 5:30 p.m. and I had to go straight to the University of Toronto to teach a class. I asked one of my students, an observant Muslim from Pakistan, what would have happened in similar circumstances in Lahore when he was still living there. "What if a person was killed right in front of you? Would you ignore the death, sigh and rearrange your flight to an all-inclusive in Punta Cana?"

"No," he said, laughing in surprise. "We would rush to tell the imams, and every mosque nearby would begin ringing bells."

If we can't even face the basic fact of death in secular North American culture, how can we be expected to understand and respect the radical profundity of it, and thus begin to sort out the "psychic fayre" (novelist Hilary Mantel's term for our indulgence in "fun-size beliefs") from the true mystical experience, the NDE, the sensed presences? We deny or we radically accept, but we have no frame. "Where is the wisdom we have lost in knowledge? / Where is the knowledge we have lost in information?"

✳

A week of rain and fog ensued, along with my encountering some unsettling teachings from *The Tibetan Book of Living and Dying*, by Sogyal Rinpoche, which I'd borrowed from the library. It is a common belief in the stone monasteries of the Himalayan foothills that when you die, you enter what are known as bardo, or transition, states. Buddhist monks prepare studiously for this experience of entering the bardos, because the states—or realms—of the bardo can be trippy in the extreme. They might be ecstatic but may also be hellish, and if you don't keep your cool as you encounter demons, wrathful deities and monstrous wolves, you will race for the nearest available exit, which could result in rebirth as a stick insect or an aloe vera plant. I simplify, but psychologically you have to run a bit of a gauntlet before you get to any kind of heaven.

I took the dog for a walk in the drizzling evening, the air redolent of rain-damp oak leaves, and wondered uncomfortably what this had meant for Katharine and Dad. NDE accounts are profoundly comforting: you die and find yourself in the best place *ever*. But Tibetans insist that that's too simple, too easy. Instead, a much more complicated and potentially frightening experience ensues that is difficult to navigate without studious advance practice. Yes, they say, your emotions are heightened times pi, but not only the good ones. And if you give in to your emotions, or at least to the negative ones, you will be swiftly ushered into your new stick-insect costume and off you go to someone's back garden in Coventry.

I contemplate this formulation as I walk along Bellwoods Avenue in downtown Toronto. My middle-aged Sheltie ambles a pace behind me, immersed in a world of immediately present scents. Urine, grass, a pizza crust—every step a marvel of information. A young man strides towards and past me, his focus glossed over by whatever is on his iPod. He is present but not present, taking advantage of what he figures is a safe external environment to space out on his musical choice. In the bardo realms, you don't space out. You *are* spaced out, literally. And you have to concentrate.

How do you get there from here? If the Tibetans are right, then only they know how to brace for the experience of death, which means that the vast majority of the world's population will be blown immediately through the portal that rebirths us as beetles. How does that make sense? Could some monk not have passed along the word?

I pass the pretty little Anglican church of St. Matthias. My children have grown up playing soccer and doing cartwheels in the grassy yard of this church. Clara even attended Sunday school a few times, but she found it hard to wrap her mind around lessons like "Job and the Fig Tree," with its archaic language and irrelevant fruits. It wasn't a frame that could hold her. Yet there needs to be some frame around all these gleanings or we won't know how to live with them, how to integrate them, and we'll slide across the enchanted boundary and start seeing fairies on the end of our nose.

As Nancy Evans Bush, the woman who spent years contemplating her frightening NDE of Taoist black-and-white circles, writes, "We have to recognize that the world is made up of darkness as well as light, so we'd better pay some attention to the implications of that." It's not just heaven or lights out. Every mystic and saint, every hero has had a more harrowing journey. On some level we know that. "The deepest enigma for human beings is learning to live with what we believe. That's the hard part," she wrote.

Well, yes, and that's also a bit of an understatement.

One day, four years after Dad and Katharine died, I took the children to our witchy Celtic cottage where the wall warns of ghoulies and ghosties. This is bedrock home to me and my clan, the place we come from and go to, the place from which we draw our strength. I was awoken that first morning by someone calling my name, or at any rate "Pat." Since my son, Geoffrey, often teasingly calls me that now, I assumed he was trying to get me out of bed. I roused myself and went out onto the porch, where he was deeply immersed in a computerized game of chess. He hadn't said a thing. Oh.

Clara woke up a few hours later. She'd been struggling to sleep on the previous couple of nights because of a respiratory infection. She discovered that an extra blanket had been laid atop her. "Did you put that on me?" she asked.

"No," I said. Oh.

In the afternoon, when Clara was having a nap, she felt

someone gently grasp her foot. A sensed presence, although she didn't know that term.

Towards midnight I was sitting at a table on the screened-in porch. There was a whine and whir of insects banging against the mesh. I watched the full moon rise through the branches of the pine tree outside, ascending with cool beauty through shadowy cloud. I was listening to choral music and thinking of my sister, who had loved Clara and would totally have snuggled her up with blankets. (Clara sang at Katharine's memorial service. Proud of her exquisite musicality, I prompted her to repeat the song later at a dinner party, and she fixed me for a fool. It was sacred, unrepeatable. It was *for Aunt Katharine.*)

In the dark, familiar quiet of my cottage I abandoned my cool defensive musings and my journalist's distance and thought about my sister open-heartedly. Had she not come to me? When I lay in bed some weeks after she died and asked in messed-up anguish for a sign that she was all right, I found a single vivid pink bloom—not a bud but a ridiculous, time-elapsed bloom—on a long-dead plant in the hallway. When I asked her to come to the Omega Institute, the medium relayed details that neatly matched me, even though I wouldn't claim them. And now I heard knocks and whispers.

We reach and reach, trying to stay connected across space and time. This is what I was reflecting upon in the dark dining room of the cottage—this genuine fidelity of Katharine's reaching out to me since I'd lost her—when the Sharpie on the table near my laptop suddenly rolled.

Almost immediately I began to doubt the truth of what I'd seen. No, I *did* see the Sharpie roll; there is no question, because it startled me. I tried breathing out a puff of air to test if it would roll again. There was no breeze, but perhaps it had to do with the way I was breathing. That's what I figured. But no, nothing since. It didn't move again, any more than the phone book or the bowl of fruit or the other pen nearby had moved.

That Sharpie had firmly and decidedly moved across the table, about three inches or so, as I was thinking about my sister's persistence in attempting to reassure me. It is difficult to fix it in my mind, this signalling pen, precisely because I am so primed by my culture to disbelieve in its significance, primed by my culture to approach it analytically, deductively, like Sherlock Holmes. I picture my sister's fond exasperation. *How much more obvious can I get??*

Never before has a pen moved across a table in front of me; never have I hallucinated. I had begun to reflect on my sudden sense of genuine gratitude for her efforts over the past four years. I had started *believing* in her. Whereupon the pen moved. Yet the walls are too high. Our cultural skepticism is too great: a stern and forbidding cliff, terribly, terribly difficult to scale. Okay, you're right. By truly believing in Katharine's continuing consciousness, I instantly conjured a hallucination, because that is the power of belief. Have I then never believed in anything before? What else could I conjure with this power of belief I possess? A forest of lollipops? A nighttime infusion of joy? How about a winning lottery ticket?

If I am to accept that my sister communicated with me, then I have to start contemplating where she is and what she has been up to. I've been trying to find out, of course, but nothing in the answers provides what you might call a specific itinerary. Is she in the bardo realms? Totally foreign—I have no cultural understanding of that. I try to keep hold of her, but she grows totemic. What would she look like now? Would she still be with her boyfriend, Joel? Would she still be in her same job? And where is she? In a new body? Is she a baby in Nicaragua; is she in China; is she doing Pilates in the ether? Has she become a formless drop of light, and if so, what is the point of this exercise—how will I find her? When American writer and philosopher Ken Wilber lost his new wife to cancer, she kept telling him repeatedly as she was dying, "Promise me that you'll find me." How do we *find* one another again?

All these questions, so painful, lead us to refusing to answer, which is so much easier. A couple of years ago I walked along the cliff edge of the Adriatic Sea, along a trail that the great German poet Rainer Maria Rilke once paced a hundred years ago. In a letter penned above these limestone rocks, he wrote:

> This is in the end the only kind of courage that is required of us: the courage to face the strangest, most unusual, most inexplicable experiences that can meet us. The fact that people have in this sense been cowardly has done infinite harm to life; the experiences that are called "apparitions," the whole so-called "spirit world," death, all these Things that are so closely related to us, have through our daily defensiveness been so entirely pushed out of life that the senses with which we might have been able to grasp them have atrophied.

Yes, they have. Of course they have.

✳

Sitting in the boat at the cottage in the autumn of last year, bailing leafy water out of the stern with a plastic jug: a rhythmic scoop and pour, scoop and pour, cool water rushing in, sloshing over, trickling, dripping, creating all this watery sound in the otherwise uncommon silence. Sun casting a pure, high light across the lake. Silence and sunlight and water.

There is sometimes a juxtaposition of those elements that approaches the sacred, and I can only imagine what the numinous light would be like. As Teresa of Avila said, this water, and this light, is but a muddy stream in comparison. If Katharine were trying to communicate with me, it would only be to say, "you have no idea—there are no words!" As palliative psychologist Kathleen Dowling Singh has noted, "the dying become radiant, and speak of 'walking through a room lit by a lantern,' or of their body 'filling with sunlight.' They share these experiences with a quiet, thankful awe. There is something about the quality of their demeanor and expression at these times that has a feeling of purity, like a world wiped clean by new snow or as seen through the eyes of an infant. Ego is not in these expressions . . . It would appear that we move into a sacred realm of Being that we recognize with faith, confidence and gratitude to be our own. One woman kept returning from this depth of being to let those of us around her know: 'I cannot tell you how beautiful this is.'"

I meet up with my sister Anne and her husband, Mark, and we spend the afternoon tucking in the cottage for its winter slumber. Much of what we do involves confounding the squirrels, which appear to have spent most of their autumn collecting acorns and carefully hiding them in our bedsheets and between the folds of swimming towels. Each time we strip a bed, acorns tumble out of hiding spots and bounce across the floor. It's like we're on an inadvertent Easter egg hunt in each room. Anne and I keep laughing. We take apart the docks by bolt and screw and use the boat to tow them around to the lee of the boathouse bay, where Mark ropes them to cedar bushes and we hope for the best.

The next day, as I shutter the windows to the cottage for the season, I wonder what will have happened when they are next thrown open to soft spring light. What will have transpired in my life, in ours, in the history of the world? Who else will have died?

But the grace I see now comes from the comfort I draw from this tribe, from my cousins and aunts and uncles and extended family and friends. Love is the coin of the realm, said Eben Alexander, and he's right. The extended family has drawn ever closer, unselfconsciously so, through the astonishments of death. It's like a footprint in the sand that needs to be filled in. Where the water rushes in, where love rushes in.

ACKNOWLEDGEMENTS

This book has been fiendishly difficult to write for a number of reasons, not least of which is the wall of skepticism I've had to scale even in my own neighbourhood, amongst my own friends. I am profoundly grateful to those who have encouraged me.

I would like to thank, above all, my mother, Landon, who permitted me to share the story of my father's and sister's deaths without attempting to control the narrative; who introduced me to various key sources, including the German theologian Rudolf Otto; who read drafts and offered incisive feedback; who supported me in every imaginable way with open-minded curiosity and heart. For a woman who has achieved international respect as an architect and advocate for the United Nations Convention on the Rights of the Child, she has practised what she preached in her own family. I have never felt anything less than completely engaged respect from her as I've fumbled my way along, seeking meaning.

Huge, respectful thanks to the women who fought for this project to come to fruition, walking around kicking shins so that contracts could come into being: my amazingly smart and witty agent, Sarah Lazin; my editors, Anne Collins at Random House Canada and Leslie Meredith at Atria; and my long-time publisher and friend, Louise Dennys. I am honoured by you all for giving me a voice. (I also hate but respect you all for making me rewrite this book so many times.) It has been the great pleasure of my career to work with such fiercely intelligent, utterly sane and uncompromising women.

None of this writing would have been possible without the foundational research of some key people who have risked their reputations to keep our inquiry into human spiritual experience going in a time of heightened materialist belief. In particular I am indebted to my fellow journalists John Geiger and Maria Coffey; to psychologists Erlendur Haraldsson and Karlis Osis; to neuropsychiatrist Peter Fenwick; to the many excellent scholars at the University of Virginia's Division of Perceptual Studies, including the late Ian Stevenson, Bruce Greyson, Emily Williams Kelly and Edward Kelly; to doctors Penny Sartori, Sam Parnia and Pim van Lommel; and to members of the International Association of Near-Death Studies, in particular Jan Holden and Diane Corcoran.

Many people contributed their experiences to this book, and I am grateful to those who allowed me to name them, as well as those who preferred to remain anonymous.

For editorial feedback and source suggestions along the way, my thanks to Ambrose Pottie, Marni Jackson, Judy Finlay, Teresa Toten, Dr. Mary Vachon, Sheila Whyte, Monique Séguin, Leah Cherniak, Manuela Jessel, Mary Mackenzie, Joanne Thomas Yaccato, Lewis Humphreys, Doug Campbell, Anne Pearson, Mark Vorobej, Sarah Jordison, Amanda Lewis, Barney Gilmore and Gillian Watts. I am forgetting a million people, I know it.

Jeff Warren has been my sounding board and musing pal from the outset and, I hope, for many years to come.

I am indebted to the Canada Council for the Arts for supporting this project.

Finally, I apologize to my husband and children for festooning the house with books about death for several years. They eventually got so used to it that Clara, at sixteen, suggested this book title: *YOLO, or Do You?*

NOTES

CHAPTER 1

2. **"extreme reality"**: Virginia Woolf, "Sketch of the Past," in *Moments of Being: Unpublished Autobiographical Writings*, ed. Jeanne Schulkind (London: Chatto and Windus, 1976).

6. **"Beauty is only the first touch of terror"**: Rainer Maria Rilke, *Duino Elegies* (New York: Vintage, 2009).

8. **"One has never seen the world well"**: Gaston Bachelard, *The Poetics of Reverie: Childhood, Language and the Cosmos* (Boston: Beacon Press, 1971).

12. **Albert Heim:** A. Heim, "Remarks on Fatal Falls," *Yearbook of the Swiss Alpine Club* 27 (1892): 327–37. In R. Noyes and R. Kletti, "The Experience of Dying from Falls," *Omega* 3 (1972): 45–52.

13. **doctors wildly overestimate:** See a discussion of this survival prognosis error in Marcus Alexander and Nicholas A.

Christakis, "Bias and Asymmetric Loss in Expert Forecasts: A Study of Physician Prognostic Behavior with Respect to Patient Survival," *Journal of Health Economics* 27 (2008): 1095–1108. See also Atul Gawande, "Letting Go: What Should Medicine Do When It Can't Save Your Life?" *New Yorker*, August 2, 2010.

17. **questionnaire for family members:** Michael Barbato, "Parapsychological Phenomena Near the Time of Death," *Journal of Palliative Care* 15 (Summer 1999): 30–37. "Our data are consistent with other studies," Barbato notes, "that show no correlations between religion, spiritual beliefs or cultural background and the occurrence of parapsychological experiences."

19. **survey of college professors:** M. W. Wagner and M. Monnet, "Attitudes of College Professors Toward Extrasensory Perception," *Zetetic Scholar* 5 (1979): 7–17.

19. **Archives of Scientists' Transcendent Experiences:** http://www.issc-taste.org/index.shtml.

19. **critical thinking skills:** C. Roe, "Critical Thinking and Belief in the Paranormal: A Reevaluation," *British Journal of Psychology* 90 (1999): 85-98. See also Dean Radin, *Entangled Minds: Extrasensory Experiences in a Quantum Reality* (New York: Pocket Books, 2006). "Other studies confirm this lack of difference," Radin reports. "A 1997 study by Uwe Wolfradt in the journal *Personality and Individual Differences* found no correlation between dissociative behavior and belief in psi. On the other hand there is a strong correlation between absorption—the ability to concentrate or focus—and experience of psi . . . in spite of evidence to the contrary, some skeptics continue to assert that belief in the paranormal is best explained by ignorance or mental deficiency" (40).

20. **people more likely to accept psi:** "The Religious and Other Beliefs of Americans," Harris Poll, February 26, 2003. http://www.harrisinteractive.com/vault/Harris-Interactive -Poll-Research-The-Religious-and-Other-Beliefs-of-Americans -2003-2003-02.pdf. In other words, it is pretty widely accepted that there is something going on in the universe that draws on another sense than the ones we've officially identified so far.

20. **Freeman Dyson:** See also F. Dyson, "One in a Million," *New York Review of Books,* March 25, 2004.

20. **"ESP exists":** Ibid.

22. **"This changes everything":** Mayer, *Extraordinary Knowing,* 3, 215.

CHAPTER 2

24. **"This is different":** C. Cornacchia, "What Happens When We Die?" *Montreal Gazette,* February 10, 2007.

25. **David Kessler:** See a discussion and examples in D. Kessler, *Visions, Trips and Crowded Rooms* (Carlsbad, CA: Hay House, 2010).

26. **James Brown:** Jeremy Simmonds, *The Encyclopedia of Dead Rock Stars* (Chicago: Chicago Review Press, 2008).

27. **comprehensive study of deathbed experiences:** Karlis Osis and Erlendur Haraldsson, *At the Hour of Death: A New Look at Evidence for Life after Death* (Mamaroneck, NY: Hastings House, 1990).

27. **"I am going":** Osis and Haraldsson, 67.

27. **Paramedics:** http://www.coasttocoastam.com/show/2009/08/28.

28. **"I'm going to die today":** Shane Sinclair, "Impact of Death and Dying on the Personal Lives and Practices of Palliative and

Hospice Care Professionals," *Canadian Medical Association Journal* 183(2) (February 8, 2011): 180–87.

28. **amazement and surprise:** Osis and Haraldsson.

29. **beginning point and end point:** Kathleen Dowling Singh, *The Grace in Dying: A Message of Hope, Comfort and Spiritual Transformation* (San Francisco: HarperOne, 2000). Writes Singh further: "The psychoalchemy of terminal illness seems to allow a natural feeling of safety as death approaches . . . or as Sogyal Rinpoche says, we move toward it 'as instinctively . . . as a little child running eagerly into its mother's lap, like old friends meeting, or a river flowing into the sea.' It is my observation, by and large, this is so. Jewish wisdom speaks of devekut, 'melting into the Divine'" (223).

29. **passport and ticket:** Maggie Callanan, presentation at the International Association of Near-Death Studies (IANDS) annual conference, Raleigh, North Carolina, 2008. See also M. Callanan and P. Kelley, *Final Gifts: Understanding the Special Awareness, Needs and Communications of the Dying* (New York: Bantam, 1992).

30. **five stages of dying:** See, for example, Elisabeth Kübler-Ross, *On Death and Dying*, first published in 1969.

30. **Moody's research:** Raymond Moody, *Life after Life: The Investigation of a Phenomenon—Survival of Bodily Death* (San Francisco: HarperOne, 2001), originally published in 1975.

31. **paranormal death-bed phenomena:** H. Lovelace et al., "Comfort for the Dying: Five Year Retrospective and One Year Prospective Studies of End of Life Experiences," *Archives of Gerontology and Geriatrics* 51, no. 2 (September–October 2010): 173–79. See also S. Brayne et al., "End of Life Experiences and

the Dying Process in a Gloucestershire Nursing Home as Reported by Nurses and Care Assistants," *American Journal of Hospital and Palliative Care* 25, no. 3 (2008): 195–206.

31. **distinct state of consciousness:** Callanan and Kelley, *Final Gifts.*

31. *Ars moriendi:* "In the Christian Monastic tradition," writes Kathleen Dowling Singh, "the dying enter three phases: separation, liminality and reincorporation. Liminality was viewed as a period of metamorphosis, the preparatory period for the emergence of the soul on its journey home to Spirit." Singh, *Grace in Dying,* 216.

32. **responsibility to tell our stories:** Callanan, presentation at IANDS conference, 2008.

33. **a deceased relative "visits":** Lovelace, "Comfort for the Dying."

33. **Penny Sartori:** Interview with the author, summer 2012.

34. **Dianne Arcangel:** D. Arcangel, *Afterlife Encounters: Ordinary People, Extraordinary Experiences* (Charlottesville, VA: Hampton Roads, 2005), 119.

34. **majority reported seeing such visions:** Osis and Haraldsson, *Hour of Death.*

35. **a woman who had come to take him away:** Osis and Haraldsson.

35. **fevers as causing hallucinations:** Osis and Haraldsson.

35. **terminal restlessness:** See, for example, A. Mazzarino-Willett, "Deathbed Phenomena: Its Role in Peaceful Death and Terminal Restlessness," *American Journal of Hospice and Palliative Medicine* 27, no. 2 (2010): 127–33.

36. **anxiety-based thing:** Brayne, "End of Life Experiences." See also P. Fenwick et al., "End of Life Experiences and

Their Implications for Palliative Care," *International Journal of Environmental Studies* 64, no. 3 (2007): 315–23.

36. **apparitions with a take-away purpose:** Osis and Haraldsson, *Hour of Death*, 86.

37. **Barbara Cane:** Peter Fenwick and Elizabeth Fenwick, *The Art of Dying* (London: Continuum, 2008).

45. **Herophilus of Alexandria:** M. Roach, *Spook: Science Tackles the Afterlife* (New York: Norton, 2005), 68–69.

45. **classic Egyptian understanding:** See, for example, The Egyptian Book of the Dead: The Book of Going Forth by Day.

45. **soul bone:** Roach, *Spook*, 67–68.

45. **"spiritus":** ibid., 67.

46. **Descartes:** See, for example, the discussion in C. Zimmer, *Soul Made Flesh: The Discovery of the Brain and How It Changed the World* (New York: Atria, 2005).

46. **Franz Gall:** Roach, *Spook*, 73–75.

47. **Duncan MacDougall:** Roach, *Spook*, 110–11.

48. **Lady Florence Barrett:** William Barrett, *Deathbed Visions: How the Dead talk to the Dying* (Guildford: White Crow, 2011), 13–14.

49. **teenager in Lithuania:** Osis and Haraldsson, *Hour of Death*.

49. **terminal lucidity:** M. Nahm and B. Greyson, "Terminal Lucidity in Patients with Chronic Schizophrenia and Dementia: A Survey of the Literature," *Journal of Nervous and Mental Disease* 197, no. 12 (2009): 942–44.

50. **schizophrenics and stroke patients:** Osis and Haraldsson, *Hour of Death*.

50. **terminal lucidity cases:** M. Nahm et al., "Terminal Lucidity: A Review and a Case Collection," *Archives of Gerontology and*

Geriatrics (2011). See also S. Haig, "The Brain: The Power of Hope," *Time*, January 29, 2007.

51. **first encounter with terminal lucidity:** Pamela Kircher, *Love Is the Link: A Hospice Doctors Shares Her Experience of Near-Death and Dying* (Pagosa Springs, CO: Awakening Press, 2013).

51. **hospice care use:** National Hospice and Palliative Care Organization, www.nhpco.org; Fenwick and Fenwick, *The Art of Dying*; Canadian Hospice Palliative Care Association, "Fact Sheet: Hospice Palliative Care in Canada."

CHAPTER 3

54. **percentage of general population:** R. A. Kalish and D. K. Reynolds, "Phenomenological Reality and Post-death Contact," *Journal for the Scientific Study of Religion* (1973): 209–21. For a review of cross-cultural prevalence, see E. Steffen and A. Coyle, "'Sense of Presence' Experiences in Bereavement and Their Relationship to Mental Health: A Critical Examination of a Continuing Controversy," in *Mental Health and Anomalous Experience*, ed. C. Murray (Hauppauge, NY: Nova Science, 2012), 33–56.

54. **grief hallucinations:** See, for example, Craig Murray and Sheila Payne, "Grief Hallucinations: A Narrative Review," *Mental Health, Religion and Culture* (in press).

54. **sixth sense:** J. M. Small, letter to the editor, *Lancet* 337 (June 22, 1991): 1550.

54. **extraordinary encounters:** Erlendur Haraldsson, *The Departed among the Living: An Investigative Study of Afterlife Encounters* (Guildford: White Crow Books, 2012).

58.   **experiences in dreams:** Cited in Dean Radin, *Entangled Minds: Extrasensory Experiences in a Quantum Reality* (New York: Pocket Books, 2006). "The truth is that to very high levels of confidence we know that information at a distance was successfully perceived in dreams under well-controlled conditions" (115).

58.   **odds against chance:** Radin, *Entangled Minds*, 110. Odds against chance with crisis apparitions were first calculated by Gurney and Myers at Cambridge. They compared the frequency with which people reported having hallucinations in a waking, healthy state with statistics regarding the incidence of death in the United Kingdom, concluding that hallucinations coinciding with death happened too frequently to be attributable to chance. This research is discussed in Edward Kelly and Emily Williams Kelly, eds., *Irreducible Mind: Toward a Psychology for the 21st Century* (Plymouth, UK: Rowman & Littlefield, 2007), 109.

58.   **Hans Berger:** David Millett, "Hans Berger: From Psychic Energy to the EEG," *Perspectives in Biology and Medicine* 44, no. 4 (Autumn 2001): 522–42.

59.   **twin studies:** Radin, *Entangled Minds*, 18. For more EEG studies, see ibid., 137–40. See also Daryl J. Bem and Charles Honorton, "Does Psi Exist? Replicable Evidence for an Anomalous Process of Information Transfer," *Psychological Bulletin* 115, no. 1 (1994): 4–18. For further discussion of methodology in PSI research, see http://www.koestler -parapsychology.psy.ed.ac.uk/Psi.html.

59.   **British twins:** Göran Brusewitz and Adrian Parker (Department of Psychology, University of Gothenburg),

Proceedings of the Annual Meeting of the Parapsychological Association, Viterbo, Italy, August 2013.

59. **Jiří Wackermann:** J. Wackerman, "Dyadic Correlations between Brain Functional States: Present Facts and Future Perspectives," *Mind and Matter* 2, no. 1 (2004): 105–22. See also J. Wackerman et al., "Correlations between Electrical Activities of Two Spatially Separated Subjects," *Neuroscience Letters* 336 (2003): 60–64.

60. **Ian Stevenson:** I. Stevenson, *Telepathic Impressions: A Review and Report of 35 New Cases* (Charlottesville: University of Virginia Press, 1973). For a retrospective analysis of Stevenson's work, see Carlos Alvarado and Nancy Zingrone, "Ian Stevenson and the Modern Study of Spontaneous ESP Experiences," *Journal of Scientific Exploration* 22, no. 1 (2008): 44–53.

60. **Myers and Gurney:** See E. Gurney, F. W. H. Meyers and F. Podmore, *Phantasms of the Living,* 2 vols. (London: Truber, 1886).

61. **storm at sea:** For a full discussion of the Wilmot case and the way in which skeptical psychologist Susan Blackmore dismissed it by overlooking certain facts, see Kelly and Kelly, *Irreducible Mind.*

62. **Myers and Gurney cases:** Stevenson, *Telepathic Impressions.*

62. **Oliver Sacks:** O. Sacks, *Hallucinations* (New York: Vintage, 2013).

62. **Myers and Gurney cases:** Stevenson, *Telepathic Impressions.*

62. **communication of joy:** Stevenson.

63. **violent death:** Stevenson.

63. **violent deaths in Iceland:** Haraldsson, *Departed.*

63. **gloomy forebodings:** Stevenson, *Telepathic Impressions.*

63. **some kind of action:** Stevenson.

63. **Mrs. Hurth:** Stevenson.

64. **agent's focus on percipient:** Stevenson.

64. **feeling of conviction:** Stevenson.

68. **propensity or giftedness:** Stevenson. See also Radin's discussion of traits and factors that seem to correlate with an enhanced capacity to receive telepathic impressions, in *Entangled Minds.*

68. **Janey Acker Hurth:** Stevenson, *Telepathic Impressions.*

69. **information gradually coming into focus:** Stevenson. This model of what's going on is reminiscent of the U.S. government–funded remote viewing experiments, about which see Russell Targ, "Why I Am Absolutely Convinced of the Reality of Psychic Abilities, and Why You Should Be, Too," presentation at the annual convention of the Parapsychological Association, Paris 2010.

70. **death-bed coincidences:** Fenwick and Fenwick, *Art of Dying.*

70. **Vincent:** Fenwick and Fenwick, *Art of Dying,* 63.

70. **Richard Bufton:** Fenwick and Fenwick, 62.

71. **hallucinations of text:** Dominic ffytche et al., "Visual Command Hallucinations in a Patient with Pure Alexia," *Journal of Neurology, Neurosurgery and Psychiatry* 75 (2004): 80–86.

72. **intuiting death and distress events:** See, for example, Radin, *Entangled Minds,* and Haraldsson, *Departed.*

72. **Kath McMahon:** Fenwick and Fenwick, *Art of Dying,* 66.

72. **buoyantly happy:** Fenwick and Fenwick, 115.

72. **Raymond Hunter:** Fenwick and Fenwick, 53.

73. **couvade:** Stevenson, *Telepathic Impressions,* 102. This has subsequently been documented a little more clearly with shared emotional symptoms. See, for example, James F. Paulson

et al., "Prenatal and Postpartum Depression in Fathers and
Its Association with Maternal Depression: A Meta-analysis,"
Journal of the American Medical Association 303, no. 19 (2010):
1961–69.

73.　**the sound of my heart breaking:** Paul Hawker, *Secret Affairs
of the Soul: Ordinary People's Extraordinary Experiences of
the Sacred* (Kelowna, BC: Northstone, 2000), 101.

74.　**fighting to breathe:** Fenwick and Fenwick, *Art of Dying,* 54.

75.　**Glennys Howarth:** G. Howarth, "Shared Near-Death and
Related Illness Experiences: Steps on an Unscheduled Journey,"
Journal of Near-Death Studies 20, no. 2 (Winter 2001): 71–85.

75.　**Derek Whitehead:** Fenwick and Fenwick, *Art of Dying,* 73.

76.　**burn victim:** Allan Hamilton, *The Scalpel and the Soul:
Encounters with Surgery, the Supernatural and the Healing
Power of Hope* (New York: Tarcher/Penguin, 2008), 71–76.

79.　**vardøger:** For a fascinating case discussion, see L. David Leiter,
"The Vardøgr: Perhaps Another Indicator of the Non-locality
of Consciousness," *Journal of Scientific Exploration* 16, no. 4
(2002): 621–34.

81.　**models for understanding:** Mayer, *Extraordinary Knowing.*

81.　**meteorites:** Mayer, *Extraordinary Knowing,* 97.

81.　**Ignaz Semmelweis:** See, for example, K. Codell Carter
and Barbara R. Carter, *Childbed Fever: A Scientific Biography of
Ignaz Semmelweis* (New Brunswick, NJ: Transaction, 1994).

81.　**John Snow:** See a brief history of his investigation into
the causes of cholera at http://www.ph.ucla.edu/epi/snow
/fatherofepidemiology.html.

82.　**Wright brothers:** Hilary Mantel, "That Wilting Flower," *London
Review of Books* 30, no. 2 (January 24, 2008): 3–6.

82.   **Ganzfeld technique:** See the discussion in, for example, Bem and Honorton, "Does Psi Exist?" Also in Radin, *Entangled Minds.*

82.   **sensory awareness:** Radin, *Entangled Minds.*

83.   **telepathy experiment:** Dean Radin, *Supernormal: Science, Yoga, and the Evidence for Extraordinary Psychic Abilities* (New York: Deepak Chopra, 2013).

84.   **Ganzfeld experiments around the world:** Radin, *Supernormal.*

84.   **Richard Wiseman:** http:subversivethinking.blogspot.com/2010 /04/richard-wiseman-evidence-for-esp-meets.html.

85.   **Robert Rosenthal:** Bem and Honorton, "Does Psi Exist?"

85.   **Henry Sidgwick:** H. Sidgwick, "Presidential Address," *Journal of the Society for Psychical Research* 1: 8.

86.   **Brian D. Josephson:** Kenneth Chang, "Do Paranormal Phenomena Exist?" *New York Times,* November 11, 2003.

86.   **Harold Puthoff:** Mayer, *Extraordinary Knowing,* 114.

86.   **quantum entanglement:** J. Matson, "Quantum Entanglement Links Two Diamonds," *Scientific American,* December 1, 2011.

87.   **Michael Persinger:** Interview by Alex Tsakiris, broadcast December 16, 2009, *Skeptiko.*

87.   **quantum theory:** Radin, *Entangled Minds,* 232.

88.   **group consciousness:** Roger Nelson and Peter Bancel, "Effects of Mass Consciousness: Changes in Random Data During Global Events," *Explore* 7 (2011): 373–83.

88.   **PEAR Global Consciousness Project:** http://noosphere .princeton.edu/.

88.   **global mind:** Roger Nelson, "Is the Global Mind Real?" *EdgeScience* 1 (October 2009): 6–8.

89.   **William Long:** W. Long, *How Animals Talk* (New York: Harper, 1919).

89. **Rupert Sheldrake:** R. Sheldrake, *Dogs That Know When Their Owners Are Coming Home*, rev. ed. (New York: Broadway Books, 2011). See also the ensuing debate between Sheldrake and Richard Wiseman, summarized by Chris Carter in "Heads I Lose, Tails You Win: How Richard Wiseman Nullifies Positive Results and What to Do about It," *Journal of the Society for Psychical Research* 74: 156–67; and Sheldrake's further discussion with Wiseman in *The Science Delusion: Freeing the Spirit of Scientific Inquiry* (London: Coronet, 2012).

89. **African bushmen:** Laurens van der Post, *The Lost World of the Kalahari*, cited in Sheldrake, *Science Delusion.*

90. **long body:** William Roll, "Psi and the Long Body," *Australian Journal of Parapsychology* 8, no. 1 (2008).

91. **unrecognized exchanges of feelings:** Stevenson, *Telepathic Impressions.*

92. **sense of danger:** Radin, *Entangled Minds*, 265.

93. **students at Bristol:** Fenwick and Fenwick, *Art of Dying.*

94. **Cornell experiments in precognition:** Daryl Bem, "Feeling the Future: Experimental Evidence for Anomalous Retroactive Influences on Cognition and Affect," *Journal of Personality and Social Psychology* 100, no. 3 (2011): 407–25.

95. **Joachim Krueger:** Peter Aldhous, "Is This Evidence We Can See the Future?" *New Scientist*, November 11, 2010.

95. **ability to anticipate danger:** Bem p. 51. This idea is also discussed in G. Hitchman et al., "A Re-examination of Non-intentional Precognition with Openness to Experience, Creativity, Psi Beliefs and Luck Beliefs as Predictors of Success," presentation at the annual convention of the Parapsychological Association, Curitiba, Brazil, 2011:

"Stanford's Psi-mediated Instrumental Response model predicts that psi can operate in the absence of conscious awareness, facilitating advantageous outcomes for the organism by triggering pre-existing behaviours in response to opportunities or threats in the environment."

95. **Hans Eysenck:** H. J. Eysenck, "Personality and Extra-sensory Perception," *Journal of the Society for Psychical Research* 44 (1966): 55–71.

96. **physiological reactions:** Radin, *Supernormal,* 165.

96. **Bengalese finches:** Radin, *Supernormal,* 176.

96. **experiments in presentiment:** See F. Alvarez, "Anticipatory Alarm Behaviour in Bengalese Finches," *Journal of Scientific Exploration* 24, no. 4 (2010); D. Radin et al., "Electrocortical Activity prior to Unpredictable Stimuli in Meditators and Non-meditators," *Explore* 7 (2011), 286–99; Bem, "Feeling the Future"; and C. Wildey, "Impulse Response of Biological Systems" (master's thesis, Department of Electrical Engineering, University of Texas, 2001).

96. **significant incidence of precognition:** Julia Mossbridge, Patrizio Tressoldi and Jessica Utts, "Predictive Physiological Anticipation Preceding Seemingly Unpredictable Stimuli: A Meta-analysis," *Frontiers in Psychology,* October 2012.

96. **Mossbridge's article:** Email conversation with the author.

97. **Lev and Sveta:** Orlando Figes, *Just Send Me Word: A True Story of Love and Survival in the Gulag* (New York: Metropolitan Books, 2012), 282.

CHAPTER 4

101. **William Bird:** Bird's memoir, *Warm Hands*, is quoted in Tim Cook, "Grave Beliefs: Stories of the Supernatural and the Uncanny among Canada's Great War Trench Soldiers," *Journal of Military History* 77 (April 2013): 523–56. See also Michael Roper, *The Secret Battle: Emotional Survival in the Great War* (Manchester, UK: Manchester University Press, 2009).

102. **George Maxwell:** Cook, "Grave Beliefs."

102. **"Who is the third?":** T. S. Eliot, "What the Thunder Said," *The Wasteland.*

103. **Ernest Shackleton:** Interview with London's *Daily Telegraph*, February 1, 1922, cited in John Geiger, *The Third Man Factor: The Secret to Survival in Extreme Environments* (Toronto: Penguin Canada, 2009).

104. **polar explorers:** D. Chan et al., "But Who Is That on the Other Side of You? Extracampine Hallucinations Revisited," *Lancet*, December 21, 2002.

104. **Henry Stoker:** Geiger, *Third Man Factor*, 61.

104. **World Trade Center survivors:** Geiger, 1.

105. **Lou and Ingrid Whittaker:** Maria Coffey, *Explorers of the Infinite: The Secret Spiritual Lives of Extreme Athletes—and What They Reveal About Near-Death Experiences, Psychic Communication, and Touching the Beyond* (New York: Tarcher, 2008).

105. **Olaf Blanke:** O. Blanke, A. Shahar, et al., "Induction of an Illusory Shadow Person," *Nature* 443 (September 21, 2006). See also O. Blanke and T. Metzinger, "Full-Body Illusions and Minimal Phenomenal Selfhood," *Trends in Cognitive Science* 13 (2009): 7–13; and M. Persinger, "Experimental Facilitation of

the Sensed Presence: Possible Intercalation Between the
Hemispheres Induced by Complex Magnetic Fields,"
Journal of Nervous and Mental Disease 190, no. 8 (2002):
533–41.

106. **sensed-presence phenomenon:** Peter Suedfeld et al.,
"The Sensed Presence as a Coping Resource in Extreme
Environments," in *Miracles: God, Science, and Psychology in the
Paranormal–Parapsychological Perspectives,* vol. 3, 1–15.
(Westport, CT: Praeger, 2008).

108. **James Sevigny:** Geiger, *Third Man Factor,* 7–10.

108. **Joshua Slocum:** Geiger, 49–52.

108. **Edith Stearns:** Geiger, 92.

109. **Brian Shoemaker:** Geiger, 94–96.

109. **Ensio Tiira:** Geiger, 199–202.

109. **Rob Taylor:** R. Taylor, *The Breach: Kilimanjaro and the Conquest
of Self* (Albany, Australia: Wildeyed Press, 1991).

111. **dying visions of William Blake:** Mary Oliver, "Blake Dying," in
A Thousand Mornings: Poems (New York: Penguin, 2013), 29.

111. **genesis of qualia:** Oliver Sacks, "In the River of
Consciousness," *New York Review of Books,* January 15, 2004.

111. **brain activation and conscious experience:** Alexander
Morelos, presentation at "The Science of Consciousness"
conference, University of Arizona, Tucson, 2012.

112. **promissory materialism:** Morelos, 2012.

112. **Julio Peres:** Tucson, 2012.

113. **transformations:** Sacks, "River of Consciousness."

113. **brainwaves of meditating monks:** See, for example, the
website of Richard Davidson's Lab for Affective Neuroscience,
http://psyphz.psych.wisc.edu/.

113. **hallucination mechanisms:** Patricia Boksa, "On the Neurobiology of Hallucinations," *Journal of Psychiatry and Neuroscience* 34, no. 4 (July 2009): 260–62.

114. **National Health Service research grant:** news release, King's College, London, June 29, 2012.

114. **Harold Puthoff:** Mayer, *Extraordinary Knowing.*

114. **epistemological modesty:** Martha Farah, "The More We Understand, the Less We Know," presentation at the Nour Foundation 2009 Symposia Series.

115. **Ann Bancroft:** Liv Arnesen and Ann Bancroft, *No Horizon Is So Far: Two Women and Their Historic Journey across Antarctica* (Cambridge, MA: Da Capo Press, 2003). Additional interview quotes cited by Geiger, *Third Man Factor.*

116. **Jerry Linenger:** Geiger, 102.

116. **presence of someone deceased:** Edith Steffen et al., "'Sense of Presence' Experiences in Bereavement and Their Relationship to Mental Health: A Critical Examination of a Continuing Controversy," in *Mental Health and Anomalous Experience: Psychology Research Progress* 3 (2012): 33–56.

116. **visual perception of the presence:** M. Barbato, *Parapsychological Phenomena Near the Time of Death.* See also the statistical breakdown in Haraldsson, *Departed.*

117. **2006 study:** Haraldsson, *Departed.*

117. **Sigmund Freud:** Freud's essay "Mourning and Melancholia" is discussed by Steffen et al. in "'Sense of Presence' Experiences."

117. **hallucinatory wishful psychosis:** Steffen et al., "'Sense of Presence' Experiences in Bereavement."

118. **not a mental disorder:** Saxby Pridmore, *Download of Psychiatry* (Hobart: University of Tasmania, 2006) [ebook].

118. **surviving AIDS partners:** T. A. Richards, "Spiritual Resources Following a Partner's Death from AIDS," in *Meaning Reconstruction and the Experience of Loss*, ed. R. A. Neimeyer (Washington, DC: American Psychological Association, 2001), 173–90.

118. **comforting and benign:** Pridmore, *Download of Psychiatry*.

119. **widows and widowers:** A. M. Greeley, "Hallucinations among the Widowed," *Sociology of Social Research* 71, no. 4 (1987): 258–65.

119. **Vaughan Bell:** V. Bell, "Ghost Stories: Visits from the Deceased," *Scientific American*, December 2, 2008.

119. **account from a lawyer:** Haraldsson, *Departed*.

123. **reactions to grief counselling:** E. Steffen and A. Coyle, "Sense of Presence Experiences and Meaning-Making in Bereavement: A Qualitative Analysis," *Death Studies* 35 (2011): 579–609.

123. **uncanny experiences in patients:** Barbato, "Parapsychological Phenomena."

123. **Johan Kuld:** Quoted by Haraldsson, *Departed*, 113.

124. **the living shared their pastures and roads:** Claude Lecouteux, *The Return of the Dead: Ghosts, Ancestors, and the Transparent Veil of the Pagan Mind* (Rochester, VT: Inner Traditions, 2009).

125. **bodies were decapitated:** See the discussion in Timothy Taylor, *The Buried Soul: How Humans Invented Death* (Boston: Beacon Press, 2002).

125. **the world was haunted:** Lecouteux, *Return of the Dead*.

126. **William of Newburgh:** William of Newburgh, *History of English Affairs*, book 5, chapter 24 (full text available from Fordham University at http://www.fordham.edu/halsall/basis/william ofnewburgh-intro.asp). Lecouteux agrees with Newburgh: "Revenants were no cause for surprise to the Germanic peoples; they fit perfectly within their mind-sets, their place has not been usurped, and we cannot dismiss these stories as 'old wives tales.' The roots of the belief are too deep" (*Return of the Dead,* 155).

126. **Augustine:** Lecouteux, *Return.*

126. **Chaz Ebert:** Interview with Studs Terkel in his oral history *Will the Circle Be Unbroken? Reflections on Death, Rebirth and a Hunger for Faith* (New York: Ballantine, 2001).

127. **vision as a construction:** Radin, *Entangled Minds.* Leaving aside for a moment the origin of the signal, the idea that we can construct visual meaning is now commonly understood within the field of perceptual studies. The most elementary example is this: Yuo mgiht aslo be srupsired to fnid taht yuo can raed tihs ntoe wtihuot mcuh trouble. (See further discussion in Kelly and Kelly, *Irreducible Mind.*)

128. **deceased moulds the perception:** Haraldsson, *Departed.*

128. **Gregory the Great:** Lecouteux, *Return of the Dead.*

129. **sensed presence with sleep paralysis:** Allan Cheyne, "Relations among Hypnagogic and Hypnopompic Experiences Associated with Sleep Paralysis," *Journal of Sleep Research* 8 (1999): 313–17. See also A. Cheyne, "A Webpage about Sleep Paralysis and Associated Hypnagogic and Hypnopompic Experiences," http://watarts.uwaterloo.ca/~acheyne/.

134. **Fukushima University research:** Jeff Warren, *The Head Trip: Adventures on the Wheel of Consciousness* (Toronto: Random House, 2007).

134. **hypnagogic experiences:** Warren, *Head Trip.*

135. **sounds made by presences:** David Hufford, interviewed for the 2008 television documentary *Your Worst Nightmare: Supernatural Assault.* Observations confirmed in email correspondence with the author. See also D. Hufford, "Visionary Experiences in an Enchanted World," *Anthropology and Humanism* 35, no. 2 (2010): 142–58.

135. **feelings of dread:** Cheyne, "Hypnagogic and Hypnopompic Experiences."

135. **pattern of sleep paralysis:** Hufford, *Your Worst Nightmare.*

135. **supernatural assault:** David Hufford, *The Terror that Comes in the Night: An Experience-Centered Study of Supernatural Assault Traditions* (Philadelphia: University of Pennsylvania Press, 1989).

137. **Japanese widows:** J. Yamamoto et al., "Mourning in Japan," *American Journal of Psychiatry* 125 (1969): 1660–65.

137. **post-bereavement hallucinations:** A. Grimbly, "Bereavement among Elderly People: Grief Reactions, Post-bereavement Hallucinations and Quality of Life," *Acta Psychiatry Scandinavia* 87 (1983): 72–80. See also W. Rees, "The Hallucinations of Widowhood," *British Medical Journal* 4 (1971): 37–41; Steffen and Coyle, "Sense of Presence Experiences"; and L. E. LeGrand, "The Nature and Therapeutic Implications of the Extraordinary Experiences of the Bereaved," *Journal of Near-Death Studies* 24 (2005): 3–20.

137. **a lasting source of comfort:** Fenwick and Fenwick, *Art of Dying.*

138. **significance for the bereaved or dying:** Barbato,

"Parasychological Phenomena."

138. **"Where is the wisdom?":** T. S. Eliot, *Choruses from "The Rock"* (1934).

CHAPTER 5

141. **elevation in mood:** Osis and Haraldsson, *Hour of Death.*

145. **study of accident survivors:** Michael Sabom, "The Acute Dying Experience," *Journal of Near-Death Studies* 26, no. 3 (2008).

146. **animal model:** Sabom, "Acute Dying Experience."

146. **Albert Heim:** Heim, "Remarks on Fatal Falls."

147. **free fall into the Pacific Ocean:** Sabom, "Acute Dying Experience."

148. **flight attendant:** Sabom.

148. **J. L. Bertrand:** Cited in Ptolemy Tompkins, *The Modern Book of the Dead: A Revolutionary Perspective on Death, the Soul, and What Really Happens in the Life to Come* (New York: Atria Books, 2012).

149. **shock thoughts:** Oskar Pfister, "Schocken und Schockphantasien bei höchster Todesgefahr," *Zeitschrift für Psychoanalyse* 16 (1930): 430–55.

149. **depersonalization as a defence:** R. Kletti and R. Noyes, "Mental States in Mortal Danger," *Essence* 5, no. 1 (1981): 5–20.

150. **interesting paradox:** Sabom, "Acute Dying Experience."

152. **accounts of the light:** C. Zaleski, *Other World Journeys: Accounts of Near-Death Experience in Medieval and Modern Times* (London: Oxford University Press, 1987).

153. **Zoroaster:** F. Masumian, "World Religions and Near-Death Experiences," in *the Handbook of Near-Death Experiences: Thirty Years of Investigation,* J. M. Holden, B. Greyson and D. James, eds. (Santa Barbara, CA: Praeger, 2009), 159–84.

153. **"everlasting light":** Isaiah 60:19.

153. **Hinduism:** Masumian, "World Religions," referencing R. Griffith, *Hymns of the Rigveda* (Benares: Medical Hall Press, 1926).

153. **Jesus:** John 8:12.

153. **Buddhism:** Masumian, "World Religions."

153. **Abdu'l-Baha:** Talk presented at 309 West Seventy-Eighth Street, New York, on July 6, 1912, 2nd ed. (New York: U.S. Baha'i Publishing Trust, 1982), 470.

153. **Pope Gregory and witnesses of the light:** Zaleski, *Other World Journeys.*

153. **Teresa of Avila:** From "The Book of Her Life," excerpted in Elizabeth Powers, ed., *Pilgrim Souls: A Collection of Spiritual Autobiography* (New York: Touchstone, 2000), 300.

154. **Monique Hennequin:** Pim van Lommel, *Consciousness Beyond Life: The Science of the Near-Death Experience* (San Francisco: HarperOne, 2010), 203–21.

154. **too much for human words:** Lommel, *Consciousness.*

157. **Rudolf Otto:** R. Otto, *The Idea of the Holy: An Inquiry into the Non-rational Factor in the Idea of the Divine and Its Relation to the Rational* (Middlesex: Penguin Books, 1959).

159. **Catherine of Genoa:** Otto, *Idea of Holy.*

159. **hallucinations:** Sacks, *Hallucinations.*

159. **the day after her mother died:** Haraldsson, *Departed.*

159. **overpowering might:** Otto, *Idea of Holy.*

160. **otherworldly feelings:** Osis and Haraldsson, *Hour of Death.*

161. **meditators and nuns:** Andrew Newberg and Eugene d'Aquili, *Why God Won't Go Away: Brain Science and the Biology of Belief* (New York: Ballantine, 2001).

161. **posterior superior parietal lobe:** Newberg and d'Aquili, 119.

161. **damage by a stroke:** Jill Bolte Taylor, *My Stroke of Insight: A Brain Scientist's Personal Journey* (New York: Plume, 2009).

162. *unio mystica:* Newberg and d'Aquili, *Why God Won't Go Away*, 126.

162. **Johannes Tauler:** E. Underhill, *Mysticism: The Preeminent Study in the Nature and Development of Spiritual Consciousness* (1911; reprint, London: Kessinger, 2010).

162. **Meister Eckhart:** Underhill, *Mysticism.*

162. **Newberg and d'Aquili:** *Why God Won't Go Away*, 147.

163. **Carmelite nuns:** Mario Beauregard and Denyse O'Leary, *The Spiritual Brain: A Neuroscientist's Case for the Existence of the Soul* (San Francisco: HarperOne, 2007).

164. **Maggie Callanan:** Interview with radio host Joan Herrmann, on *Change Your Attitude, Change Your Life*, 2011.

CHAPTER 6

167. **David Bennett:** D. Bennett, *Voyage of Purpose: Spiritual Wisdom from Near-Death Back to Life* (Scotland: Findhorn Press, 2011).

171. **Ptolemy Tompkins:** P. Tompkins, *The Modern Book of the Dead.*

172. **Sogyal Rinpoche:** *The Tibetan Book of Living and Dying* (San Francisco: HarperOne, 1993), 124.

173. **incidence of near-death experiences:** See discussions about prevalence and incidence in Lommel, *Consciousnsess*, 9, and Sam Parnia, *Erasing Death: The Science That Is Rewriting the Boundaries Between Life and Death* (San Francisco: HarperOne, 2013), 173.

173. **cardiac-arrest survivors:** Parnia, *Erasing Death.*

173. **Carlos Alvarado:** See discussion in N. Zingrone and C. Alvarado, "Pleasurable Western Adult Near-Death

Experiences: Features, Circumstances and Incidence," in *Handbook of Near-Death Experiences*, 34.

173. **Near-Death Experience Scale:** Bruce Greyson, "The Near-Death Experience Scale: Construction, Reliability and Validity," *Journal of Nervous Mental Disorders* 171 (1983): 369–75.

175. **arms dealer struck by lightning:** The story of Dannion Brinkley is featured in the 2009 documentary film *Act of God*, directed by Jennifer Baichwal.

175. **small kindnesses:** Eben Alexander, public talk in Syracuse, New York, May 15, 2013.

177. **"We have lingered in the chambers of the sea":** T. S. Eliot, "The Love Song of J. Alfred Prufrock," in *Prufrock and Other Observations* (1920).

177. **"Brain's Last Hurrah":** Anil Seth, *The Guardian Weekly*, August 28, 2013, 20.

177. **post-mortem electrical activity:** http://www.uofmhealth.org/news/archive/201308/electrical-signatures-consciousness-dying-brain.

178. **objections to hypotheses:** Bruce Greyson, "Cosmological Implications of Near-Death Experiences," *Journal of Cosmology* 14 (2011): 4684–96. It has been argued, for instance by John Horgan, author of *Rational Mysticism*, that brain imaging can identify the wiring but doesn't explain the source current for these perceptions. We know that people enter into a different realm of consciousness, but not why.

178. **Jayne Smith:** Talk at the annual meeting of the International Association of Near-Death Studies, Raleigh, North Carolina, 2008.

179. **unconsciousness during anesthesia:** Greyson, "Cosmological

Implications." Further, "anecdotal reports that adequately
anesthetized patients retain a significant capacity to be aware
of or respond to their environment in more than rudimentary
ways—let alone hear and understand—have not been substanti-
ated by controlled studies"; M. Ghoneim and R. Block,
"Learning and Consciousness During General Anesthesia,"
Anesthesiology 76 (1992): 279–305.

181. **NDEers encountering deceased people:** E. W. Kelly, "Near-
Death Experiences with Reports of Meeting Deceased People,"
Death Studies 25 (2001): 229–49.

181. **boy with meningitis:** Kelly, "Near-Death Experiences."
See also Bruce Greyson, "Seeing Deceased Persons Not
Known to Have Died: 'Peak in Darien' Experiences,"
Anthropology and Humanism 35 (2010): 159–71.

181. **recognizing photographs of dead relatives:** C. Sutherland,
"Trailing Clouds of Glory: The Near-Death Experiences of
Children and Teens," in *Handbook of Near-Death Experiences*,
87–108.

181. **people with a deep NDE more likely to die:** Lommel,
Consciousness, 145.

181. **NDEs and out-of-body experiences:** Chris Carter, *Science and
the Near-Death Experience* (Rochester, VT: Inner Traditions, 2010).

182. **child who spent months in a coma:** Sutherland, "Trailing
Clouds of Glory."

182. **Maori account:** Allen Kellehear, "Census of Non-Western
Near-Death Experiences to 2005: Observations and Critical
Reflections," in *Handbook of Near-Death Experiences*, 135–58.

183. **Pele's Pit:** Kellehear, "Census."

183. **Australian Aborigine:** Kellehear.

183. **journeys:** Kellehear.

183. **individuals are no more responsible:** Kellehear.

183. **post-traumatic amnesia and NDEs:** Hou Yongmei et al., "Infrequent Near Death Experiences in Severe Brain Injury Survivors: A Quantitative and Qualitative Study," *Annals of the Indian Academy of Neurology* 16, no. 1 (2013): 75–81. Commenting on what is known to date about NDEs, the authors state: "Although no theory to date has been able to even come near to providing a complete explanation of NDE, a wide range of physiological processes have been targeted for this purpose . . . At best, these physiological findings can be stated as correlates of NDE, rather than its causative biological underpinning."

184. **India:** Allan Kellehear, *Experiences near* "Census of Non-Western Near-Death Experiences."

184. **assortment of social beings:** Ibid.

184. **Ellie Arroway:** Carl Sagan, *Contact* (New York: Doubleday, 1997).

184. **Nancy Evans Bush:** Interview by Amy Stringer, "Reflections from Three Decades with IANDS," *Vital Signs* 28, no. 4 (Fall 2009).

185. **Steven Laureys:** Thonnard et al.

185. **unique, unrivalled memories:** Marie Thonnard et al., "Characteristics of Near-Death Experiences Memories as Compared to Real and Imagined Events Memories," *PLoS ONE* 8, no. 3 (March 2013).

185. **flashbulb memories:** Thonnard et al., "Characteristics."

186. **Penny Sartori:** Telephone interview with the author. See also P. Sartori, "A Prospective Study of NDEs in an Intensive

Therapy Unit," *Christian Parapsychologist* 16, no. 2 (2004): 34–40.

186. **confabulated over time:** Bruce Greyson, "Consistency of Near-Death Experience Accounts over Two Decades: Are Reports Embellished over Time?" *Resuscitation* 73 (2007): 407–11.

187. **hallucinatory interludes:** Newburgh and d'Aquili, *Why God Won't Go Away,* 112.

187. **Teresa of Avila:** Underhill, *Mysticism.*

187. **Carl Jung:** C. G. Jung, *Memories, Dreams, Reflections* (New York: Vintage, 1989).

187. **aftermath of NDEs:** Yolaine Stout, in *Back to Life: Six Challenges Faced by Near-Death Experiencers,* documentary presented at the International Association of Near-Death Studies conference, 2008.

188. **David Bennett:** Bennett, *Voyage of Purpose.*

188. **synesthesia:** Maureen Seaberg, *Tasting the Universe: People Who See Colors in Words and Rainbows in Symphonies—A Spiritual and Scientific Exploration of Synesthesia* (Pompton Plains, NJ: New Page Books, 2011).

189. **Moses on Mount Sinai:** Exodus 20:18.

190. **Carlos Carsolio:** Maria Coffey, *Explorers of the Infinite.*

191. **Abraham Abulafia:** Seaberg, *Tasting the Universe.*

191. **meditation and synesthesia:** Roger Walsh, "Can Synaesthesia Be Cultivated? Indications from Surveys of Meditators," *Journal of Consciousness Studies* 12 (2005).

191. **David Bennett:** Interview with the author.

191. **synesthetic after-effects:** See the discussion in Mahendra Perera, Karuppiah Jagadheesan and Anthony Peake, *Making*

Sense of Near-Death Experiences: Handbook for Clinicians
(London: Jessica Kingsley, 2011), 72.

191. **Willoughby Britton:** W. B. Britton and R. R. Bootzin, "Near-Death Experiences and the Temporal Lobe," *American Psychological Society* 15, no. 4 (2004): 254–58.

191. **hyperconnectivity in the temporal lobe:** http://blogs .scientificamerican.com/literally-psyched/2013/02/26 /from-the-words-of-an-albino-a-brilliant-blend-of-color/.

192. **changes to perception of the world:** Stout, *Back to Life.*

192. **NDE during a motorcycle crash:** Stout.

192. **Yvonne Kason:** Described in Y. Kason, *Farther Shores: Exploring How Near-Death, Kundalini and Mystical Experiences Can Transform Ordinary Lives* (Toronto: HarperCollins, 1994).

193. **Tony Cicoria:** Panel discussion at annual meeting of the International Association of Near-Death Studies, Washington, 2013.

193. **problems after NDEs:** I. Corbeau, "Psychological Problems and Support after an NDE," in *Return: Journal of Near-Death Experiences and Meaning* 15, no. 2 (2004): 16–22.

193. **"you can't talk freely about it":** Presentation on after-effects by psychologist Yolaine Stout, annual meeting of the International Association of Near-Death Studies, 2008.

194. **Saint John of the Cross:** Powers, *Pilgrim Souls,* 308, citing "On a Dark Night," in *The Collected Works of St. John of the Cross,* trans. Kieran Kavanaugh and Otilio Rodriguez.

194. **platoon commander:** As reported by Col. Diane Corcoran, annual meeting of the International Association of Near-Death Studies, 2008.

194. **group NDEs:** Corcoran.

195. **shared death experience:** See, for instance, Howarth, "Shared Near-Death and Related Illness Experiences."

195. **Joan Borysenko:** Borysenko described her experience at the Omega Institute in Rhinebeck, New York, October 2011.

196. **Raymond Moody's cases:** R. Moody, *Glimpses of Eternity: Sharing a Loved One's Passage from This Life to the Next* (San Francisco: HarperOne, 2010).

197. **perceiving places in NDEs:** Moody, *Glimpses.*

198. **mist emitted from the body:** Moody, *Glimpses.*

199. **Roger Ebert:** R. Ebert, "I Do Not Fear Death," *Salon,* September 15, 2011.

200. **cardiac-arrest victim found lying in a field:** Lommel, *Consciousness,* 21.

200. **error-free descriptions by NDE patients:** Michael Sabom, *Recollections of Death: A Medical Examination* (New York: Simon & Schuster, 1982).

201. **five-year study of hospitalized intensive care patients:** Penny Sartori et al., "A Prospectively Studied Near-Death Experience with Corroborated Out-of-Body Perceptions and Unexplained Healing," *Journal of Near-Death Studies* 27, no. 1 (2008). It is estimated that 10 percent of the general population and perhaps up to 25 percent of children have had a spontaneous sensation of being outside their bodies. This mirrors the percentage split between children who have sensed presences and adults who have, suggesting that consciousness is less firmly entrained in the body in childhood, or that children are more fantasy-prone, depending upon your point of view; Lommel, *Consciousness,* 77).

201. **accurate details of their resuscitations:** Sabom, *Recollections of Death.* Sabom has been criticized for his control group, who were seasoned cardiac patients but not necessarily those who had undergone cardiac arrest and rehabilitation without experiencing an NDE. See the discussion in J. M. Holden, "Veridical Perception in Near-Death Experiences," in *Handbook of Near-Death Experiences,* 185–212.

201. **above myself looking down:** Sabom, *Recollections.*

201. **cardiac surgeon flapping his arms:** E. W. Kelly et al., "Can Experiences near Death Furnish Evidence for Life after Death?" *Omega* 40, no. 4 (2000): 513–19.

202. **OBE perceptions corroborated:** Holden, "Veridical Perception," 197. Holden reserves judgment on what these reports lead us to conclude, wary of being definitive until there are better-designed and -controlled investigations. "The sheer volume of AVP [apparent veridical perception] anecdotes that a number of different authors over the course of 150 years have described suggests that AVP is real," she notes. But she believes that "if the controlled investigation of AVP is to continue, it will likely be a complex and protracted—and therefore, costly—process"; ibid. The Horizon Research Foundation has been funding such efforts in participating cardiac wards in the United States and Europe. Known as the AWARE Study, the wards (ER or cardiology) have placed boards with random symbols high up, facing the ceiling. Parnia discusses the research objectives in his 2013 book, *Erasing Death.*

202. **Jeff Warren:** Conversation with the author.

202. **Sam Parnia:** *Erasing Death,* 228.

202. **Richard Mansfield:** Parnia, *Erasing Death.*

203. **Tom Aufderheide:** Parnia, *Erasing Death.*

204. **detailed accounts of conversations and events:** Parnia, *Erasing Death.*

205. **critical-care nurse in the Netherlands:** Lommel, *Consciousness,* 21.

206. **Pam Reynolds:** Case summarized by Michael Sabom, *Light and Death: One Doctor's Fascinating Account of Near Death Experiences* (Grand Rapids, MI: Zondervan, 1998).

206. **enhanced mental functioning:** J. E. Owens et al., "Features of 'Near-Death Experience' in Relation to Whether or Not Patients Were near Death," *Lancet* 336 (1990): 1175–77.

207. **"Hotel California":** See the BBC television documentary *The Day I Died: The Mind, the Brain and Near-Death Experiences,* directed by Nick Broome, 2002.

208. **Keith Augustine:** K. Augustine, "Does Paranormal Perception Occur in Near-Death Experiences?" *Journal of Near-Death Studies* 25, no. 4 (2007): 203–36.

208. **Ms. Reynolds's brain was being monitored:** Minden, "Veridical Perception," 199.

209. **Susan Blackmore:** S. Blackmore, *Dying to Live: Science and the Near-Death Experience* (London: Grafton Books, 1993), 177.

210. **experimental studies and bird's-eye view:** See Blackmore, *Dying to Live,* and then the critique by C. Carter in *Science and the Near-Death Experience,* 202.

210. **simple theory of OBE:** Blackmore, *Dying to Live.*

210. **Olaf Blanke:** O. Blanke et al., "Out-of-Body Experience and Autoscopy of Neurological Origin," *Brain* 127 (2004): 243–58. See also O. Blanke et al., "Stimulating Illusory Own-Body Perceptions: The Part of the Brain That Can Induce Out-of-Body Experiences Has Been Located," *Nature* 419 (2002): 269–70.

210. **empirical findings of Blanke:** Kelly and Kelly, *Irreducible Mind,* 223. Kelly's rebuttal is as follows: "The interpretation of the empirical findings of Blanke and his colleagues is controversial. First, the purported localization of neurologic abnormalities is less than clear. The TPJ is only a region of 'mean overlap' of individual lesions that are distributed much more widely. Furthermore, the appearance of localization derives partly from mapping results from the very different brains of all five patients onto the left hemisphere of only one of them. In one patient, no overt anatomical or functional default could even be identified. Among the 29 additional patients for whom any information was available, the seizures of two were specifically localized to the anterior temporal lobe, and only about a dozen were characterized in terms even loosely consistent with the hypothesis. Furthermore, there was no clear evidence of lateralization; among their patients, the location of identifiable foci was evenly split between the left and right hemispheres. Second, the generalization from these few patients with neurological problems to all persons experiencing an OBE, most of whom have no known neurological problem, is purely conjectural. Abnormal activity in the TPJ region or some other location may sometimes be sufficient for occurrence of an OBE; to conclude that any such activity pattern is necessary is dubious. Five of the six patients of Blanke and his colleagues suffered moderate to severe neurological pathology, but such pathology appears generally to be absent in the vast majority of persons spontaneously experiencing OBEs . . . Moreover, the vast majority of patients with seizures do not experience OBEs . . . Finally, even if OBEs

were shown to be associated with a certain region of the brain—something that is far from established—such localization cannot account for the occurrence of any complex perception or mentation at a time when the abnormalities in brain functioning would ordinarily abolish consciousness."

210. **Ernst Rodin:** Quoted in Kelly and Kelly, *Irreducible Mind.* Position confirmed in email correspondence with the author. See also the discussion in Holden, Greyson and James, *Handbook of Near-Death Experiences,* 220.

211. **pushing the boundaries:** Parnia, *Erasing Death,* 169.

211. **study done with student volunteers:** Parnia, *Erasing Death,* 169. For more on the study, go to http://www.time.com/time /health/article/0,8599,1655632,00.html.

211. **reproduced an out-of-body experience:** Parnia, *Erasing Death,* 170.

211. **Parnia's research:** Email correspondence with the author. Parnia has had two OBE cases in his hospital during the AWARE study so far, but neither took place on wards where the boards were set up. One woman, he says, saw a nurse whom she'd never met before; *Erasing Death,* 255.

212. **hippocampus sensitive to damage:** E. M. Vriens et al., "The Impact of Repeated Short Episodes of Circulatory Arrest on Cerebral Function," *EEG Clinical Neurophysiology* 98 (1996): 236–42.

212. **low oxygen levels and NDEs:** Parnia, *What Happens When We Die,* 21.

213. **akin to a waking dream:** Kevin Nelson, *The Spiritual Doorway in the Brain: A Neurologist's Search for the God Experience.*

213. **NDEs can be scientifically accounted for:** See, for example, Nelson's interview with Alex Tsarkiris of *Skeptiko* on January 27, 2010, http://www.skeptiko.com/kevin-nelson-skeptical-of-near -death-experience-accounts/.

214. **NDErs in Nelson's survey:** J. Long and J. Holden, "Does the Arousal System Contribute to Near-Death and Out-of-Body Experiences? A Summary and Response," *Journal of Near-Death Studies* 25, no. 3 (2007).

214. **NDE and REM sleep:** Britton and Bootzin, "Near-Death Experiences."

214. **what's not delusional:** Bruce Greyson, at United Nations symposium on the launch of the Human Consciousness Project, New York, November 9, 2008.

215. **Nancy Bush:** Interview in *Vital Signs.*

216. **no blood levels for enlightenment:** Greyson, UN symposium, 2008.

216. **religious affiliation and NDE:** C. Sutherland, *Transformed by the Light: Life after Near-Death Experiences* (Sydney, Australia: Bantam, 1992).

216. **Lommel's study:** Lommel, *Consciousness,* 57.

217. **integrating deep NDE:** Stout, IANDS meeting, 2008.

217. **David Bennett:** Interview with the author.

219. **Eben Alexander:** Talk presented May 2013 in Syracuse, New York.

222. **"Where death is, I am not":** Epicurus. See, for example, Simon Critchley, *The Book of Dead Philosophers* (New York: Vintage, 2009).

222. **"Death is not extinguishing the light":** This is widely attributed to Tagore but I haven't been able to find it in his work. I have found it in a much humbler source: an American

Catholic priest named Floyd Lotito who wrote a short book of inspirational thoughts, *Wisdom, Age and Grace: An Inspirational Guide to Staying Young at Heart* (Mahwah, NJ: Paulist Press, 1993).

223. **"the more impoverished life becomes":** Jung, *Memories, Dreams, Reflections*, 302.

224. **Raymond Moody:** Talk presented at the Omega Institute, Rhinebeck, New York, October 2011.

230. **Carl Jung:** from *Memories, Dreams, Reflections.*

233. **"Where is the wisdom we have lost?":** Eliot, *Choruses from "The Rock."*

CHAPTER 7

235. **Nancy Evans Bush:** N. Bush, "Distressing Western Near-Death Experiences: Finding a Way Through the Abyss," in *Handbook of Near-Death Experiences*, 87–108.

239. **Ken Wilber:** K. Wilber, *Grace and Grit: Spirituality and Healing in the Life and Death of Treya Killam Wilber* (Boston: Shambhala Press, 2000).

239. **"the only kind of courage":** Rainer Maria Rilke, Letter 8 (1904), in *Letters to a Young Poet* (1929).

BIBLIOGRAPHY

Arcangel, Dianne. *Afterlife Encounters: Ordinary People, Extraordinary Experiences.* Charlottesville, VA: Hampton Roads, 2005.

Aries, Philippe. *The Hour of Our Death.* New York: Vintage Books, 2008.

Bachelard, Gaston. *The Poetics of Reverie: Childhood, Language and the Cosmos.* Boston: Beacon Press, 1971.

Barrett, William. *Deathbed Visions: How the Dead Talk to the Dying.* Guildford, UK: White Crow Books, 2011.

Beauregard, Mario, and Denyse O'Leary. *The Spiritual Brain: A Neuroscientist's Case for the Existence of the Soul.* San Francisco: HarperOne, 2007.

Bennett, David. *Voyage of Purpose: Spiritual Wisdom from Near-Death Back to Life.* Scotland: Findhorn Press, 2011.

Blackmore, Susan. *Dying to Live: Science and the Near-Death Experience.* London: Grafton Books, 1993.

Callanan, Maggie, and Patricia Kelley. *Final Gifts: Understanding the Special Awareness, Needs and Communications of the Dying.* New York: Bantam, 1992.

Cardena, Etzel, Steven J. Lynn, and Stanley Krippner, eds. *Varieties of Anomalous Experience: Examining the Scientific Evidence.* Washington, DC: American Psychological Association, 2000.

Carter, Chris. *Science and the Afterlife Experience.* Rochester, VT: Inner Traditions, 2012.

———. *Science and the Near-Death Experience.* Rochester, VT: Inner Traditions, 2010.

Coffey, Maria. *Explorers of the Infinite: The Secret Spiritual Lives of Extreme Athletes—and What They Reveal about Near-Death Experiences, Psychic Communication, and Touching the Beyond.* New York: Tarcher, 2008.

Davis, Wade. *The Wayfinders: Why Ancient Wisdom Matters in the Modern World.* Toronto: CBC Massey Lectures/House of Anansi Press, 2009.

Ecklund, Elaine Howard. *Science vs. Religion: What Scientists Really Think.* London: Oxford University Press, 2010.

Eliot, T. S. *Choruses from "The Rock," a Pageant Play.* New York: Harcourt, Brace, 1934.

———. *Prufrock and Other Observations.* 1920. Reprint, Whitefish, MT: Kessinger, 2010.

———. *The Wasteland.* New York: W. W. Norton, 2000.

Fenwick, Peter, and Elizabeth Fenwick. *The Art of Dying.* London: Continuum Books, 2008.

Figes, Orlando. *Just Send Me Word: A True Story of Love and Survival in the Gulag.* New York: Metropolitan Books, 2012.

Furlong, Monica. *Visions and Longings: Medieval Women Mystics.* Boston: Shambhala, 1996.

Geiger, John. *The Third Man Factor: The Secret to Survival in Extreme Environments.* Toronto: Penguin Canada, 2009.

Gratton, Nicole, and Monique Séguin. *Les rêves en fin de vie : 100 récits de rêves pour faciliter la grande traversée.* Montreal: Flammarion Québec, 2009.

Grof, Stanislav. *Spiritual Emergency: When Personal Transformation Becomes a Crisis.* New York: Tarcher, 1989.

Gurney, E., F. W. H. Meyers, and F. Podmore. *Phantasms of the Living.* 2 volumes. London: Truber, 1886.

Hamilton, Allan. *The Scalpel and the Soul: Encounters with Surgery, the Supernatural and the Healing Power of Hope.* New York: Tarcher/ Penguin, 2008.

Haraldsson, Erlendur. *The Departed among the Living: An Investigative Study of Afterlife Encounters.* Guildford, UK: White Crow Books, 2012.

Hawker, Paul. *Secret Affairs of the Soul: Ordinary People's Extraordinary Experiences of the Sacred.* Kelowna, BC: Northstone Publishing, 2000.

———. *Soul Survivor: A Spiritual Quest Through 40 Days in the Wilderness.* Sydney, Australia: Lion Books, 2001.

Holden, Janice Miner, Bruce Greyson, and Debbie James, eds. *The Handbook of Near-Death Experiences: Thirty Years of Investigation.* Santa Barbara, CA: Praeger, 2009.

Horgan, John. *Rational Mysticism: Spirituality Meets Science in the Search for Enlightenment.* New York: Houghton Mifflin, 2003.

Hufford, David. *The Terror That Comes in the Night: An Experience-Centered Study of Supernatural Assault Traditions.* Philadelphia: University of Pennsylvania Press, 1989.

Huxley, Aldous. *The Doors of Perception.* New York: Harper, 1954.

James, William. *Varieties of Religious Experience.* New York: Modern Library, 1902.

Jorgensen, Rene. *The Light Behind God: What Religion Can Learn from Near-Death Experiences.* Montreal: Createspace, 2010.

Jung, C. G. *Memories, Dreams, Reflections.* New York: Vintage, 1989.

———. *Psychology and Religion.* New Haven, CT: Yale University Press, 1938.

Kason, Yvonne. *Farther Shores: Exploring How Near-Death, Kundalini and Mystical Experiences Can Transform Ordinary Lives.* Toronto: HarperCollins, 1994.

Kellehear, Allan. *Experiences Near Death: Beyond Medicine and Religion.* London: Oxford University Press, 1996.

Kelly, Edward, and Emily Williams Kelly, eds. *Irreducible Mind: Toward a Psychology for the 21st Century.* Plymouth, UK: Rowman & Littlefield, 2007.

Kelly, Emily Williams. *Science, the Self and Survival after Death: Selected Writings of Ian Stevenson.* Plymouth, UK: Rowman & Littlefield, 2012.

Kessler, David. *Visions, Trips and Crowded Rooms.* Carlsbad, CA: Hay House, 2010.

Kircher, Pamela. *Love Is the Link: A Hospice Doctor Shares Her Experience of Near-Death and Dying.* Pagosa Springs, CO: Awakening Press, 2013.

Kübler-Ross, Elisabeth. *On Life after Death.* Toronto: Celestial Arts, 2008.

Kuhl, David. *What Dying People Want: Practical Wisdom for the End of Life.* Toronto: Anchor Canada, 2003.

Kuhn, Thomas. *The Structure of Scientific Revolutions.* Chicago: University of Chicago Press, 2012.

Lagrand, Louis. *Love Lives On.* New York: Berkley Books, 2006.

Lecouteux, Claude. *The Return of the Dead: Ghosts, Ancestors, and the Transparent Veil of the Pagan Mind.* Rochester, VT: Inner Traditions, 2009.

Lommel, Pim van. *Consciousness Beyond Life: The Science of the Near-Death Experience.*
San Francisco: HarperOne, 2010.

Mayer, Elizabeth Lloyd. *Extraordinary Knowing: Science, Skepticism and the Inexplicable Powers of the Human Mind.* New York: Bantam, 2007.

McLuhan, Robert. *Randi's Prize: What Sceptics Say about the Paranormal, Why They Are Wrong and Why It Matters.* Leicester, UK: Matador, 2010.

Meyers, F. W. H. *Human Personality and Its Survival of Bodily Death.* London: Longmans Green, 1903.

Moody, Raymond. *Glimpses of Eternity: Sharing a Loved One's Passage from This Life to the Next.* New York: Guideposts, 2010.

———. *Life after Life: The Investigation of a Phenomenon—Survival of Bodily Death.* San Francisco: HarperOne, 2001.

Nelson, Kevin. *The Spiritual Doorway in the Brain: A Neurologist's Search for the God Experience.* New York: Dutton, 2012.

Newberg, Andrew, and Eugene d'Aquili. *Why God Won't Go Away: Brain Science and the Biology of Belief.* New York: Ballantine Books, 2001.

Oliver, Mary. *A Thousand Mornings.* New York: Penguin, 2013.

Osis, Karlis, and Erlendur Haraldsson. *At the Hour of Death: A New Look at Evidence for Life after Death,* rev. ed. Mamaroneck, NY: Hastings House, 1990.

Otto, Rudolf. *The Idea of the Holy: An Inquiry into the Non-rational Factor in the Idea of the Divine and Its Relation to the Rational.* Middlesex, UK: Penguin, 1959.

Parnia, Sam. *Erasing Death: The Science That Is Rewriting the Boundaries Between Life and Death.* San Francisco: HarperOne, 2013.

———. *What Happens When We Die: A Groundbreaking Study into the Nature of Life and Death.* Carlsbad, CA: Hay House, 2006.

Perera, Mahendra, Karuppiah Jagadheesan, and Anthony Peake, eds. *Making Sense of Near-Death Experiences: A Handbook for Clinicians.* London: Jessica Kingsley, 2011.

Powers, Elizabeth, ed. *Pilgrim Souls: A Collection of Spiritual Autobiography.* New York: Touchstone, 2000.

Radin, Dean. *Entangled Minds: Extrasensory Experiences in a Quantum Reality.* New York: Pocket Books, 2006.

———. *Supernormal: Science, Yoga, and the Evidence for Extraordinary Psychic Abilities.* New York: Deepak Chopra Books, 2013.

Rilke, Rainer Maria. *Duino Elegies.* New York: Vintage, 2009.

Roach, Mary. *Spook: Science Tackles the Afterlife.* New York: Norton, 2005.

Roper, Michael. *The Secret Battle: Emotional Survival in the Great War.* Manchester, UK: Manchester University Press, 2009.

Sacks, Oliver. *Hallucinations.* New York: Vintage, 2013.

———. *Musicophilia: Tales of Music and the Brain.* Toronto: Vintage Canada, 2007.

Sagan, Carl. *Contact.* New York: Doubleday, 1997.

Seaberg, Maureen. *Tasting the Universe: People Who See Colors in Words and Rainbows in Symphonies—A Spiritual and Scientific Exploration of Synesthesia.* Pompton Plains, NJ: New Page Books, 2011.

Sheldrake, Rupert. *Dogs That Know When Their Owners Are Coming Home,* rev. ed. New York: Broadway Books, 2011.

———. *The Science Delusion: Freeing the Spirit of Scientific Inquiry.* London: Coronet, 2012.

Singh, Kathleen Dowling. *The Grace in Dying: A Message of Hope, Comfort and Spiritual Transformation.* San Francisco: HarperOne, 2000.

Slocum, Joshua. *Sailing Alone Around the World.* Barnes and Noble Classics, 2005.

Sogyal Rinpoche. *The Tibetan Book of Living and Dying.* San Francisco: HarperSanFrancisco: 1993.

Stevenson, Ian. *Telepathic Impressions: A Review and Report of 35 New Cases.* Charlottesville: University of Virginia Press, 1973.

Tart, Charles. *The End of Materialism: How Evidence of the Paranormal Is Bringing Science and Spirit Together.* Oakland, CA: New Harbinger, 2012.

Taylor, Jill Bolte. *My Stroke of Insight: A Brain Scientist's Personal Journey.* New York: Plume, 2009.

Taylor, Rob. *The Breach: Kilimanjaro and the Conquest of Self.* Albany, Australia: Wildeyed Press, 1991.

Taylor, Timothy. *The Buried Soul: How Humans Invented Death.* Boston: Beacon Press, 2002.

Terkel, Studs. *Will the Circle Be Unbroken: Reflections on Death, Rebirth and Hunger for a Faith.* New York: Ballantine Books, 2001.

Tompkins, Ptolemy. *The Modern Book of the Dead: A Revolutionary Perspective on Death, the Soul, and What Really Happens in the Life to Come.* New York: Atria Books, 2012.

Underhill, Evelyn. *Mysticism: The Preeminent Study in the Nature and Development of Spiritual Consciousness.* 1911. Reprint, London: Kessinger, 2010.

Warren, Jeff. *The Head Trip: Adventures on the Wheel of Consciousness.* Toronto: Random House, 2007.

Wilber, Ken. *Grace and Grit: Spirituality and Healing in the Life and Death of Treya Killam Wilber.* Boston: Shambhala Press, 2000.

Zaleski, Carol. *Other World Journeys: Accounts of Near-Death Experience in Medieval and Modern Times.* London: Oxford University Press, 1987.

Zimmer, Carl. *Soul Made Flesh: The Discovery of the Brain and How It Changed the World.* New York: Atria, 2005.

INDEX

INDEX

PATRICIA PEARSON is an award-winning journalist and novelist whose work has appeared in *The New Yorker*, the *New York Times*, *Huffington Post* and *Businessweek*, among other publications. She is the author of five books, and was a long-time member of *USA Today*'s Op-Ed Board of Contributors. She also directed the research for the 2009 History Channel documentary, *The Science of the Soul*. Known for upending conventional wisdom, Pearson's first book, *When She Was Bad*, questioning our simplistic understanding of violent women, won the Arthur Ellis Award for best non-fiction crime book of 1997. Her most recent book, *A Brief History of Anxiety (Yours and Mine)*, challenges the notion that mood disorders are purely brain-based, with no relationship to culture and personal circumstance.

www. pearsonspost.com/wp